POLICE IN
THE HALLWAYS

· · · ·

Discipline in an Urban
High School

Kathleen Nolan

Foreword by Paul Willis

University of Minnesota Press
Minneapolis
London

Copyright 2011 by the Regents of the University of Minnesota

All rights reserved. No part of this publication may be reproduced, stored in a retrieval system, or transmitted, in any form or by any means, electronic, mechanical, photocopying, recording, or otherwise, without the prior written permission of the publisher.

Published by the University of Minnesota Press
111 Third Avenue South, Suite 290
Minneapolis, MN 55401-2520
http://www.upress.umn.edu

LIBRARY OF CONGRESS CATALOGING-IN-PUBLICATION DATA
Nolan, Kathleen.
Police in the hallways : discipline in an urban high school /
Kathleen Nolan; foreword by Paul Willis.
p.   cm.
Includes bibliographical references and index.
ISBN 978-0-8166-7552-4 (hc : alk. paper)
ISBN 978-0-8166-7553-1 (pb : alk. paper)
1. School discipline—United States. 2. Urban high schools—United States.
I. Title.
LB3012.2.N65 2011
371.5—dc22
2011011283

Printed in the United States of America on acid-free paper

The University of Minnesota is an equal-opportunity educator and employer.

18 17 16 15 14 13 12 11   10 9 8 7 6 5 4 3 2 1

To my parents, Gerard and Shirley,
and to the loving memory of my sister, Maureen

Contents

Foreword

Paul Willis

IN *Police in the Hallways: Discipline in an Urban High School,* Kathleen Nolan updates our understanding of urban schools in light of a changing political economy and the turn toward penal institutional practices in American schools as exemplified, for instance, in zero-tolerance approaches to student behavior. Nolan's fine-grained ethnography operates at the frontiers of larger questions about how social structure relates to local practices and cultures. As schools begin to resemble prisons, the disappearance of any reasonable prospect of decent-paying jobs for most also makes the context of this study very different from that in which I wrote *Learning to Labor.*

I do not think that anyone has gotten really adequate theoretical and procedural answers for understanding how cultural responses relate to external structuring forces, and there is always the danger of seeming somehow to "blame the victim" for self-limiting, apparently self-directed behaviors rather than attributing everything to the automatic results of outside domination. The problems are obviously increased when dealing with racial minorities, especially in writings from an author outside the ethnic group. This author treads these lines with great care and sophistication. I always remember Pierre Bourdieu's point: the aim of a good presentation and analysis is to make the readers realize that, if they were in the subjects' shoes, they would behave in a very similar fashion. This book had that effect on me.

This foundation of understanding in the context of Nolan's acknowledgment of larger contextual factors places her very well in a position to make a particular contribution in her careful policy recommendations that promise to make real contributions to educational debate and practice at a crucial juncture. Her range of suggestions aimed at producing a morally and socially ballasted pedagogic approach to retrieve school discipline and the educational initiative from the penal and policing apparatus must command attention. Nothing is more important than arresting and reversing the surreptitiously normative drift of the school (and perhaps the whole society) into an omnipresent culture of control and aggressive policing practices. The daily immersions of school pupils in this world allows the quite alarming but apparently seamless escalation of "disrespect" into "disorderly conduct" into "court summons" into wholesale criminal identity.

An important part of Nolan's argument is that microbehaviors and microstructures matter. This is crucial. It is too easy to take up a kind of resistance, "scorched earth" perspective where everything is reduced to class and political opposition and to a kind of primal (if overwhelmingly one-sided) battle between oppressive outside structures and the creative cultural agency of the oppressed. Though I am sometimes put in that bag (and sometimes deserve it when reacting to people for whom the broader context seems to be lost!), I take a broader "cultural production" perspective that has to do with a general meaning making and identity construction from below, which is only partly about reaction to oppressive social structures. In this perspective, collective cultural development (not individual cognitive thought) and complex relations to artifacts and expressive forms have some real degree of autonomy, and results often produce unintended consequences with respect to social constraints and outcomes, but those results cannot be read back for simple class-reductive meanings. *Learning to Labor* takes institutions seriously and analyzes the "lads" culture not as an elementary socialist form of working-class culture (as I am taken to mean so often) but as a culture specifically produced through "differentiation" of the education paradigm then on offer.

Nolan must be right to say that in school the students she came to know do not somehow experience naked oppression from social forces directly—whatever that would mean. In contrast to such a "scorched earth" position, Nolan shows how her students, in part at least, experience their positions in the bottom of social space through fundamental mediations of current educational forms and how they react, often collectively and culturally rather than cognitively, to their *immediate* situational and contextual problems, finding dignity and human traction in those reactions. The disappearance of formal economic opportunities makes the school and its terms of trade actually much more important, and the prison-cell shadow cast across the school makes it even more desperately important—that I have learned from Nolan. There is enormous ambiguity in the students' responses, reflecting the ambiguity of what they are provided with. They are thinking several contradictory things at once: an individual, more bourgeois subject feels the pull of individualism and a possible personal stake in a meritocratic society, so that opportunities for advancement through the educational system can seem tantalizingly and strangely close (more so than for "the lads"). At the same time, the students' collective behaviors—the release and frisson of running down the school corridor—show something of the logic of a collective subject that "knows" that they cannot all be "saved" individually but that they can have some power as an expressive group articulating something important about their shared social situation in the school as it drifts alarmingly toward the police school.

Kathleen Nolan is an educator as well as a social scientist. She occupies a joint vantage point from which not only to insist that "empirical facts" be incorporated into how social science theorizes social processes at the micro level, but also to advance the public face of sociology into practical arenas such as the school, offering there pedagogic insights and new avenues for approaching the intractable problems of "what to do" in the classroom on Monday morning. It is not good enough for social scientists to wind up effectively in a position where the only thing to do on Monday morning is to wait for the revolution. By showing the importance of mediations, even tipped as they are now dangerously toward the penal state, surely Nolan is also showing the continuing worthwhileness of institutional-level initiatives, which might have a chance of properly responding to institutionally forged reactions in the student body. She argues that there is a misrecognized and displaced educational (not class or penal) dialogue taking place, which, if decoded carefully from a qualitative perspective, might offer educational ways forward not only to "hear" the educational (not class or deviant) voice of the students but also to show what a future dialogue of respect might sound like—partly to limit the most "self-destructive" results but also to open avenues to genuinely positive outcomes. Perhaps social chasms really can be bridged in school, or at the very least there may still be a better chance there than on the street or in the prison or in the illegal economy. The student voice is so poignant, and the yearnings carry beyond the penal frame and cry out for more ethnographically grounded educational perspectives based on the respecting of dialogue and of both the students' and the institution's voices. Nolan shows that here is a site, a platform, a stage not reduced immediately to, and foreclosed by, class forces and class antagonism. Read this book also in the opposite direction, for what it can hold out for emancipation.

Studying Urban School Discipline

A Bronx Tale

ONE AFTERNOON, I was checking my mailbox in the main office of the high school where I worked in the South Bronx. Suddenly, the quiet that settled upon the school late in the day was shattered as three police officers pushed a small black boy through the office door about ten feet from where I stood. A stocky white male officer pinned the boy, who appeared to be no older than thirteen, against the wall. The officer yelled directly into the boy's face and pressed on his chest. The boy was letting out loud sobs, unable to speak. A female officer tried unsuccessfully to ease her colleague away from the student. I stood in shock, unable to respond. The only other person in the room, a Latina school aide in her late fifties—a grandmotherly figure—who had been sitting at one of the desks, slowly and calmly stood up and walked over to the commotion. Stepping between the student and the officer, the woman slipped her arms around the boy and asked him what he needed to do. The officer backed off, and the boy, still sobbing, uttered his first comprehensible words: "I wanna call my mother."

This confrontation took place in 2000, just a few years before the commencement of the study that has culminated in this book. The incident did not typify my experience as a teacher, but my colleagues and I wondered whether such events were evidence of a change happening in schools like ours—so-called poorly performing schools serving low-income Latino/a and black students. We were aware that in the mid-1990s, educational policy makers had mandated a national policy of "zero tolerance," which calls for swift and harsh punishment—usually suspension or expulsion—even for first-time offenders of minor school infractions and tends to increase the likelihood of police involvement in disciplinary cases.[1] Then, in 1998, the mayor placed the New York City Police Department in charge of security and discipline in the city's public schools. From that point on, security agents came to work under the auspices of the police department, and law enforcement became more visible in schools.

The bulk of our conversations in the teachers' room were mainly about the daily frustrations of getting struggling students to pass the standardized tests, mice running around in the classrooms, textbooks that weren't aligned to the new standards, a student in special education throwing a chair out a second-floor window. But soon our discussions turned to the new police presence in the building and the proposed installation of a metal detector at the front entrance. Some teachers thought the new security measures were necessary to restore order to troubled schools and reduce violence; others worried that they created, as one of my colleagues put it, "a negative psychology" that would make students feel resentful and unwelcome in their own school. The teachers whom I knew best largely agreed that policy makers did not appear to have a clear understanding of daily life inside our schools. Nor were they aware of the lived experiences of the students—the pressures and the lack of resources with which teachers contended and the struggles, both in and out of school, that poor students of color faced.

Our students came from some of the poorest urban districts in the country—Mott Haven, Melrose, Morrisania, Hunts Point—known collectively as the South Bronx. The view from the windows of the upper floors of the school revealed the poverty of the area: garbage-strewn lots, broken sidewalks, and, a few blocks away, a shopping district with a variety of discount stores, street vendors, an army recruiting station, and several fast-food restaurants. Just on the other side of the run-down playing field stood the only new and impressive building in the area: a youth prison. Teachers with sardonic senses of humor warned students that they would end up there if they continued to misbehave and didn't pass their classes.

As a teacher, I could not help but observe that urban schools could be doing much more to lessen inequality. The literature on social reproduction in schooling—that is, the idea that schools are structured to reproduce social hierarchies—resonated with me as I contemplated my students' futures and wondered what outcomes their educational experiences would yield.[2] I considered my own struggle to secure basic resources for my classroom, and I could not forget the image of the young black student pinned up against the wall by armed police officers. What was high school doing for him? What was high school doing to him?

Paul Willis's classic study of cultural reproduction seemed particularly salient, as my students' oppositional behavior—cutting classes, hallway antics, and noncompliance with the dress code, for instance—seemed implicitly to demonstrate their critique of schooling while at the same time hindering any possibilities for social mobility.[3] But, unlike Willis's working-class lads, my students no longer had a shop-floor culture to embrace, and without such work options, the potential costs of oppositional behavior—which were reflected in the image of the imposing youth prison—became more severe.

It was with these concerns in mind that I left teaching in June 2001 to begin a PhD program in urban education. While I attended graduate school, zero-tolerance school discipline and school-based policing became a front-burner issue in public discussions of urban school reform. Many feared where the policies might lead, but others, including New York City mayor Bloomberg, embraced them. Indeed, school discipline became a central issue for the mayor, and in 2003 he announced the Impact Schools Initiative, a school-based policing program modeled after the former mayor Rudolph Giuliani's "quality of life" order-maintenance street-policing campaigns—an approach wherein heavy policing in targeted neighborhoods is used to crack down on low-level violations of the law in an effort to instill order and reduce crime. Just as the previous mayor had "taken back the streets," Mayor Bloomberg was intent on "taking back the schools" through a systematic and increased use of policing.

After three years of studying urban schooling and reading what the best scholars had to say about these issues, I returned to the Bronx to study a high school where zero-tolerance policies were in full force and law-enforcement officials patrolled the hallways to instill order. I wanted an on-the-ground understanding of how students made meaning of schooling in this context and how they negotiated school-based policing. Additionally, in the tradition of critical educational ethnography,[4] I wanted to gain insight into the relationship between the students' lived experience and educational trajectories and current economic and social realities.

Going Back to School

In the fall of 2004, I began my study in a high school about three miles from the one where I had taught and within walking distance from the neighborhood where I had lived for most of the 1990s. I call the school simply Urban Public High School, or UPHS. At the time of the study, UPHS was a large comprehensive neighborhood high school with about three thousand students. The student body was about 99 percent nonwhite, and 85 percent of students came from low-income homes. There was a large Jamaican and Dominican population in the school—immigrants and second-generation children of immigrants. The school was considered "poorly performing," with higher-than-average rates of disruption and violence. It was widely known as a rough school, and most of the young people I met there described it in those terms. Yet, despite the "roughness" some exhibited, I was often moved by the students' friendliness, sincerity, and courage in the face of overwhelmingly difficult circumstances.

Although the school had a rather notorious reputation for disruption and violence, it was typical, in many ways, of large racially segregated urban public schools around the United States. It was experiencing some of the most common contemporary reforms in education, such as the use of high-stakes standardized tests; the transition to small, theme-based schools; and, of course, the latest in "get tough" disciplinary policies.

Under the new Impact Schools Initiative, UPHS was assigned twelve police officers from the local precinct and another four officers from the special task force set up to implement the initiative. Additionally, twenty "safety agents" were assigned to the school. It was the job of these officers and agents to patrol hallways and other common areas of the school and to maintain order.

Despite my many years living in the Bronx and teaching high school there, I was not quite prepared for what I found when I first entered UPHS. The atmosphere at UPHS was markedly different from that of the school where I had worked. An institution that in its early days had purported to serve in loco parentis, taking on some of the functions and responsibilities of parents, appeared instead to have taken on responsibilities of the criminal-justice system. In a building full of struggling and alienated students, order-maintenance policing took precedence over educative aims, and a culture of control permeated the building. Hallways were heavily patrolled. Police officers and agents would routinely confront students for taking too long to get to class, shouting too loudly, or wearing a hat. Additionally, many spaces within the school had taken on precinct, or even prison, characteristics. The security apparatus—for example, metal detectors, scanners, and cameras—transformed the physical spaces of the building, and their use became a normal part of daily routines. Police and prison language was commonplace. Students got "picked up" in the hallways and "did time" in the detention room. Many were getting arrested and summoned to juvenile or criminal court (for anyone sixteen or older), often for what seemed like minor infractions.

Police officers and safety agents had a good deal of authority and influence over daily life in the school. They did not entirely run the school, but they set the tone and were often the first to confront rule breakers. When they became involved in a disciplinary incident, even a minor one, the situation immediately became a "police matter," and school personnel would need to defer to them. At times, educators at UPHS found ways to subvert the authority of the police by not reporting an incident, and they used educational solutions to disciplinary problems when they could. Nevertheless, school personnel also "learned to cooperate" with the police and became invested in the success of police intervention to curtail disorder. The school, devoid of any culture of learning, had become a kind of auxiliary penal institution in which some of the city's most marginalized youth spent their days under heavy police surveillance.

Meeting the People

My gaining entrance into UPHS was not difficult. As a former teacher, I had a contact at the Bronx superintendent's office who offered to help. This person suggested UPHS as a field site because the school had a history of violence and disorder and thus was part of the city's new policing program. It also appeared that the new principal had had a positive effect on the school climate, and incidents of violence were on the decline. UPHS also seemed like a good fit for me. I was very familiar with the area surrounding the school and the neighborhoods where the students lived, given that I had lived nearby. In fact, around the time my research subjects were born, I had been working as a community organizer in the area, and I later worked for a local social service agency before becoming a teacher. I had been inside dozens of homes in the area and had taken countless opportunities over the years to speak with residents about their experiences and the struggles they faced. This personal history, along with my teaching experience at another Bronx high school nearby, provided some immediate context for understanding students' lived experiences and perspectives.

I visited UPHS for about five hours a day, several days a week, as an observer. On my first morning in the building, I met the principal, whom

I will call Ms. Alvarez. (All the names of students, school personnel, and law-enforcement officials are pseudonyms.) Alvarez, in her late thirties, had become the principal of UPHS only a year before. Many people, teachers and students alike, told me that she had brought new energy to the school. She was well liked, a friendly but no-nonsense woman with little time to spare for entertaining the questions of a researcher. She quickly passed me off to the assistant principal of school safety, Mr. Juarez, who brought me to the deans' office.

The deans were the team of about thirteen teachers who had been granted a reduced teaching load in order to take on disciplinary responsibilities. As the center of disciplinary life, their office became a home base for me. I was part outsider, part insider. I connected with the deans as a Bronx teacher, and they frequently included me in their daily banter. Lorraine, the secretary in the deans' office, provided me with a key to the staff bathroom and a locker to keep my things in. Thus, I became part of the deans' daily life, and I believe my background allowed them to develop a good deal of trust when we spoke of disciplinary matters. To that extent, I was an insider. But, unlike the deans, I had no reason to invest in the disciplinary protocols and no responsibilities other than recording my observations in my notebook, so I remained a visitor in their space, and there were occasional moments of hushed conversation in the corner of the room to which I was not privy.

I often spent a couple of hours during my visits to the school moving between the deans' office and the adjoining detention room, where students involved in disciplinary cases were brought. Initially, some students mistook me for a teacher, but that did not quite make sense to them. There were spaces, like the detention room and the cafeteria, where teachers almost never ventured, so I was a curious sight. One day early in the school year, while I was sitting in a seat in the middle of a crowded detention room, the girl next to me leaned over to my desk and asked, in an incredulous tone, "Hey, do you go here?" She just could not fathom who else besides a student would come to sit in that dank room. I also was incredulous. I was more than twice some of the students' age and, in a school where students were overwhelmingly black or Latino/a, I was white. Just as I did on countless other occasions, I introduced myself and explained that I was a researcher studying school discipline and that I was interested in students' perspectives. This was almost always enough to start a conversation with a student.

My earliest relationships with students were established in these two rooms. It was there where I first encountered Carlos. I spotted him slumped over Dean Dempsey's desk, resting his head on his hands. He looked bored, so I introduced myself to him. He had had his ID card taken from him during a confrontation with a police officer and was waiting to get it back. His frustration over the situation and my interest in his experience allowed for an easy flow of conversation. We quickly moved past disciplinary matters. I learned he lived in an apartment with his mother on a block I knew well from my organizing days. He wasn't working at the time, but he helped take care of his grandmother and had worked at a day camp with young children during the previous summer, an experience that had inspired an interest in a career working with children.

I also met other students whom I would get to know very well in the deans' office. Dean Jackson introduced me to Duane and Wanda. They were both frequent visitors to the deans' office, and Dean Jackson correctly suspected that they would be willing and happy to speak with me. One of the police officers, Officer Hoffmann, introduced me to Zack, another student I got to know very well. Duane and Zack were both members of a gang and had notorious reputations in the school. In fact, both boys reported having been initiated into a gang before they had reached age eleven. As a young child, Duane, the son of Jamaican immigrants, had dreamed of being a police officer, but he had become disillusioned with that goal when he started running into trouble with the law. In contrast, Zack, who was Puerto Rican, was born into a family with gang affiliations and never really imagined another life. Both young men frequently got into trouble, but they had also endeared themselves to a number of the deans and even a couple of law-enforcement officials. Similarly, they endeared themselves to me. I was aware of the violence in which they had participated, but as I got to know them, I came to appreciate their warmth and humor and the ease with which they spoke to me. Wanda, a tall, light-skinned black student with a friendly smile, had a history of being involved in disciplinary problems in school and had had a few run-ins with the law but was working hard to "turn things around." When we spoke, Wanda would often bring up her efforts to do well in her classes, but she also discussed her frustrations, such as when she began having difficulties in her math class. All three of these young people seemed to come to the deans' office as much to seek the guidance and company of the caring adults who worked there as they did to "do time" after a disciplinary incident.

Besides the deans' office and the detention room, I also spent considerable time attending classes and hanging out in the hallways, the stairwells, the lunchroom, the library, and the student government office, where I got to know dozens of other students. I met Jennifer in her Global Studies class, which I attended regularly. It turned out that she and Carlos were dating, so I often spent time with the two of them together outside the school. By getting to know students in these various parts of the building, I began to develop a broad sense of the overall student body. I built relationships with the "typical" UPHS students, who were getting by in their classes; the ones frequenting the detention room; and the student leaders. In all, there were six students with whom I developed close ongoing relationships that extended outside the school. There were another two dozen or so with whom I had a friendly ongoing connection—students I would speak with if I bumped into them in the lunchroom or the hallway—some of whom I eventually interviewed more formally. And there were a few hundred others with whom I spoke only once or twice during the school year.

It was sometimes difficult to know what the students thought of me, a white woman whom they immediately assumed was not from the area. I presume that many did not trust me and perhaps did not always tell me the truth. Some probably questioned my motives. One young man whom I met early in the school year and with whom I would occasionally chat when we saw each other, for example, never seemed comfortable enough to give me a formal interview. In fact, he liked to tease me by telling his friends that I was an FBI agent. I do not think he really believed this, but there was an implicit "I don't trust you" in his ongoing joke. Nevertheless, the vast majority of students I met were friendly and appeared happy to share their experiences and present their views. The students sometimes told me that no one seemed to care about their perspectives, and they expressed appreciation that I did. Students also frequently seemed glad to hear how well I knew the Bronx and that I was not scared to walk through their neighborhoods, as they often surmised I would be upon meeting me.

Along with just "hanging out" in the hallways, lunchroom, and offices, I attended twelve different classes, four of them on a regular basis, and I conducted audio-recorded interviews with students, school personnel, and a few law-enforcement officials. In all, I interviewed thirty-three students. I interviewed most students alone, but I also conducted three group interviews. Seven students granted me more than one audio-recorded interview. I had dozens of other lengthy conversations with students during which I took ample notes. I formally interviewed (on audio recording) six deans, two of them twice, but my knowledge of the deans and their perspectives came mainly from spending time with them and interacting with them in more informal ways. Besides the deans, nine teachers granted me interviews. Additionally, I interviewed one department head (assistant principal) and one guidance counselor. Assistant Principal of School Safety Juarez and Principal Alvarez also granted me audio-recorded interviews, as did Officer Hoffmann and the head of the safety agents. I gained further insight into daily life in the school from speaking with school aides. There were three in particular with whom I became friendly: one stationed in a stairwell, another in the lunchroom, and a third in the detention room. Finally, I was able to access school records and occurrence reports that provided written documentation of all disciplinary incidents from the institutional perspective.

One issue that frequently emerged during my conversations with students was the number of summonses they were accumulating. Some were getting summoned to criminal court for incidents that occurred in the school; some were getting summoned to transit court for jumping the subway turnstile or littering in the station. The summons, it turned out, was a fairly prominent theme in many students' lives. So, once students began to share their perspectives with me, it seemed (to me, at least) a logical next step for me to ask those who had gotten summoned to court whether I could accompany them. Invariably, they thought my request was a bit odd. Often a student would shrug his or her shoulders and say, "Sure," but then the student would say something like, "You know, it's really boring." Going to court with students was often an entrée into their lives outside the school. At other times, I would invite a student to do an interview in a local restaurant to establish a connection outside the school. Eventually, I spent time with certain students in their homes and neighborhoods, in the local commercial districts, and in activities like catching a movie or going bowling. I spent many an afternoon in Carlos's living room with him and Jennifer, listening to hip-hop or Reggaeton CDs while Carlos narrated his life through the lyrics of the music, or riding a crosstown bus with Duane while he explained the meaning of the gang-related graffiti on the buildings we passed.

By following several of my research subjects to locations outside the school, I was able to trace ethnographically the relationship between various parts of the students' lives. For example, by going to criminal court with a student who was answering a summons received in school and observing his or her day in court, I was able to document the lived experience of the link between school and court. Likewise, employing a multi-sited strategy allowed me to observe such things as neighborhood conditions, family circumstances, and students' means of negotiating the streets—all of which provided context for making sense of students' in-school experiences. In a sense, by spending time with students across various spaces, I was able to study the relationship between everyday practices and the social and economic forces that are mediated through these various spaces.[5]

Looking back, however, I believe I was not fully cognizant of the harsh realities in which the students often grew up, and I was perhaps a little dismissive of the amount of violence that occurs in the Bronx, an area historically known for having some of the country's poorest and most crime-ridden neighborhoods. In fact, given its almost mythical reputation, I had often found myself defending the Bronx to middle-class whites who lived elsewhere—like the suburban neighborhood some twenty miles away where I grew up—claiming it wasn't really dangerous. I had to confront the fact that although I occupied almost the same physical world as UPHS students, I certainly did not occupy the same social world. I would become painfully aware of this fact at particular moments during my research, such as when Carlos and Jennifer were "jumped" one night by a group of youngsters who knew Jennifer from school—a reminder to me that I, as a white adult, could walk the same streets in relative safety.

One day I argued with Carlos at the entrance to the subway. He was attempting to sneak past the turnstile by manipulating his MetroCard. (A MetroCard is a prepaid subway pass.) I wanted to pay his fare, but he was refusing to let me do so. My anxiety grew as I imagined a police officer approaching. Carlos finally managed to get past the turnstile without paying. Then, looking back at me, he smiled slightly and said, "This is the way we live." He and I had once discussed the term "research subject" and he said he didn't like it, so I suggested he come up with another term. He pondered for a while then decided he preferred the term "living proof." He also liked to think of himself as my "guide." Despite my own familiarity with the Bronx, I still had much to learn from all of my "guides" concerning the social world and the material conditions in which they lived.

Living Proof: Multiple Perspectives and Lived Experiences at UPHS

In this project, ethnography is, in part, an attempt to uncover the voices of those who are most often excluded from public debate: the living proof, as Carlos would say, of what it means to grow up in a poor urban community and attend a "bad" school with punitive disciplinary practices. It is also my goal to describe actions I observed, stories students shared, and conversations we had, and to help make explicit the connections between their lived experiences and social and institutional forces that provide context for those experiences. In the process, I introduce real individuals, although their names have all been changed. There are no composite characters, and the words they speak are their own, with only very minor changes made on occasion to make certain quotations more readable. The perspectives and actions of the students appear most prominently in the pages that follow, but throughout this book I have attempted to include a variety of subjectivities and multiple perspectives in order to provide a nuanced account of life at UPHS.

After those of the students, the perspectives of deans and administrators involved in school discipline were the most central to this study. There is a tendency sometimes, among critical scholars, to view and represent teachers, school administrators, deans, and police officers as "agents of the state" who willingly carry out unjust policies, to the detriment of oppressed groups. However, I had too much empathy for the adults I met to cast them in such a light. After all, I had been one of them—a teacher— and throughout my adult life I had served in several roles as a direct-service provider in a homeless shelter, a mental health agency, and a school, charged with enacting policies designed for "regulating the poor,"[6] so I had insight into the contradictory nature of these roles. As I began the writing process, my goal was to provide a nuanced portrait of these individuals. I recognized that they were working within very difficult circumstances, and virtually all of them, I believe, wanted what was best for the students. My hope is that I have done them justice in the pages that follow by revealing their predicaments and depicting their compassion and complexities.

Classroom teachers offered their perspectives mainly of classroom life. Many teachers spoke eloquently about the difficulties they faced in the classroom. They lamented the underpreparation of their students, and some mentioned the difficult home lives and the impoverished conditions in which they lived. Many also complained that they had to rush through material that often seemed irrelevant to the students in order to prepare them for the New York State Regents Exams (high-stakes standardized tests). Finally, teachers spoke about the problem of classroom disruption, and they usually related it to students' underpreparation and the curricular mandates that failed to engage students. However, teachers did not usually have much to say about the disciplinary process beyond the classroom. This was because most teachers spent very little time outside their classrooms or department offices. I rarely saw a teacher in the hallway when students were changing classes. Thus, teachers had a very limited view of the disciplinary process once students left their rooms, and they had virtually no time to learn about policing practices. Most teachers did express that the school appeared to be more orderly than it had been in the past, and they attributed the changes both to the new principal and to the expanded police presence. The teachers whose perspectives were most informative were those working as deans. These were the teachers who had an insider's view of disciplinary practices as well as a deep understanding of classroom dynamics.

My efforts to gain a police perspective were sometimes frustrated. One September morning, as I was sitting in the deans' office soon after I arrived at the school, several law-enforcement agents ushered a young man into the room. Placing the student's hands on top of an empty desk, one officer began to frisk him while another searched through the student's backpack. I began taking notes—too brazenly, apparently. The police sergeant who was in charge whispered to one of the deans to tell me to put away my notebook. He was definitely not comfortable with my presence. It took a few months to develop a friendly rapport with him. Ultimately, only Officer Hoffmann granted me a formal audio-recorded interview. Several others spoke to me informally on a regular basis. The head of the safety agents (who worked under the auspices of the police department) did not permit his staff to be interviewed. He himself, however, did grant me an interview, which I could only describe as "textbook" in that it seemed to reflect the official discourse of the department regarding the training his agents received and official policy. Despite the limited access I had to officers' and agents' testimonies, their perspectives are not completely missing. I had the opportunity to observe them in action, and some of what I learned came from what I saw.

As for the students, I sought the greatest possible variations in perspective. I spent time with a wide range of students, including many who were doing well academically and were not frequently getting into trouble. Part of my reason for doing so was to seek out an alternative subjectivity to that of the chronic "troublemaker": that of students who might welcome law enforcement in the school. I was aware that initially there had been considerable public support for Mayor Bloomberg's disciplinary agenda, as many parents and students were frustrated by and fearful of the persistent violence and disorder that pervaded their schools. Nevertheless, to my surprise, no matter how hard I tried to represent that alternative perspective, the definitions of the situation reported by academically engaged, compliant students were not very different from those of students who were frequently getting in trouble. That is, regardless of their position in the school, most students had a critique of law enforcement and lived with some level of fear of the police. Even when they recognized that violence and disorder had declined in the school over the previous couple of years, they attributed this primarily to the new principal and her team of deans; although some also conceded that the heavy presence of law enforcement may have made the school safer, they ultimately returned to the view that policing practices were unfair.

Of course, given the focus of the study, I spent the majority of my time observing and speaking with students who were regularly getting into trouble. These were the students who were most affected by the policies yet whose perspectives, I believe, had been most absent from public debates on the issue. Thus, to gain the greatest possible understanding of perceptions of the disciplinary process and policing practices, it was crucial that I excavate these students' perspectives and experiences.

The chapters that follow present a partial yet wide-ranging view of the culture of control that I found inside the school, a culture that reflects our societal culture of control.[7] In chapter 1, I start out by explaining how a school like UPHS, with its heavy police presence, comes into existence. Then, to illuminate how we got to a point where zero tolerance and order-maintenance policing inside certain schools are deemed necessary, I trace the political, economic, and cultural developments of the last several decades and the subsequent punitive turn that has occurred in crime-control policy and urban education reform.

In chapter 2, I illuminate the material and spatial dimensions of the culture of control in which everyday disciplinary rituals took place at UPHS. The school appeared in many ways to be a typical urban public school, but there were marked changes with the installation of the security apparatus—such as the metal detector, cameras, and scanners—and the kinds of interactions the apparatus inspired.

Chapter 3 draws on data derived from a systematic review of occurrence reports, interviews, and observations of student–law-enforcement interactions to illustrate that within the framework of zero tolerance and order maintenance, students tended to get summoned to criminal court for incidents that began with the breaking of a minor school rule, not the law. Cutting class, wearing a hat, or being disruptive did not directly lead a student into the criminal-justice system; the behavior that resulted in an arrest or summons—behavior the school labeled as "insubordination" or "disrespect"—frequently came *after* the student was confronted by law-enforcement officials. At other times, students' behaviors, such as fighting, may have been considered a violation of the law or a crime in any circumstance, but school disciplinarians could have handled these matters internally, as they had in the past. In either case, what became clear was that aggressive policing practices and police surveillance prevailed over other types of responses to disorder and often created a flow of students into criminal court. To illustrate this process, I use a combination of two stories, one of two young men, Terrell and James, getting arrested at school, and another that describes a trip to court with Carlos for a summons he received in school.

In chapter 4, I present a detailed examination of students' contestation of policing practices and their rationales for noncompliance. I show how the process began with the use of order maintenance to establish control, but when students were confronted by law-enforcement officials for minor school infractions or when they were approached in a manner they considered unnecessarily harsh, they sometimes chose not to comply. I describe how their rationales for noncompliance were multifaceted but most often reflected students' assertion of self and their indignation. Wanda, for example, would tell me, "I know my rights!" In this way, students maintained a sense of dignity, but unfortunately, by contesting law enforcement, they inevitably reinforced media images of urban students as incorrigible and took part in the production of themselves as a criminalized class—in need of being policed.

I also illustrate throughout the book that it was not merely the number of police–student confrontations that resulted in arrest, nor summonses and trips to the courthouse that concretized the culture of control. The culture had much to do with the appropriation of a wide range of criminal-justice-oriented disciplinary practices and their supporting discourses. Such practices included hallway stops, sweeps, and getting threatened with a summons.

School officials—administrators and deans, the subject of chapter 5— often accepted order-maintenance policing not necessarily as the *ideal* but as the *norm* and the legitimized response to disruption. Their own more constructive disciplinary strategies were constrained and overshadowed by the prevailing framework as incidents came to be defined by the actions and language of the police. In essence, I observed that school officials relied upon the moral rationales that support aggressive street policing as they struggled to "reach the students" and make sense of the new disciplinary policies while maintaining their identities as educators.

These findings suggest that the relationship between the urban public school and the prison system is not a simple one, nor is there necessarily a direct path from one institution to the other, as the school–prison track or "pipeline" metaphor used by advocates suggests.[8] The school–prison track is a well-documented phenomenon, but what it looks like "on the ground" needs to be illuminated. Students do not generally go from school to prison based on one run-in with the law in the school hallway. Instead, students are subjected to heavy policing in various domains of their lives—in the streets, on public transportation, and, in the case of UPHS, in the hallways of their school. As they accumulate summonses for minor violations of the law and school misbehavior, they ultimately miss court appearances, and warrants are then put out for their arrest. In some cases, students have another confrontation with police in school. At other times, they get caught up in low-level criminal activity on the street, and when it is discovered that they missed a court appearance (after receiving a summons in school), they spend time in jail. So although it is true that disproportionately high numbers of poor and working-class youth of color face prison sentences, it is equally important to note that many more are subjected to low-level forms of penal management without ever doing serious time behind bars.[9] Urban schools like UPHS have come to play a significant role in this phenomenon.

In chapter 6, I examine the most pervasive forms of oppositional behavior in the school—classroom misbehavior, cutting classes, disruption, hat wearing, gambling, and fighting—and document students' perspectives and rationales for their misbehavior. I learned that although students often found themselves entangled with law enforcement and deans as a result of their oppositional behavior, they tacitly sought certain personal benefits through these actions that made them appear more reasonable. Building on Erving Goffman's analysis of human behavior in tightly controlled institutional settings,[10] I demonstrate that within a context of a deep sense of educational and economic exclusion and penal control, students found ways to regain a sense of ownership over the self and develop identities that they could be proud of, to identify as part of a particular community, to manage the violence in their lives (which official policies often did little to mitigate), to make a little money, and to have some fun.

In the tradition of critical school-based ethnography, I sought to understand the nature of the dialectical interplay between students' cultural practices and daily life inside the school, and external political, economic, and cultural forces. Additionally, for me, part of the critical ethnographic endeavor was an attempt to understand the shifting functions of the racially segregated urban public school in the context of high unemployment, pervasive poverty, and what David Garland has called a societal culture of control, and to reconsider the relevance of theories of social reproduction and resistance in schooling within this new context. In chapter 7, I take up this task. My goal is to draw on critical educational theory in conjunction with students' statements concerning their relationship to schooling and the job market and my observations of the microinteractions of everyday life in the school to provide an up-to-date analysis of the significance of reproduction and student resistance. First, I describe how the process of social reproduction at this historical moment has become complicated in new ways. Gone are the days when the bulk of urban students attended large neighborhood high schools with either a college-preparatory or a vocational focus. Instead, urban school restructuring has created a wide range of possibilities. Some students, for example, may receive a college-preparatory education; others may attend schools where they receive preparation for service or technical jobs that require some college. And still others—those who fare the least well in the current system of sorting and tracking—are tracked into schools like UPHS whose primary function appears to be the penal management of excluded youth.

Like reproduction, the notion of oppositional behavior as resistance also needs to be placed in the current context. For one thing, low-income black and Latino/a students face more serious repercussions than ever before for their oppositional behavior in school. That is, when they misbehave, they participate in the production of themselves as a criminal-ized class. In addition, in light of my findings, I contend that we can no longer simply take note of the social critique embedded in oppositional behavior, and we need to move beyond a resistance framework in which oppositional behavior is understood, and perhaps celebrated, for its politi-cal implications. I argue that it is more useful to examine microlevel dy-namics of oppositional behavior and the ways young people make sense of it within the changed context—or, more specifically, in the context of a deep sense of economic and educational exclusion and penal manage-ment. My findings reveal, first, that students did not view their opposi-tional behavior as a wholesale rejection of schooling (as some scholars have suggested), and second, that their behaviors brought certain social and psychological benefits, despite the heavy price they paid.

In the Conclusion, I argue that an analysis of oppositional behavior from students' perspectives and at the micro level can serve as a diagnostic of institutional practices and can reveal the shortcomings of current pol-icy. Moreover, implicit in a description of students' experiences and per-spectives is a vision of alternative possibilities. The possibilities become clear when we pay close attention to the people most affected by the poli-cies and practices.

CHAPTER 1

How the Police Took Over School Discipline

From Policies of Inclusion to Punishment and Exclusion

IN 2007, IN AVON PARK, FLORIDA, six-year-old Desre'e Watson, who was black, had a tantrum in her kindergarten classroom. As children generally do during a tantrum, she cried, kicked, screamed, and became even more upset when the adults present tried to physically constrain her. School officials opted to call the police. When Desre'e saw the police, she cowered under a table in fright, but the officers quickly managed to grab her and pull her out of her hiding spot. Because her tiny wrists were too small for the adult-sized handcuffs, the cops placed the cuffs on her biceps. She was taken to central booking at the county jail and fingerprinted. Little Desre'e posed for mug shots and was charged with battery on a school official, disruption of a school function, and resisting arrest.[1] In Los Angeles that same year, a sixteen-year-old was arrested in her school lunchroom for dropping a piece of birthday cake and failing to clean it up to the satisfaction of the school safety officer. During the arrest, a security guard forced the girl's head onto a desk and broke her wrist.[2]

The following year, five-year-old Dennis Rivera from Queens, New York, who suffered from speech problems, asthma, and attention deficit disorder, was handcuffed by police and taken to a psychiatric ward at a local hospital after having a tantrum at school.[3] In Florida, a schoolboy was arrested for continually passing gas and turning off his classmates' computers.[4]

In 2009, on the South Side of Chicago, twenty-five children between the ages of eleven and fifteen at a predominantly black middle school were arrested for "reckless conduct" for participating in a food fight in the school cafeteria. Newspapers reported that some students spent eight hours in jail after being fingerprinted and having their mug shots taken.[5] That same year, Texas newspapers reported two incidents—one that took place in a Dallas school and the other in an El Paso school—in which boys with Asperger's syndrome were charged with misdemeanors and fined. Their offense? Cursing.[6]

Such news stories from around the country may represent the most shocking incidents of zero tolerance at its worst, but at the same time they speak to the nation's acquiescence to police intervention as a response to normal student misbehavior. At UPHS, however, the arrests of youngsters for misbehavior aren't usually considered newsworthy. In a school where law-enforcement officials patrol the hallways, arrests occur too frequently for every incident to make the news. The consistently heavy police presence and the resulting culture of control that I encountered at UPHS, in fact, may represent an extreme—a sort of "perfect storm"—of social forces and policy decisions that helped to create the precinct, or even prison, atmosphere. Only schools with similar profiles—high rates of racial segregation and poverty, an inner-city location, low levels of academic performance, and a commitment to order-maintenance policing—are likely to take on, with the same intensity, the characteristics of a penal institution. Nevertheless, the nation's collective sentiments about crime and safety that have led to the culture of control at UPHS are pervasive. These sentiments drive national policy and shape the experiences of schoolchildren around the country, children like six-year-old Desre'e Watson, five-year-old Dennis Rivera, and the twelve-year-old in Chicago who threw a hamburger at his classmate.

How did we come to a place where it seems reasonable, perhaps even necessary, to handcuff and fingerprint a six-year-old? Why have we allowed children with special needs and disproportionately high numbers of children of color to experience the fullest impact of such punitive disciplinary practices? Finally, what has led to the existence of urban schools like UPHS, where our national obsession with criminal-justice disciplinary control of black and Latino/a youth has become so manifest? These are not simple questions to answer. To understand fully how we got to where we are, it is necessary to take a step back and examine the social-historical forces that have given rise to the widespread use of zero-tolerance approaches, school-based police intervention, and the existence of heavily policed schools like UPHS.

Where We Came From: Public Schools and Crime Control in the Industrial Era

The current trends in punitive school discipline, and social policy more generally, are not an entirely new phenomenon. Historically, numerous scholars have described public schools, as well as prisons, as repressive institutions.[7] The drive toward institutionalization that began in the latter half of the nineteenth century, through the prison system and the establishment of public schools, was largely a response to the massive influx of poor immigrants into U.S. cities, an attempt to instill social order by disciplining and containing "the dangerous classes."[8] Prisons were generally horrid places, and incarcerated blacks suffered some of the most brutal treatment. Likewise, public schools were often extremely regimented and harsh places. In the 1930s, sociologist Willard Waller described schools as despotisms.[9] Historian Michael Katz wrote about early industrial public schools before the establishment of the juvenile-justice system, finding they were not simply institutions charged with disciplining young people from the working classes but also, in some cases, both educational and involuntary custodial facilities for children of the poor who were deemed incorrigible.[10]

Yet, despite the repressive elements of schools and prisons, throughout the industrial era these institutions operated largely under an ethos of students' and prisoners' inclusion into society, at least for the majority of working-class immigrants hailing from Europe, for whom public schools offered vocational training and the possibility of social mobility. UPHS, from its inception in the 1910s through the 1950s, fit this description.

At the same time, from the early industrial era to the 1970s, the criminal-justice system was premised on what David Garland terms penal-welfarism, a paradigm that views the criminal offender as economically and socially disadvantaged and emphasizes individual treatment, social welfare, and reintegration into civil society.[11] Thus, both school and prison sought to preserve social cohesion by preparing the so-called dangerous classes to be productive members of what was then a growing labor market. Black men, women, and children, of course, did not benefit in the same ways as their white counterparts from the benevolent intentions of schools and the rehabilitative goals of prisons. Indeed, blacks were initially entirely excluded from schooling and then were segregated in schools with the poorest resources and limited to nonacademic tracks.[12] Nevertheless, the integrative goals of schools and prisons would eventually extend to blacks and other people of color. The social movements of the 1950s and '60s brought the ethos of inclusion to its height, during which time the social and economic advancement of people of color was finally addressed. During this liberal period, prisons were used relatively discriminately and emphasized drug treatment, job training, and, in some cases, opportunities to pursue higher education in order to prepare individuals for reintegration into society. At the same time, schools were experiencing a transformation through such reforms of inclusion as open college admissions, bilingual education, and the implementation of racial desegregation plans. But within a decade or so, policies of inclusion were fiercely challenged and began to lose sway. A new paradigm was about to emerge in both education and criminal justice.

Where We Are: The Punitive Turn in Social Policy

Crime Control

Today (as of 2010), the United States has the highest incarceration rates in the world. There are 2.3 million people in the United States in prison—a 500 percent increase over the past thirty years. This dramatic increase in imprisonment has had its greatest impact on poor black men and other people of color. One in ten black men between the ages of twenty-five and twenty-nine is behind bars. For Latinos in the same age group, the ratio is one in twenty-six, and for white men, one in sixty-three.[13] High school dropouts are particularly vulnerable. Some 60 percent of black male high school dropouts born in the late 1960s served time in prison by the end of the 1990s—a rate four times higher than that of their college-educated counterparts.[14] David Garland and other scholars have used the term "mass imprisonment" to describe this phenomenon. The term is meant to denote incarceration rates that are markedly above the historical and comparative norm for societies like the United States, as well as the demographic concentration and systemic imprisonment of whole groups of people.

The most direct cause for the rise in incarceration rates was the punitive turn in sentencing and parole policies, including longer and more fixed prison sentences, the incarceration of increased numbers of nonviolent offenders under new drug laws, and more stringent parole regulations. These policy changes, however, did not come about in a vacuum. They were rooted in the massive transformations of the political economy that have occurred over the last several decades. In the postwar decades, U.S. cities were depleted of vital economic resources and opportunities through deindustrialization, corporate and manufacturing relocations abroad, and the growth of low-wage service industries.[15] The national fiscal crisis of the 1970s compounded problems, leaving cities like New York in dire economic circumstances.

These economic shifts have translated into the loss of thousands of jobs in many U.S. cities and millions in total. Jobs in the service industries have increased; however, they have not made up for lost manufacturing jobs in either number or wages. Nationally, unemployment rose and real wages have decreased, disproportionately affecting blacks and Latinos/as. Although the national economy and employment rates have taken more positive turns in recent decades, unemployment and underemployment have remained persistently high in inner-city neighborhoods. The financial crisis of 2009 also added to already high rates of joblessness. The Bronx, home of UPHS, has the highest unemployment rates and lowest reported incomes in New York City. Additionally, the borough includes some of the poorest districts in the entire country.[16] There is significant empirical evidence of a strong correlation between living in impoverished areas and the increased likelihood of incarceration,[17] so with circumstances as they are in the Bronx, it is not surprising that the most northern borough of New York City has disproportionately high rates of juvenile and adult incarceration.

Throughout the 1970s and 1980s, inner-city neighborhoods were ravaged by the changes in the economy, deep cuts in social services, a growing drug trade, and the subsequent rise in street violence. In the mid-1980s, I observed the devastation in the Bronx firsthand as an undergraduate at Fordham University. The homeless population was rapidly growing, as was the influx of crack cocaine into the community.

Conservative political discourses have blamed urban plight on poor blacks and other people of color. In the 1980s, Charles Murray, for example, was a vocal public critic of New Deal policies that targeted structural sources of poverty.[18] He, along with many other conservatives, contended that such policies fostered a "culture of poverty" characterized by lack of self-respect and responsibility. In a similar vein, Ronald Reagan's rhetoric attacked both liberal politicians who were "soft on crime" and "undeserving welfare recipients" (read: poor black women) for the "breakdown of law and order." These economic circumstances and political and public discourses inspired a new way of thinking about crime and punishment, what Garland calls criminologies of "the dangerous other."[19] In this framework, prison has become the commonsense solution to the social problems of the time, no matter what the cost. And as blame has been placed on poor blacks and other people of color, the old notions of rehabilitation and integration of economically marginalized individuals have been replaced by the more compelling themes of punishment and exclusion. As the new criminologies of the dangerous other began to shape crime policy in the early 1980s, the prison population soared among urban communities of color.

Throughout the last twenty years, the U.S. prison population has remained at unprecedented levels. However, the neoliberal language of "cost-benefit" and "fiscal responsibility" has influenced another strand of thinking within the criminal-justice system: what Garland refers to as "criminologies of everyday life." In an effort to create an efficient and less expensive system, these criminologies, which view crime as a normal and inevitable part of society, emphasize preventive measures and the extension of crime-control responsibilities beyond the boundaries of the prison system and into the streets and institutions of civil society.[20]

Aggressive order-maintenance street policing, Garland argues, has obvious affinities with criminologies of everyday life. Order maintenance, as I described in the Introduction, involves a heavy police presence and the cracking down on low-level violations of the law and general disorder in targeted neighborhoods.[21] The approach is premised on the "broken windows" theory, according to which serious crime is a result of social and physical disorder in neighborhoods. Therefore, according to the theory, if police officers focus on low-level violations of the law, such as fare evasion in the subway, and "quality of life" offenses, such as graffiti or loitering, they can have a significant impact on bringing down overall crime rates. In the early 1990s, the New York City Police Department, a leader in order maintenance, began huge neighborhood policing campaigns to "take back the streets," apparently from the criminal element that had been wreaking havoc. Neighborhoods with concentrated poverty, the subways, and gentrifying residential and commercial districts all became prime locations for the implementation of order maintenance. Critics, however, argued that the new tactics amounted to a war on the poor, on the growing

numbers of chronically unemployed city residents, and on those working in the informal economy: car-window washers, street vendors, homeless individuals, and young people with nowhere to go.[22] Some academics
were also critical of the new initiatives, noting that aggressive street policing had had much less effect on lowering crime rates than its proponents
claimed.[23]

About a decade after the adult prison population soared, the juvenile
prison population followed in the same direction, in part as a response
to growing youth gun violence throughout the 1980s. Still, rates of youth
gun violence peaked in 1993 and remained level throughout much of the
next decade, yet youth incarceration rates for nonviolent offenses rose
considerably.[24] Indeed, the majority of youth in custody today are doing
time for nonviolent offenses.[25] The increased use of juvenile incarceration
has been supported by an increasingly retributive attitude toward urban
youth reflected in slogans such as "Adult time for adult crime" and John
DiIulio's now-notorious proclamation that we have a new breed of "superpredator" in our midst—black and Latino city youth.[26] This occurred, as
Pedro Noguera points out, despite the fact that urban youth have no control over society's disinvestment in education, social services, and job creation, nor over the influx of guns and drugs into their neighborhoods.[27]

Not surprisingly, black and Latino/a youth, especially boys, have been
disproportionately affected by our growing reliance on incarceration. National data show, for example, that youth of color, especially black boys,
are more likely to do time than their white counterparts for the same offense; they tend to remain in the system longer; and they are more likely
to be waived to adult court and thus sent to adult prisons.[28] In New York
City, there is similar evidence of racial disparity.[29] Additionally, a disproportionately high number of incarcerated youth in New York City come
from the poorest neighborhoods, providing further evidence of a correlation between living in areas of concentrated poverty and increased
chances of incarceration.[30] The youth prison across the street from the
school where I taught—a gleaming white edifice rising out of the rubble
and decay of the South Bronx—stood as testimony to this new investment
in locking up youth of color in poor urban neighborhoods.

Bringing about the rise in juvenile incarceration were a host of tougher
crime-control laws aimed at urban youth, for example, curfews, strict
truancy laws, and antigang loitering ordinances. Order maintenance, although not always explicitly linked to juvenile-justice policy, has become

a key component in the enforcement of the new laws and, more generally, in the management of urban youth. On a daily basis, UPHS students, like other youngsters living in similar neighborhoods, find themselves caught up in police sweeps in front of and near their school building. They are picked up during school hours for truancy, shooed away from street corners and out of parks after dusk, and summoned to court for loitering. They are also stopped and frisked by police more often than their white counterparts, even when there is only a negligible level of suspicion.[31]

In short, we have witnessed political and economic transformations that have inspired a punitive turn in crime-control policies: a dramatic rise in the prison population and new forms of aggressive street policing. These trends have had a particularly negative impact on low-income black and Latino/a youth living in depleted urban communities with few resources and bleak job prospects. At the dawn of zero-tolerance school discipline, popular political discourses had already begun to demonize the young urban "superpredator." Additionally, crime-control policies aimed at urban youth—drug laws, truancy laws, curfews, loitering ordinances, and order maintenance—became more punitive. As policy makers continued to expand their focus on the control of urban youth, the next logical target was the hallways of racially segregated, poorly performing urban schools.

Urban Public School Reform and School Discipline

"Tough on crime" policies, particularly the popular order maintenance, are the most direct precursors to punitive school discipline. Yet there has been a long history of administrative practices in urban school districts that have helped to set the conditions for violence and disruption in certain schools and, subsequently, the perceived need for zero tolerance and order-maintenance policing in these schools. Additionally, national education reform, influenced by the same set of ideological forces as crime-control policy, has created a context conducive to the appropriation of zero-tolerance school discipline. In urban districts, education reform and restructuring have often worked hand in hand with an expanded form of zero tolerance that relies heavily on the use of law enforcement.

Just as we have observed in the field of crime control, education policy over the last few decades has been influenced by both neoconservative and neoliberal agendas. Michael Apple argues that although the neoliberal and the neoconservative agendas are distinct, recent policy and school restructuring initiatives have satisfied both. The neoliberal project emphasizes aligning the curriculum with economic exigencies and labor-market needs. Additionally, there is a push toward privatization and the adoption of a corporate logic dedicated to increasing productivity while minimizing spending. Proponents of such market-based reforms view the creation of competition through choice as the remedy for low-performing urban schools, and standardized high-stakes testing becomes the means by which success is measured. At the same time, neoconservatives have concerned themselves with issues of pedagogy and curriculum, calling for tighter controls on what is taught. For conservatives, Apple contends, standardized high-stakes testing provides the means for establishing what constitutes official knowledge.[32]

The landmark 1983 report *A Nation at Risk*, commissioned by the Reagan administration, was a springboard for contemporary U.S. school reform. In tough (some would say alarmist) language, it presented a dire warning that the U.S. economy would be in peril if the nation did not dramatically improve academic standards and teacher quality. Within the context of this heightened sense of urgency to improve education, conservatives attacked multicultural education and pushed for a return of the Western canon and a "back to the basics" curriculum. Vouchers were also politically popular at the time, the first sign of a trend toward market-based reforms.

The Clinton administration brought market-based school reforms to new heights. In her thoughtful critique of our current accountability-and-testing regime, educational historian Diane Ravitch explains how the Clinton administration championed a "third way," a policy agenda that was informed by neither orthodox left policy nor orthodox right policy.[33] Schools were to be restructured through market reforms. Competition would be created through choice so that good schools, it was believed, would proliferate, and bad schools would close down under market forces. All the while, the private sector would have an increasing hand in running schools, to the detriment of public education. Additionally, the Goals 2000 program provided federal money for states to develop their own standards, but, as Ravitch explains, developing meaningful curricular standards that were acceptable by both sides of the political spectrum became a nearly impossible task. What was initially intended to be a focus on the creation of rigorous academic standards became an obsession with standardized testing.[34]

In 2001, George W. Bush's No Child Left Behind initiative (NCLB) was passed. The bill, which Ravitch describes as a policy bereft of any educational ideas and lacking any vision other than testing of math and reading, ensured that education policy would remain fixated on accountability and high-stakes testing—something all states were required to implement.[35] NCLB provides perhaps the most explicit example of how education and punitive crime-control policies have been driven by the same ideological forces: implicit blame is placed on those with the weakest performance. Schools in poor urban communities thus become a prime target. Policy makers have gotten tough and hold "out-of-control" students and their teachers accountable. And the consequences for continued failure are going to be severe. For instance, Ravitch, in a chapter in her latest book entitled "NCLB: Measure and Punish," describes how NCLB requires that poorly performing schools raise standardized test scores or face a host of progressively more punitive sanctions and ultimately close down.[36] (Individual failing students, of course, are denied a diploma.) This system of accountability and testing, besides being punitive, opened the door for massive restructuring and the creation of new "schools of choice," often in the form of privately run charter schools.

The case of New York City serves as an illustrative example of a long history of administrative practices that led to current circumstances. Of course, it is not surprising that poorly performing (and disorderly) schools often exist in the most economically depressed areas, serving students from poor families. Indeed, an abundance of research illustrates the positive relationship between socioeconomic status and academic achievement.[37] In New York, an informal system of sorting and tracking has also led to high concentrations of the most structurally marginalized and academically alienated students in particular schools. Such schools tend to be the most poorly funded, with the fewest offerings of college-preparatory classes.[38] Together, such factors help set the conditions under which school disorder and violence flourish.

Alvarez, the principal of UPHS, believed that over time certain schools in the system became repositories for the most underprepared, most vulnerable youth, whereas others closed their doors to troubled youth. The latter group of schools, she maintained, also frequently were better resourced than the former—a contention that was substantiated in a 2005 report by the Drum Major Institute. Sitting in her office with me one day, Alvarez explained, "Some schools historically have been given the opportunity to be more selective with their kids and have had the backing of several key members, whether they're from the DOE [Department of Education] or the community, which has both financially [supported those schools] and provid[ed] resources that they need, [whereas] other schools have just been totally abandoned and have not received that support and have been dumping grounds not just for students but for faculty and administrators who were incompetent. 'Just put them in that school and we'll deal with it later on.'" I had developed a similar perspective myself while teaching in the South Bronx. I used to think of the school where I worked as one of the forgotten ones. It was as if no one in the administration remembered we even existed, with our broken windows that didn't open and pathetic selection of outdated books.

As with other highly policed schools in the city, UPHS was almost entirely racially segregated, and the number of students living in poverty was significantly higher than the poverty rate in the surrounding community, suggesting that through a system of sorting and tracking, the most economically disadvantaged students in the borough of the Bronx were concentrated in this and similar schools.[39] Additionally, UPHS, along with the other most highly policed schools in the city, had disproportionately high numbers of students with poor academic records, students with special needs, students with disciplinary records, and formerly incarcerated students.[40] It is really no wonder, then, that these schools would have bad reputations and be perceived as places in need of tight police control. This especially holds true in places where city officials have been quick to credit order-maintenance street policing for "cleaning up the streets."

When New York City mayor Bloomberg first took office, in 2002, a host of public high schools all over the city resembled UPHS; some were worse off than others in performance and rates of disorder. Taking control over the school system, Bloomberg quickly put into motion sweeping changes: mandated instructional programs in reading and math; an ongoing, massive governance restructuring; and, most relevant to this analysis, a high school restructuring plan. The new, tougher disciplinary policies were actually an extension of what the previous administration had started when, in 1998, then-mayor Giuliani placed school discipline under the auspices of the New York City Police Department. In the new context, tough school discipline would support the educational reforms and restructuring schemes being implemented.

The move toward punitive school discipline had begun several years before the commencement of Bloomberg's first term. On the national level, zero-tolerance school discipline was first instituted in the mid-1990s, after a number of isolated school shootings in predominantly white suburban schools, as well as high rates of youth gun violence in urban areas throughout the 1980s and early 1990s, spurred a heightened national focus on school violence and discipline. With the burgeoning criminal- and juvenile-justice systems as a backdrop, the Clinton administration passed the 1994 federal Gun-Free Schools Act. The act ushered in a new era of school discipline. "Zero tolerance," a term appropriated from the criminal-justice system, took an aggressive stance against guns and drugs in schools. It called for swift punishment in the form of suspension, expulsion, and, at times, police intervention for all violators. Federal funding became contingent on states' adoption of a zero-tolerance policy, so it is now used widely, in some form, throughout the United States. State and local versions of zero tolerance have often extended the federal legislation by broadening the definition of "weapon" to include any sharp or potentially dangerous object and such things as a butter knife innocently stowed inside a lunch box. Additionally, district-level zero-tolerance policies around the country have been broadened so that today even students who commit small infractions may be subject to the consequences of zero tolerance.[41]

Since its implementation some fifteen years ago, zero-tolerance school discipline has been widely critiqued for its exclusionary practices. For example, the U.S. Department of Education projected that there were almost 250,000 more students suspended out-of-school in 2006–2007 than there were during the 2002–2003 school year. In Texas alone, under zero tolerance, suspensions increased by 43 percent within five years, and during the 2007–2008 school year, there were more than 128,000 referrals of students to alternative disciplinary schools. In another shocking statistic, 40 percent of ninth graders in Milwaukee public schools were suspended during the 2006–2007 school year.[42] Yet, although the negative consequences of zero tolerance have been widespread, the policies have played out differently across racial, class, and geographic contexts.

It has been shown that zero-tolerance school discipline disproportionately targets students with special needs and black and Latino/a students, especially boys.[43] Research shows that zero tolerance's use of exclusionary punishment increases the likelihood of dropping out, a problem that is disconcertingly high among black and Latino/a students.[44] Additionally, the overrepresentation of students of color in disciplinary cases, combined with zero tolerance's reliance on suspensions and expulsions, appears to contribute to the racial achievement gap.[45] But perhaps the most troubling aspect of zero tolerance is its reliance on police intervention for school infractions that traditionally were handled by school personnel. The increased use of police intervention under zero tolerance has created a flow of students—disproportionately students of color—into the criminal- and juvenile-justice systems,[46] a development which, like suspension and expulsion, increases a student's chances of dropping out of school.[47] In urban districts, where there are large concentrations of low-income students of color, control has become a major theme, and zero tolerance often includes some kind of formal partnership with local law enforcement.

As with street-based order-maintenance policing, New York City has been a leader in the use of school-based order maintenance. Mayor Bloomberg has made school discipline a major part of his educational agenda, and he has borrowed heavily from the practices and discourse of the previous mayor, Rudolph Giuliani, who championed the city's aggressive street-policing campaigns popularized in the 1990s. As a major part of his plan, Bloomberg instituted the Impact Schools Initiative. A computerized database known as SchoolSafe, which was modeled after New York City's crime-tracking system, CompStat, was used to identify the schools with the highest rates of criminal incidents. These schools were then labeled "high-impact" schools. A School Safety Taskforce of about 200 police officers was established, and these officers were distributed among the high-impact schools. Additionally, these schools received extra security agents, who since 1998 have worked directly under the auspices of the police department. As of 2008, more than 5,000 school safety agents have been hired by the New York City Police Department, up from 1,600 in 1998, the year the police department took control of school discipline.[48]

A December 2003 press release from Mayor Bloomberg and then–schools chancellor Joel Klein, which called for a "cultural transformation" in New York City schools, announced the Impact Schools Initiative. Initially, twelve schools were chosen for the Impact program. In local newspapers, they were dubbed "the dirty dozen," and UPHS was on the list. Explicitly adopting the language of the NYPD policing programs, the release said, "These 'Impact Schools' will receive targeted deployment of school safety agents and [double the number of] police officers to prevent criminal behavior. . . . School-based police officers will report to school safety sergeants in local precincts in order to forge closer ties between Impact schools and local precincts." The release went on to say, "The 'broken windows' approach to crime fighting will also be applied. Just as the NYPD has successfully preempted major crimes by paying close attention to areas with frequent minor quality of life offenses, the new school safety plan will focus on areas where there is frequent disorderly behavior, such as cursing or taunting other students."[49]

The media initially played a significant role in the construction of certain public schools as very scary places in need of heavy policing. In the months preceding the implementation of the policing program, several articles in local newspapers used provocative headlines, such as "Security Cams to Watch Horror Highs," "Crackdown at Mayhem High," "Thugs Run Wild in Troubled HS," and "Stop the Violence: Fearful Teachers Protest Students' Reign of Terror."[50] UPHS received much of the media's attention, largely because of two school stabbings and an attack on a teacher, incidents which occurred in the years before my study.

Although everyone was well aware of the violence that had occurred at UPHS and its continuing problems, I quickly learned that students and teachers alike were often defensive when it came to the reputation of their school. Students would often ask me why the media didn't report the good things. One particularly critical teacher asked, "Why don't [the media] ever focus on the lack of resources here or the way we set students up to fail?" Principal Alvarez told me during one of our first meetings that, on more than one occasion during the previous year, she found reporters from local papers and a Fox News correspondent perched on the curb in front of the building, hungry for a horrifying story from inside "the blackboard jungle." She told me that she would go outside to meet the reporters and would joke with them that the borough president must be doing a phenomenal job if camping in front of a school was the most productive use of the reporters' time. As she spoke, I could imagine the sharply dressed, always-dignified principal, who was sensitive to the media's depiction of her school and her students, descending the front steps to shoo the vultures away.

The Impact Schools Initiative worked in conjunction with and supported Bloomberg's sweeping reform-and-restructuring plan. In fact, it was presented as a first step or an auxiliary plan that would facilitate education reform. The media mogul–turned–politician mayor fully embraced the business model of education reform, with accountability, testing, and choice driving his agenda. One of his major goals was to close down large, low-performing traditional high schools and create schools of "choice." Although there has been a growing number of privately run charter schools in New York, the creation of small, theme-based schools, until recently, has played an even larger role in the restructuring.[51] Under Mayor Bloomberg and then–Schools Chancellor Klein, virtually every low-performing high school in the city has been broken up into smaller, theme-based schools. During the time I spent at UPHS, the school was transitioning into smaller schools. The entire second floor of the building housed five different schools, each with its own director and staff. Small schools—so named for their limited number of students—are publicly run schools that are affiliated with some outside entity, such as a community-based organization or institution. Many of these schools, based on their affiliation, have some career-oriented theme so that, in theory, students attending a particular small school will be prepared for a particular segment of the labor market. At UPHS, a military-themed school and a health-careers-themed school were established, for example.

Charter schools and small schools in New York City appear to have had a modicum of success, but their potential for transforming education more broadly is still unknown. Some appear to offer higher-quality educational experiences than the traditional neighborhood public schools, and some probably create opportunities for certain students from low-income families who otherwise would be stuck in a failing school. Small schools, in particular, offer great promise. Significant research demonstrates that small schools tend to provide better learning environments than large schools, and foster teacher–student relationships and lower rates of conflict and violence.[52] But while conducting my fieldwork, I came to think of my project as an examination of the flip side, or rather the underside, of the promising (yet problematic in its implementation) small-schools movement. Proclamations of widespread success have been misleading.

One issue overshadowed by the mayor's claims of success is whether or not small schools that have shown improvement are really serving the same population as their large-school predecessors. For example, when UPHS surrendered the last of its building space to small schools (two years after I completed my fieldwork), educators boasted that the students attending the new small schools at the UPHS "campus" showed improved reading scores. (More than 80 percent of the incoming freshmen at the old UPHS read at the level of fourth grade or below.) However, a local newspaper reported that the small schools at the new UPHS campus were actually admitting cohorts of freshmen with reading scores above those of previous incoming freshmen who attended UPHS. In essence, then, the "success" of the new small schools may have been simply a result of new admission practices. Moreover, there are still children entering high school with lower reading scores than those of previous UPHS students, and as more and more of these children populate the new small schools and the small-school population becomes more representative of the system as a whole, graduation rates and attendance will decline.[53]

The proliferation of small schools and charters does not, in itself, set the context for the establishment of zero tolerance and school-based policing. Rather, the restructuring process has led to uneven and unequal outcomes in an already highly stratified system and has undermined other possible reforms that could be more effective. Some small schools (and charter schools) are well resourced, have strong academic programs, and have managed to create a culture of nonviolence and a sense of community without a heavy police presence. Many others, though, have not experienced such a positive transformation. Without an explicit focus on added resources, pedagogy, and social and academic supports, these schools often reproduce the problems found in larger schools, only with more administrators and new tensions over space and resources shared among different schools in the same buildings. In the midst of all this reorganization, the considerable media attention placed on the "trouble spots" has lent legitimacy to zero tolerance and school-based policing.

The expanded form of zero tolerance that we find in New York was touted as the initial means of gaining control over troubled schools, but the policies have remained in place with the apparent goal of maintaining order in newly "reformed" schools and targeting regular "hot spots." The appeal of school-based order maintenance to reformers (besides being in sync with the tough discourses and policies of the educational reforms) is that, like its street-based counterpart, it is designed to be mobile, to target newly troubled as well as persistently troubled areas. So, if a particular school shows signs of disorder or encounters a publicized incident of violence, law enforcement is ready to move in to protect the reform efforts. This process has also helped to keep media attention on "unruly youth," rather than the lack of any substantive educational and enrichment plan, as the source of problems in schools.

In New York, particularly in the lowest-income areas, "choice" is undermined by many factors, including an extremely confusing school-grading system,[54] a dearth of "good" options, institutional push-out practices that simply refer struggling or overage students to GED programs,[55] and a complicated system of district-wide sorting and tracking. In my experience in the Bronx as a teacher, a neighbor, and a researcher, I have found that students and their parents do not often actively pursue opting out of their neighborhood high school in search of a better one. Students are frequently shuffled around to different schools, placed in a suspension center, or referred to a GED program, but there is rarely much choice involved. The experience of one of my research subjects, Jennifer, serves as an example. Jennifer, who was fifteen when I met her, dreamed of being a doctor and so applied to the small school with a health-careers focus. At the time, Jennifer was living in a foster home several miles from the school, because of her mother's chronic illness and frequent hospitalizations. So, at fifteen, she was left to negotiate the system of choice by herself. This didn't faze Jennifer at all. She was accustomed to doing things on her own, given that her father had died when she was nine and her mother was ill, but she told me that she was disappointed in the outcome of her efforts. She had spoken to her guidance counselor and expressed her wishes but was told there was no room in the health-themed school. She was placed on the list of prospective students for another small school that was to open the following year, one with a focus on law enforcement. Jennifer didn't give the possibility of attending a law-enforcement academy much thought, as her hope was to transfer out of UPHS the coming year to attend a small school closer to where she had been placed in foster care.

Some parents who lived in the immediate vicinity of UPHS did manage to negotiate for their children admission into a new small school or another neighborhood high school with a better reputation, but more often, students from other zones would be sent to UPHS because they had some kind of problem in their neighborhood schools, such as involvement in a bullying incident. Students released from custodial institutions and not accepted by their neighborhood schools would likewise be admitted to UPHS.

Another central aspect of contemporary school reform that interacts with school discipline is the use of high-stakes testing and its subsequent impact on classroom practice. Research demonstrates that high-stakes testing narrows the curriculum, fosters teacher-centered instruction, and tends to undermine culturally relevant teaching.[56] But perhaps the most troubling aspect of high-stakes testing is the attention it draws away from enrichment, relevance, and actual high standards. Testing has become the reform itself rather than simply one means of measuring achievement; it has become, in most cases, the sole measure of achievement.

In New York State, high-stakes testing in high schools comes in the form of the New York State Regents Exams. The Regents Exams became required for high school graduation while I was teaching high school ESL in the late 1990s. Months before the exams, my colleagues and I were directed to focus solely on test preparation. I observed firsthand the negative repercussions of test prep. In the case of the English–language arts exam, we quickly learned that it was possible to teach the students how to pass; the result was boring classes and increasingly nervous and frustrated students who could manage to meet the minimum grade required for graduation even with relatively low levels of English proficiency and virtually no development of their critical-thinking skills.

At UPHS, teachers spoke candidly about their belief that high-stakes testing influenced their teaching practices to the detriment of engaging, sound pedagogy. When asked about the exams, Ms. Jenkins, an English–language arts teacher, said, "We're kind of forced to teach to the test."

"So would you say it has more of a negative or positive impact, or both?" I asked.

"Realistically, if the kids really do learn the skills that are necessary to pass the Regents, those are good skills. I mean, I'm not against that, but I think that the emphasis [on exam preparation] is a kind of negative thing for them to get through. They actually don't get an education. They get prepared to take the Regents. So they don't leave high school being enlightened about the world and having an opinion about what goes on in the world and about policy and about how [they] could make [their] neighborhood different."

Mr. Garvey, a history teacher, lamented that there was just far too much material on which students could be tested, which left no time to go into any depth on a single topic—a common critique of high-stakes testing. He said of the exams, "They'll ask questions on the 1930s, but I can't spend much time on it. I mean, just jazz itself, right? I mean, I think that would be very interesting for the kids. We could spend a few days listening to some jazz recordings. But there's no way to do that because I'm expected to at least get up to the Reagan years. . . . You could spend weeks on this, but there's [only] going to be maybe two or three questions on the Regents [on this period,] so you can't spend weeks on one topic."

Overall, I observed varying levels of classroom engagement at UPHS, but for the most part engagement was low. On one occasion, for example, I attended a science class where students became enthralled in dissecting rats, but I also attended other classes where most students chatted or dozed over worksheets they were required to do so that the teacher could ensure comprehension after some dry reading. In some classes, I witnessed lively discussion in which connections were made between students' lives and course content, but I attended many others where teachers plowed through the curriculum using a teacher-centered approach, losing students' attention along the way for the sake of covering all the material that might appear on the exam, in the same way that Mr. Garvey attempted in his mad dash to get to the Reagan years.

Teaching toward the test was certainly not the only problem inside UPHS classrooms. Students were often underprepared or stressed out or otherwise distracted; resources were limited; content often seemed irrelevant and decontextualized; and the quality of teaching varied from what I would describe as valiant under the circumstances to abysmal. Yet even though there are multiple factors leading to student disengagement, it is high-stakes testing that has become the cornerstone of school reform, detracting from the kinds of innovation and classroom transformations needed to reengage alienated students.

Alienating classroom experiences were not the sole source of misbehavior and violence, of course. However, they played a central role in the creation of a flow of students out of classrooms and into the hallways, giving local educational policy makers cause to argue that students were "out of control" and in need of being policed.

Recently, in the face of overwhelming evidence of the negative consequences of zero tolerance and growing public critique, a number of states have begun to modify their zero-tolerance laws, giving more discretion and the ability to consider extenuating circumstances to school personnel. However, this new development appears only to keep zero tolerance in check. It does not challenge the nation's overall response to school disorder and violence or our thinking about how best to address disciplinary matters. Nationally, zero-tolerance school discipline remains the prevailing model, and the daily presence of law-enforcement officials in some urban schools appears to be on the rise.

As crime-control responsibilities expand beyond the boundaries of the criminal-justice system, is there a more likely place than the low-performing, racially segregated, disorderly urban school to take on those responsibilities? From a crime-control perspective, such developments are predictable. Order-maintenance policing inside UPHS is simply an application of the "preventive measures" of the criminologies of everyday life and the penal control and partial containment (through truancy laws) of the "dangerous other." Having police patrol the hallways of a racially segregated, disorderly school thus satisfies both the neoconservative and neoliberal strands of criminological (and ideological) thinking. From an educational-reform and restructuring perspective, order maintenance inside some schools also has its own logic. Zero-tolerance school discipline and school-based order-maintenance policing help to shift the locus of blame onto the most disengaged and structurally marginalized students while reformers, lacking any transformative educational vision for the classroom, applaud their own efforts to "take back our schools."

CHAPTER 2

Signs of the Times

Place, Culture, and Control at Urban Public High School

U RBAN PUBLIC HIGH SCHOOL is a large public high school that has served the surrounding communities for nearly one hundred years. It is located on a rather typical thoroughfare—part commercial, part residential. Along the street, there are several take-out restaurants selling Chinese and Jamaican food, a few bodegas that cater to the vast numbers of local English- and Spanish-speaking Caribbean immigrants, a Subway sandwich shop, a Dunkin' Donuts, and other small storefronts, most with dingy exteriors, that occupy the ground floors of residential dwellings. Despite the variety of shops near the school, there is little in the way of a thriving local business community.

For me, a person who spends considerable time in the bustling commercial districts of Manhattan, the neighborhood surrounding the school seems quiet, almost remote (except in the early morning and mid-afternoon, when hundreds of students fill the sidewalks). There are no skyscrapers or famous cultural institutions in sight, just a landscape made up of six-story apartment buildings, some marked with colorful graffiti and murals in honor of the young dead. There is an elevated subway line that cuts through the sky as far as the eye can see, heading toward the city center, which appears through the haze at a seemingly insurmountable distance. Some residents make the hour-plus trek to midtown and beyond for work; others rarely, if ever, visit "the city."

When I first visited UPHS, I noticed that it had taken on police-precinct, in some ways even prisonlike, characteristics as criminal-justice-oriented disciplinary practices and high-tech security apparatus permeated the building. To an extent, I had a sense of familiarity at UPHS, given my years in a similar high school, but there was a different "feel" to both physical structures and the daily social exchanges inspired by those structures. In many ways, the interactions that I observed were typical of any school—joking, teasing, and paternal and maternal admonitions—but the nature and kinds of interactions appeared to have changed as new security technologies were installed and police officers became fixtures in the hallway. Handcuffs, body searches, backpack searches, standing on line to walk through metal detectors, confrontations with law enforcement, "hallway sweeps," and confinement in the detention room had become common experiences for students. This contrasted significantly from my experience as a teacher, when the atmosphere was generally more welcoming and interactions did not remind me of the alienating and anxiety-provoking experience of walking through airport security, as they often did at UPHS.

The school was still a school, but its prevailing culture had shifted from the period when I had taught. This phenomenon has been noted in the New York City–based research of Jennifer McCormick, who observes that as schoolchildren are subjected to these new security technologies, there is a loss of what Erving Goffman might call "identity equipment" that makes previous conceptions of self impossible: "The loss is achieved, in part, when an 'inmate' is forced to assume [criminal] postures that conflict with societal notions of propriety."[1] At UPHS, the high-tech security apparatus, police presence, and disciplinary practices influenced how students made sense of their school and themselves. Penal management had become an overarching theme, and students had grown accustomed to daily interactions with law enforcement. In this chapter, I examine the intersections of place and culture by highlighting the spatial dimensions of control and the quotidian experience of daily life that occurred within those spaces.

Welcome to UPHS

The front of the school building extended about the length of two football fields, and its sides stretched back about the same distance, forming an immense square. The school was built in the early years of the twentieth century, the era of rapid expansion of public secondary education, to serve about five thousand students. For decades after its opening, the school was known as a fine institution of learning. But, over the years, its reputation diminished as academic performance and graduation rates went down and disorder and incidents of violence increased.

It was about 9:30 on a mid-September morning in 2004. I arrived at the school for one of my first visits. It was a quiet time, which allowed me to stand momentarily on the wide landing of the steps to take in the enormity of the building. I pulled open one of the heavy exterior doors and entered the building. There was another set of doors in front of me. A sign read:

TAKE OFF YOUR BELTS, BRACLETS AND WATCHES PUT IT IN YOUR BOOK BAG. YOU CANNOT BRING FOOD INTO THE BUILDING NO HOT ITEMS OR GLASS BOTTLES ALLOWED.

As I passed through the interior doors, I found myself in a cordoned-off section set up to direct bodies toward a large gray-blue box with a conveyor belt running through it—a metal detector—like those found at an airport. Two police officers stood beside the box, as well as two security agents (whom I could not yet distinguish from the police officers). I felt uncomfortable, imagining my embarrassment if my bags were to set off the alarm. I never got the chance to grow accustomed to the metal detector, however, because soon after my initial arrival, I was presented with a "staff" ID card, which allowed me to bypass it.

I picked up my backpack on the other side of the conveyer. The clunky security apparatus belied the quiet dignity of the entrance area's dark woodwork and brass fixtures. The walls were painted a muted yellow, and a soft light bathed the area. Directly in front of me were the heavy doors to the auditorium. Above the doors hung a multicolored neon sign shouting Bienvenidos and another to the side, repeating the greeting in English: Welcome.

Beyond the doors, the backs of several hundred wooden seats were flanked by rows of stately marble columns leading to a large stage—a typical school auditorium, worn and dusty, but still scholastic in its appearance. A sprinkling of students occupied some of the seats. Presumably they had arrived late, so now they had to wait for the bell to ring before heading to their next class.

At the very front, near the stage, four handsome brass chandeliers hung from the high ceiling. On the back wall of the auditorium, portraits of erudite men holding leather-bound books and wearing tiny, metal-rimmed spectacles were mounted inside heavy gold frames. A small gold plate under the first painting to the left read, "Randolph Beasley, principal, 1913–1919."

The entrance area, like the auditorium, had a high ceiling. Cavernous hallways lined with sturdy oak doors extended off each side, contributing to the expansive feel of the space. Two more police officers could be seen about midway down one of the hallways.

The walls to the side of the auditorium doors were lined with glass trophy cases filled with small monuments honoring victorious student athletes. One case was filled with wallet-sized photos of the graduating class of 2004—proud, smiling brown and black faces framed by shiny blue caps and gowns.

Across from the glass cases to the right side of the metal detector, bronze plaques were mounted on dark wood panels hanging on the wall. They were engraved with the names of hundreds of honor students, dating back to 1916. The sea of names reflected the various waves of immigrants that had made their way into this corner of the Bronx, starting with the European immigration of the early twentieth century: Silverman, Miller, Klein. By the 1950s, there was a spattering of names not previously seen: Rucci, McLeod, Camacho. And by the 1970s, the names began to speak of the northern migration of southern blacks and others from the Caribbean: Saunders, Richards, Melendez, Rodriguez. The subdued plaques hung like ghosts, almost fading into the wall.

There are a number of famous graduates from UPHS—politicians and business leaders, and a well-known actor and filmmaker. To this day, one may come across a story in the newspaper highlighting the latest achievements of a UPHS graduate from decades past, but it is not likely anyone would anticipate the alumnus's affiliation with the notorious school. Today, a small percentage of UPHS students make the honor role and go off to college, some perhaps bound to achieve great things, but more than 60 percent won't make it to graduation.

Morning Scanning

Most students entering the building hardly took notice of the subtle signs of the school's long history, as their attention was given to the morning security rituals. Starting at about 7:30, for almost two hours, there were two lines of students, divided by gender, waiting outside the building. The boys' line started at the eastside entrance to the school and extended down to the corner. At peak times, it wrapped around the corner to the front of the building. The girls lined up at the main entrance. Their line extended down the steps and along the sidewalk in front of the west side of the building. Deans, police officers, security agents, and school aides monitored the lines.

At another high school, about two miles away, students protested when their school installed a metal detector. One morning, almost 1,500 students demonstrated outside the school, indignant that they would have to walk through a metal detector every day and concerned that the long lines would cause them to be late for class—a common complaint heard at many of the schools with metal detectors. But at UPHS, I did not hear many complaints about the long wait to get into the building. The process had been normalized. Students were ornery sometimes, as were staff members, particularly on bitterly cold winter mornings. And in the late spring, arguments erupted between the school aides and students who showed up in tank tops and midriffs, which were against the school dress code. But, for the most part, the lines were characterized by a mixture of sleepy students and lively, innocuous banter. The students eventually proceeded to remove their belts, jewelry, hats, and do-rags, and plop their book bags on the conveyor.

The boys' line led to a long, narrow basement hallway on the east side of the building. The area was known as "boys' scanning." It had beige walls and a gray floor. Just inside the exterior doors, there were posters listing school rules. One read,

STUDENTS WHO ARE CAUGHT IN THE HALLWAYS AFTER THE LATE BELL WILL BE SUBJECT TO AFTER-SCHOOL DETENTION THE SAME DAY. THEY WILL BE TAKEN TO [ROOM] B-40 AND A DETENTION FORM WILL BE GIVEN TO THEM AND THEIR IDs CONFISCATED.

Another warned that students should have a book bag, notebook, and writing utensil or they would be sent directly to the deans' office. In the late spring, another sign was added to inform students of the new hat and "head cover" policy: "AS OF MAY 2ND ALL WILL BE CONFISCATED AND NOT RETURNED." There was also a poster of Tony the Tiger telling kids,

GET OUT THERE. EAT A SCHOOL BREAKFAST, AND STAY ACTIVE.

Between the exterior and interior doors, there were two computers for ID scanning and two walk-through body scanners—one set for the UPHS boys, one for the boys attending the small schools on the second floor—and just beyond the doors was the metal detector, where students from all the different schools dropped their bags for inspection. The bulky security equipment and cadre of uniformed officers seemed to define the narrow, gray corridor.

Beyond the metal detector, a few tables were pushed against the walls, and about twenty feet farther was the office of the police and security agents. Several more feet down the hallway was the entrance into the stairwell where the boys headed up to their classes. If classes were in session, the boys (and girls, who entered through the main entrance) were ushered into the auditorium to wait for the next bell.

When the boys entered the building, they were greeted by Dean Dempsey, a young black woman who had grown up a few miles from the school. Dempsey's style was a mixture of warmth and abruptness. She could joke with the boys, but she was tough and unbending when it came to the rules. Practically all of the students I spoke with liked her and had great respect for her. A dozen or so others milled about in the area: school aides, security agents, and police officers. Some worked the security equipment; others just stood around.

One morning in late May, I sat on a table with Dempsey during boys' scanning to see how the new hat policy was being implemented. Each of the boys passed his ID card to the aide working the computer. As the student's card was swiped, his picture and some written information appeared on the screen. If the young man had been suspended, a low siren would go off, indicating a "hold" on the student's card, and a computerized voice would announce that this student had been suspended. At other times, the voice said something like, "Report to Ms. Rosa's office." (Ms. Rosa was a counselor.) Below the student's picture, in bold red writing, there would be a brief explanation for the hold on the student's card.

Under the computer stand on the floor was a box with about twenty do-rags inside. I did not immediately recognize its function until a young man stepped through the outside doors with a do-rag on. As he placed one foot in the building, he realized his mistake. He smiled, grabbed his head, and took a giant step backward, but it was too late. Dempsey said, "Don't leave the building now. You were already in. Put it in the bin." The young man reluctantly dropped his do-rag in the box and proceeded past the metal detector, down the hall, and up the stairs.

From my first day at the school, I heard critiques of these security practices from school personnel. One teacher who had worked for more than thirty years at UPHS said, "I think walking through that metal detector every morning completely brings hostility into the building before [the students] even start the day. It makes people feel like they're walking into a prison. It makes life very difficult for everyone." Nevertheless, my observations told me that the practices had become routinized. In large part, students, deans, and law-enforcement officials appeared to carry out this ritual with a kind of unconscious acceptance.

The First Floor and the Detention Room (B-40)

To the west of the main entrance on the first floor were several administrative offices, including that of Alvarez, the principal. Around the corner, in the west corridor, were the counselors' offices, some other administrative offices, the history department, and several classrooms. Off of the south corridor were the gymnasiums, fitness rooms, and the nurse's station. The special-education wing took up the rest of the first floor, including the east corridor and extending around to the east side of the main entrance. The students who took classes in the special-education wing were generally contained in that area of the school unless they were headed to lunch or to the library or science lab. Many students in special education, who tended to be some of the most alienated students in the school, navigated their way through the stairwells and hallways of the labyrinthine building, avoiding classes.

These students were generally rounded up and brought down to the detention room—commonly known as B-40—a large, stark room in the basement on the west side of the building. There was a fairly steady flow of traffic into B-40, especially from the special-education wing, but, as I learned quickly, the room had many functions. At any given moment, the detention room was filled with a wide variety of students with myriad reasons for being there.

Early in the school year, I spent the day with Dean Jackson, whose job it was to patrol the first floor. Jackson, an athletically built black man in his late twenties, walked swiftly through the hallways, responding to calls on his hand-held radio. He had warned me beforehand to wear sneakers. The first stop of the day was a classroom on the first floor, where Jackson picked up Steven, one of the regulars in B-40. Steven, who was Puerto Rican, was tall and plump with a short buzz haircut. He had small eyes and a wide smile. Jackson didn't ask questions. He knew Steven would deliberately cause a little disruption at the beginning of each class so that the teacher would likely dismiss him to the detention room. Instead, he introduced Steven to the white lady walking with him—me—but Steven looked down with his head tilted to the side, sheepishly smiling. I would eventually get to know Steven and the struggles he faced, his difficulties in learning and his incarceration. But in that first encounter, he remained shy. Jackson chided him for not "steppin' up his game." Steven's smile grew even wider, and his eyes turned into crescent moons. He giggled and his round cheeks burned red.

Next, Jackson picked up a student whose teacher had evidently slammed the door on his hand. He was black, with a light complexion. His hair was neatly braided into rows. He walked with his shoulders back and a stoic look on his face, cradling his bloody hand. When he was asked to explain what happened, the squeaky voice of a wounded child bubbled up. "I wasn't doing anything. Another student was just handing me the hall pass and . . ."

As the day went on, Jackson picked up a student who wasn't prepared for gym class and had gotten angry when the teacher kicked him out of the room; then he nabbed another regular, Evan, who preferred roaming the hallways to going to class. Next, he spent a few moments talking with a large, awkward freshman who had been kicked out of class for talking back to his teacher. The student claimed his teacher had picked on him. Jackson orchestrated an apology from the boy, who, defeated, went back into the classroom. The radio crackled again. Jackson was called to the front entrance, where he found a group of four young men. It was unclear what they had done wrong, but their ID cards had been "flagged," so Jackson had to immediately escort them to B-40. It was the first encounter of the day where hostility was evident; Jackson did not introduce them to me.

B-40 had gotten crowded, with about thirty students in all. It was the middle of the fifth period. The aide who worked in the room sat behind his big table, conversing with two female students. There were a lot of latecomers who had been barred from their classes or picked up in the hallway sweep. One group was engaged in a lively conversation, but most of the students sat quietly with bored looks on their faces. Some stared directly to the front; others rested their heads on their desks.

On Steven's third trip of the day down to B-40, he had two companions, Marcus and Calvin. Steven peered in the small window on the door and declared he wasn't going in, because he had "beef in there." He looked at the others, widening his small eyes. "Those guys," he said, referring to the ones escorted from the main entrance, "are Crips." As Jackson brought the three boys around the corner to B-42, Assistant Principal Juarez's office, he poked fun at gang rules, saying in a high-pitched voice, "Oh, I can't go in there. They're purple and I'm pink," feminizing the actual gang colors, red for Bloods, blue for Crips. Jackson dropped the boys off in B-42 despite the protests of the women who worked there.

On another day early in the school year, I sat at one of the desks in the middle of the detention room. I had learned that it was a convenient place to get away from the action and tension of daily life and catch up on field notes. At that moment, the room contained only a few students and was, thankfully, quiet. As often happened, a girl struck up a conversation with me, during which I asked her why she was in B-40. "Oh, well, I have math right now, but I didn't feel like going," she said. With this, I learned of yet another common use of B-40. Ironically, the room that might have been considered the center of disciplinary life also served as the ideal place for a student to go if he or she wanted to cut class or to be left alone.

The Brains and Heart of School Discipline

Juarez's office, number B-42, was known as "Base" and functioned as the brains of the security apparatus.[2] It was a large, cluttered office with desks for Juarez, his secretary, and a school aide in charge of the computer system that held all of the students' information. (It was here where notes were attached to students' profiles that appeared on the screen during morning scanning when their cards were swiped.) As in a typical school office, there were a photocopy machine and several filing cabinets lining the walls behind the desks. Inside these cabinets were copies of students' disciplinary records and occurrence reports. Across from the desks, next to the door was a large freestanding monitor with selected images captured by the numerous security cameras mounted in the corners of the hallways and the lunchroom. Behind the monitor on the wall hung a bulletin board with several signs and memos and a Navy recruitment calendar with a pocket full of business cards. Juarez didn't spend much time in his office, but when he was at his desk, he was likely to be found on the phone or meeting with a student or a parent, and often had several other people waiting to meet with him.

If Base was the brains of the security apparatus, the deans' office was the heart. This was the room where police and security agents escorted handcuffed students, whether in the aftermath of a fight or simply as a result of a student–law-enforcement confrontation. During a quiet moment, it resembled any other school office. The walls were lined with filing cabinets and bulletin boards covered with administrative memos explaining new procedures and regulations. There were a secretary's desk, a photocopy machine, and a storage closet. There were two desks for the deans to use facing each other in the center of the room, another against the wall next to the entrance, and three more along the back wall, separated by partitions. Behind that set of desks was the door to the adjoining detention room.

Often there were three or four deans in the room doing paperwork, talking to a parent on the phone, or talking with a student who had come by in an attempt to retrieve his or her ID card that had been confiscated the day before. At times, a cherished stillness fell over the office, but at least once a day, and often several times, the stillness was jarringly disrupted as several police officers and security agents poured into the room, escorting handcuffed students. Shrill static peppered with police lingo emanating from the officers' hand-held radios suffused the room. Angry voices of students, cops, and agents rose above the radio static. In each corner of the room, there would be a different interaction.

On one day, a young man stood over one of the desks in the center of the room with his legs spread and his hands placed on the desktop while one officer conducted a body search and another went through the young man's bag. The officer took interest in some red and white beads he found. As he raised them up, I wondered if the boy could be a practitioner of Santeria, a spiritual system originating in the Caribbean that merges Yoruba religion and the worship of Catholic saints. Beads can be used to represent different deities. But the officer identified them as gang paraphernalia.

Next to the adjacent desk, another student flipped through the binder of student photos in an attempt to find a student who had hit him. At one of the desks in the back, yet another young man sat quietly with his hands cuffed behind his back. The deans seemed to have sprung into a new mode of action. One was on the phone, attempting to contact a parent. A few agents stood around, waiting. The boy with the red and white beads was arrested and brought to the police precinct.

Days later, I observed a student getting frisked as several officers stood around the room. The boy dropped his bracelet on the floor, and the police officer inadvertently stepped on it. When the student brought this to the officer's attention, the officer was slow to move his foot. The boy asked in a low, angry voice, "Why do you have to disrespect me?" The officer said nothing but motioned to the boy to pick up his bracelet.

On another day, I walked into the room to find three officers standing over a student. The buzz of the radios provided a constant backdrop to the activity. One officer was writing up a court summons to give to the student. Another officer said, "Pray today is not like yesterday." Just then, a "fifty-two" (code for a fight) was called over the radio. Two officers ran out of the room, and I spotted another darting through the hallway to join them as they ran past the drone of tuning tubas and trumpets coming from the music room next door.

These kinds of scenes were common, as there was frequent interaction between law enforcement and students. A student in handcuffs became a familiar image, and the threat of police intervention, summons, and arrest was even more likely to occur in the deans' office. "Do you want a summons?" a dean barked on one occasion when a student was angrily trying to explain his situation from his perspective. "Calm down or you're gonna end up getting yourself arrested," I heard on another day, when a student sat complaining about the treatment he had received from a teacher.

The Upper Floors

On the third floor of the school (UPHS students were barred from the second floor, where the small schools—new theme-based "academies" with their own principals and staff—were located), one found the second-language and art department offices on the west side, along with one of the small schools, which had encroached upon UPHS's space. The library could be found off the south corridor, and the English and math departments were located on the east side. While walking through the hallways, one would notice the typical display of student projects, artwork, and inspirational posters. Most were likely to be found hanging in Any School, USA; others were more specific to the school, such as flags and drawings representing students' national origins or local cultures.

On this floor, where many classes were held, several security agents and police officers always seemed to be standing around. Usually clusters of two or three could be found in the corners or strolling down the hallway. During the change of classes, the security team formed a blue wall and corralled students in one direction. Most of the time when I observed this process, it would go smoothly. Students seemed to be willingly directed to class, chatting and joking as they moved along. Most ended up in their proper classes. Some, however, used the moment when the students far outnumbered the security team to slip unnoticed into the stairwell and disappear into some hidden corner of the building or out a side door.

The fourth floor housed the science department, more classrooms, and labs on the west side, and the "freshman academy" on the east side. The cafeteria, or lunchroom, extended along the whole north side.

The lunchroom was an extremely long room broken into three sections. There were dozens of tables on both the east and west sides and an open space in the middle, where, I was told, students had played dominoes and cards until games were banned in order to discourage gambling. Doors in this middle section led to the food counter. There were entrances on both sides of the enormous room. At each entrance, there was a computer and scanning machine, and usually an aide and a couple of security agents were standing around. There was also a dean assigned to the lunchroom. At the beginning of each lunch period, students would line up at both entrances. One by one, their cards were swiped through the computer to verify that they were assigned to the lunchroom for that period.

The lunchroom smelled of grease and the fare of the day—typically burgers or pizza. I learned to step carefully while traversing the large room so as not to step on a knocked-over juice carton or a streak of ketchup or some already-stepped-on French fries. The students generally sat chatting and eating their lunches in a relaxed manner. There were usually so many of them in the room at once—clowning around, laughing, and yelling across the tables to their friends—that I quickly came to understand why some students chose to go to the detention room during their lunch periods: to avoid the assault on one's senses. (Still others chose the deten-tion room over the lunchroom to avoid other kinds of assaults.) Indeed, I occasionally found myself heading to the detention room rather than the lunchroom to "take a break" and strike up conversations with students.

The lunchroom was one of the most common areas in the school for a fight to break out. It is difficult to describe an actual fight, one student hit-ting another, as I found it nearly impossible to get near such a conflict. The first sign of imminent fisticuffs would be the soft rumbling of anticipation. Then, as the first punch was thrown, a wave of spectators rolled in the di-rection of the dueling students. Sometimes someone yelled, "Fight!" The crowd formed quickly. The security team moved into action, rounding up students. Many of the bystanders got swept up along with the fighters and were hauled down to the deans' office in the basement, down the dark hallway and past the music room. But although fights were rather com-mon, fighting did not define the lunchroom. Generally, the cafeteria ap-peared to be simply a lively social scene, with lots of students eating their lunches off of Styrofoam trays. As I got to know the students better, I came to know the lunchroom more intimately, particularly through the eyes of one of my frequent companions, Zack, who later in the school year ex-plained the layout in his own terms.

Bloomberg's "Cultural Transformation"

The mayor and schools chancellor, as I mentioned in chapter 1, had re-leased a memo upon the creation of their new policing program. They called for a cultural transformation of disorderly schools, and, indeed, a transformation had occurred. By its appearance, UPHS was undeniably typical in many ways of a large, old, urban public high school. Artifacts of the past—graduation pictures, athletic awards, wooden doors chosen decades ago to give the hallways a learned feel—and newer displays of student projects, posters, and school rules offered visible signs of a long, evolving scholastic history. Yet by the time I entered the school, new signs of the changing times had been layered with the old: the clunky metal de-tectors, the security cameras tucked into the corners, the large monitor projecting images from around the school, scanning machines and com-puters that contained all sorts of student information stationed at the building and cafeteria entrances, and armed law-enforcement officials patrolling the hallways. These signs of the times constitute the spatial and material dimensions of the culture of control and reflect how the criminal-justice system operated through the school. They are manifestations of new policies and ways of thinking about social order and punishment, and consequently they shaped daily interactions and disciplinary rituals inside the school.

CHAPTER 3

Instituting the Culture of Control

Disciplinary Practices and Order Maintenance

ALTHOUGH A VARIETY OF POLICIES AND PRACTICES were part of the culture of control inside UPHS, the most central was the systematic use of order-maintenance-style policing. This included law-enforcement officials' patrolling of the hallways, the use of criminal-procedural-level strategies,[1] and the pervasive threats of summonses and arrest, which together led to three essential consequences. First, the heavy policing of students on a daily basis and an official policy of police intervention for minor school infractions led to the criminalization of misbehavior. In fact, frequently the police intervention itself triggered the behavior that was ultimately considered criminal. Second, disciplinary incidents that could have been considered violations of the law but had once been handled internally by educators, such as fighting, came to be defined as serious crimes and were often handled through police intervention, summonses, and the arrests of students. Third, as school discipline merged with an ideology of street policing, the boundaries between once-separate domains—the school, the street, and institutions of the criminal-justice system—became blurred. As David Garland suggests, as crime-control responsibilities move beyond the boundaries of the criminal-justice system, institutions of civil society, such as the urban public school, assume explicit roles in the larger societal project of the penal management of marginalized, low-income youth of color.[2]

What Does "Disorderly" Mean, Anyway? The Policing of Misbehavior and the Criminalization of Disrespect

How did the new disciplinary plan work in actual practice? One way to find out was to look carefully at the kinds of acts that became defined in everyday practice as the appropriate domain for police action. With this question in mind, I undertook a systematic examination of the school occurrence reports for the 2004–2005 school year, during which time at least 113 summonses and 58 youth referrals were meted out and more than 50 arrests were recorded, 221 occurrences in total.[3] My careful examination of the reports led to one striking finding: 52 percent of the offenses were for "disorderly conduct." Given that so many students were charged with this offense, it was important to examine the actual behaviors that led to it. My experiences at UPHS shed light on the definitional process, from the initial interaction between police and students that led to the charge of disorderly conduct, to the hours students spent in court.

It was late September. I was standing in the office of the assistant principal of school safety, Juarez. I was there to pick up an ID card that had been made for me. Only the secretary, the aide, and I were present. The quiet morning lull of office work was broken suddenly when three police officers escorted two handcuffed boys into the office. For me, the experience was still new. I had not yet grown accustomed to the scene, and it seemed jarringly out of place in a school. The boys were forcibly pushed down into two chairs. Two more police officers entered the room, which suddenly felt much smaller. Their anger was palpable. The secretary and the aide did not seem fazed. The aide began to print out information on the two students. One was nineteen years old. "He needs to go to the precinct," one of the officers said.

The five officers stepped to one side of the room near the door to confer. This strange moment of waiting and conferring I would see again and again over time. They appeared to be making decisions on the fly. The secretary continued to work. The aide quietly said to me, "Your card won't be ready until tomorrow," cuing me to leave.

"I'm watching this," I said.

"I don't think you have permission."

"I have the principal's," I assured her.

The two young men were talking to each other. The older one whispered, "They're beasts," referring to the officers. Their chairs were about three feet apart. They leaned close to each other with their cuffed wrists behind their backs and continued to complain in low voices about the treatment they had received. I later learned that they were brothers—Terrell and James. The older one claimed that he had come to the defense of his younger sibling. The occurrence report, which I obtained later, described the incident like this:

Two male students were arrested by PO [police officer] —— of the
XX pct for Disorderly Conduct and Resisting Arrest. One student
refused to provide identification. They were both disorderly and
disrespectful when stopped. Parental contact unsuccessful. Suspensions are pending.

One of the officers glanced at me; I felt very conspicuous. More angry
words were exchanged between the boys and the officers as they waited for
the police van. I pretended not to notice. Finally, my awkwardness got the
better of me and I left the room. Just then Assistant Principal Juarez came
rushing in. He was a smallish, well-dressed Dominican man with a charm-
ing disposition and a mild manner. But at that moment he was not happy
and, like the mood in his office, he had transformed. From just outside the
doorway, I heard his stern voice shouting, "I know what I'm doing. . . . If
you don't like it, leave! I can't have all these people in my office. Get out!"
"Okay, okay," one of the officers said. "We'll step outside."
I walked toward the side entrance of the building where I predicted
the boys would be taken out. A few moments later, the police escorted
them past me out to the police van. Juarez followed. He looked at me as
he passed and said, "Sometimes we don't always see things the same way."
Although the tension between the school administrator and the police
was evident, what struck me most about the incident was how it confused
me. I could not understand why the boys were arrested. What had they
been caught doing? It was the beginning of the school year, and I had not
quite figured out the process by which small disciplinary matters escalated
into police matters.
The story continued two months later, on a cold November morning,
when I arrived at the Bronx Criminal Court House at 8:30. Unbeknown to
me, it was the day that Terrell and James were to appear before the judge.
I was there to meet Carlos, who had also received a summons at school
for disorderly conduct. The courthouse was an immense stone building
that extended the length of a block. A wide, shallow set of steps led up to
the main entrance on 161st Street, a busy commercial strip with several
government buildings in the vicinity. I figured Carlos would be late, as he
found it difficult to make it to school before 10:00 AM, so I waited on
the corner of 161st and Sheridan, propped against some scaffolding, and
began to read.
Periodically, I looked up from my book to scan for Carlos. The streets

were alive with morning shoppers, vendors, and people starting out for the day. By 9:00, the line into the courthouse extended along the front of the building and wrapped around the corner where I was standing. It was made up predominantly of young men, but there were women too, many alone, some with mothers and small children, a few with older men. Some people had arrived in pairs, others by themselves, some in suits, others in baggy jeans and do-rags. Virtually all were black or Latino/a, except for one recognizably white woman, scantily clad, with a haggard face and teased hair dyed platinum blond. The line had a calm energy and was sprinkled with small pink papers clutched in people's gloved hands.

At 9:45, I felt a light squeeze on the back of my arm. I turned to see Carlos's impish smile and large almond-shaped eyes looking up at me. He told me he got them from his Peruvian father. ("But don't tell anyone. My mom is Puerto Rican, so I just tell people I'm Puerto Rican," he said half jokingly one day during one of our first talks.) He was dressed in his typical style—extremely baggy clothes that made his small frame appear even smaller, a do-rag, and his favorite Yankees baseball cap.

Carlos apologized for being late as we walked toward the entrance. There was no longer a line to join. Carlos assured me that the last time he was at court, he wasn't called into the courtroom until after 10:00. I realized then that he was unaware that names were called in the order people arrived at the courthouse and handed in their summonses. Submitting a summons after 10 AM assured us a long day!

As we entered the courthouse, we were directed toward different lines to pass through the metal detectors. I was still uncomfortable with the process. I felt somehow exposed standing with my arms stretched out, the officer guiding the hand-held scanner over the contours of my body. We couldn't figure out why I kept beeping. At last, I found Carlos slipping his belt back through its loops. We had stood like that before, but still I was embarrassed and diverted my eyes.

"I hate that process," I said.

"Imagine how the girls at school feel doing that every day," he responded in a quiet voice.

Carlos handed in his summons at the window, and we slid into one of the long rows of benches arranged like church pews facing the large double doors into the courtroom. We sat for hours, intermittently in easy silence and casual conversation. We talked about our favorite movies and musicians, school, family, his urban childhood memories and my suburban ones. I showed him the book I was reading—a book about homeless men. "I don't understand how people become homeless," Carlos said. (Later in the year, his mother would take in his uncle for a couple of months while he was in transition.)

We bumped into Terrell and chatted briefly. Like Carlos, he and his brother James had received summonses for disorderly conduct. Carlos knew Terrell from the neighborhood. I recognized him from that late September day in Juarez's office. He smiled warmly and said, "I know you. You're the lady writing a book or something."

At some point during our wait, I asked Carlos, "So, how did you end up getting this summons, again?" He explained how a police officer had found him in the hallway of the school after the bell had rung. It was going into fourth period and Carlos was on his way to lunch. Carlos claimed that the stairwell was too crowded, so he decided to take another route, but the bell rang before he was able to work his way through the building to the cafeteria. Carlos believed that the police officer had disrespected him by demanding to see his ID and refusing to listen to an explanation for why he had been in the hallway when he wasn't supposed to be. As with so many students in similar situations, Carlos decided not to cooperate, because he did not believe he had done anything wrong, so the officer cuffed him, brought him to the detention room, and gave him a summons for disorderly conduct.

It was after 1:30 in the afternoon when we returned from a lunch break. The court officer shouted out another round of names. Finally, we heard, "Carlos Mendoza!"

We went through the double doors and quietly took seats in another set of benches. About twenty people inside the small courtroom were waiting to see the judge, most of whom had received summonses evidently in the streets of their own neighborhoods. Terrell and his brother were already inside. They smiled at us. The officer bellowed out the names of the offenders and their offenses.

"Jose Rodriguez, public urination. . . . Fifty dollars. Can you pay it today?" The lawyer mumbled something. Jose did not have the money that day.

"Hector Media, open bottle, twelve-ounce Budweiser, and public urination. . . ."

"Thomas Jones, disorderly conduct." A young black man from another Bronx high school presented himself before the judge. "What high school do you go to?" the judge asked from behind his large wooden desk on a high perch.

On that particular day, the judge decided he wanted to see the school-boys on another day with a parent. Of the four in the room, none was accompanied by a parent that day. This was not always how a judge handled such cases. On another of my visits to court, with Duane, the judge took a different approach. Instead of requesting to meet with parents, he made a tired attempt to engage each offender.

"Duane Gordon, disorderly conduct!" the officer called out. I scooted over to give Duane room to pass.

The judge seemed confused by the charge of disorderly conduct. "So, what did you do?" he asked.

"Disorderly conduct," the lawyer replied as if that would clarify things.

The small judge, in his early sixties with thick, round glasses, was growing irritable. "Whatever you did, just don't do it again. Dismissed," he said with a slight sigh. As the courtroom doors closed behind Duane and me, we looked at each other and giggled at the judge's reaction.

But on that November afternoon, the judge's request to see a parent worried Carlos. He hadn't experienced this strategy. He asked me if I thought he'd be locked up. I said, "No, I think he just wants to speak to your mother." And I hoped that was really the case. (The next month we learned that that indeed was the case. Carlos missed another day of school and his mother, a counselor in a group home for developmentally disabled adults, missed a day of work to attend court and hear the judge rehash why her son needed to behave in school.)

After checking out the movie listings at the Concourse Plaza across the street, we walked along 161st Street toward the subway. Carlos was not his playful self; he was still worried about having to return to court with his mother, so we walked in silence. As we stepped off the curb at the Grand Concourse, he asked, "What does 'disorderly' mean, anyway?"

Given the ambiguity surrounding the events that led to police interventions, Carlos's question was not easily answered. In the context of UPHS, what *did* "disorderly" mean? I wondered. In his case, it referred to the acts of being in the hallway after the bell had rung, refusing to hand over his ID in an attempt to get a security agent to listen to his explanation, and arguing when the security agent refused to listen. Likewise, the arrests of and summonses given to Terrell and James arose from their being in the hallway when they were not supposed to be there. But how did the breaking of a school rule escalate so quickly into a police matter resulting in the issuance of a court summons?

When I first arrived at UPHS, I did not quite understand the behaviors that would lead to an arrest or summons for disorderly conduct. I remember asking one day in the deans' office, "What was that student arrested for?" The answer I received was resisting arrest. I persisted. "But why was he arrested in the first place?" The dean with whom I was conversing gave me a confused look and after a moment conceded, "Oh, I don't know. I wasn't there."

I began to explore the issue and learned from my examination of the occurrence reports that generally there were two types of behavior labeled disorderly conduct: altercations between students (total number: 45 out of about 110, covering twenty-two separate incidents); and students' insubordination during an exchange with an adult, usually involving the refusal to show identification (total number: 65).[4] So the refusal to show ID was landing all of these kids in front of a judge? It was hard to believe, but several individuals I interviewed gave similar accounts. One dean explained that students cut classes and hung out in the hallways, wearing hats and do-rags and fooling around. Then, when they were approached by security, they acted in an inappropriate manner. They wouldn't give up their IDs, they wouldn't go to class, and they just refused to do what they were told. Then they were brought downstairs (to the deans' office) and given a summons. It was the same process Carlos told me about, except that the story was now told from the perspective of an adult who was tired of students not being where they were supposed to be and disrespecting police officers.

An examination of the occurrence reports submitted by the deans helps to provide an understanding of what often transpired between a student and a school safety agent or officer leading up to an arrest or summons for disorderly conduct.[5] We see from the samples I quote here that the reports also reveal the interplay between an institutional demand for respect and the culture of penal control—one feeding the other.

(September 22, 2004) Sarah Watkins was issued a summons by PO —— of the XX pct for misbehaving.

(October 4, 2004) A male student Jonathan Walker was arrested by PO —— of the XX pct for insubordination. Jonathan refused to show ID to Officer ——.

(October 15, 2004) A male student was issued a summons by School Safety Task Force for Insubordination. He refused to identify himself. When SSA's [school safety agents] continued to ask him for identification he became irate. A suspension is pending.

(October 29, 2004) A male student was arrested by SSA —— and transported to the XX [precinct] for Disorderly Conduct and Resisting Arrest. He was observed with glazed eyes and an odor. It was suspected that he might be under the influence of a controlled substance. He was being escorted to the office when he became irate and resisted authority. A suspension is pending.

(November 5, 2004) A male student was issued a summons by PO —— of the XX pct for Disorderly Conduct and insubordination. He refused to show ID and was cursing at staff members. PO —— also arrested the student for a outstanding warrant.

(November 10, 2004) A male student was issued a summons by SSA —— for Disorderly Conduct. He refused to show ID and became irate and disorderly. A suspension is pending.

(November 23, 2004) A male student was issued a summons by PO —— of the Task Force for Disorderly Conduct. He was asked for his ID by an SSA, but he refused. A suspension is pending.

(December 17, 2004) A male student was issued a YD [youth referral] by PO —— of the School Safety Task Force for Insubordination. He refused to ID himself and was found loitering in the hall more than once. A suspension is pending.

(December 17, 2004) A female student was issued a YD for Disorderly Conduct by PO —— of the XX pct. She refused to present identification when asked to do so. A suspension is pending.

(December 23, 2004) A male student was issued a summons by PO —— of the XX pct for Disorderly Conduct. He refused to produce ID and became verbally abusive toward the officer. A suspension is pending.

(January 19, 2005) Two male students, Donald and Steven was issued a Summons by PO —— of the XX pct for Disorderly Conduct. They refused to show ID when asked by the officers. A suspension is pending.

(February 11, 2005) A female student was issued a YD by PO —— of the XX for Disorderly Conduct. She refused to show identification and cursed out a Dean. A suspension is pending.

(February, 14, 2005) A male student was issued a summons by PO —— of the School Safety Task Force for Insubordination. He was being uncooperative towards a police officer and refused to show his identification. Student, Quinton Willis, was found on the 3rd floor stairwell with a female student. PO —— approached Quinton and requested his ID card. Quinton claimed he didn't have one and became very defiant and insubordinate towards the police officer. Quinton was taken downstairs to the dean's office and was issued a summons.

(March 3, 2005) A male student was issued a summons by PO —— of the XX pct for Disorderly Conduct. He was asked to stop by PO —— and became irate and uncontrollable. He had to be restrained. A suspension is pending. At the time of occurrence, defendant was asked to stop and present ID, refused and became verbally abusive to PO —— and did public alarm and disturbance on the 3rd floor.

(March 21, 2005) A male student was issued a YD by PO —— of the XX pct for Disorderly Conduct. He was verbally abusive towards the PO's and he refused to comply with their instructions. A suspension is pending. Student was insubordinate and verbally abusive.

(March 30, 2005) A male student was issued a YD by PO —— of the School Safety Task Force for Insubordination. He was insubordinate with SSAs and PD. A suspension is pending. Shane Tompkins attempted to enter the student cafeteria and was told to go to class. Shane became uncooperative to school safety agent —— and SSA —— requested for assistance. PO —— approached Dean —— and SSA ——. Shane was told to leave but became belligerent and insubordinate to PO ——.

(March 31, 2005) A female student was issued a YD by PO —— of the XX pct for Disorderly Conduct. She was insubordinate towards a female SSA —— and used profanity towards her. A suspension is pending. Student was insubordinate to SSA —— and used abusive language when given a directive.

(April 6, 2005) A female student was issued a summons by PO —— of the XX pct for Disorderly Conduct. She refused to show identification and she verbally abused SSA ——. Suspension is pending.

(April 6, 2005) A female student was issued a YD by PO —— of the XX pct for Disorderly Conduct. She was approached by PO —— and was disrespectful and used inappropriate language towards him. A suspension is pending.

(May 25, 2005) A male student was issued a summons by PO —— of the XX pct for Disorderly Conduct. He refused to obey the directions of officers and became verbally abusive. A suspension is pending. Student Marcus Brown was issued a C-Summons for disorderly conduct by NYPD. He refused to follow directions and was verbally disrespectful.

(May 25, 2005) A male student was issued a YD by PO —— of the XX pct for Disorderly Conduct. During scanning he refused to follow directives and punched the glass in the door causing injury to his hand. EMS transported [student] to the hospital. A suspension is pending. Student Juan Garcia was defiant with Dean —— and SSA agents —— and —— when asked to take off his "Doo-Rag" and step into the vestibule before entering school. After several minutes of insubordination and defiant behavior, Juan punched through the glass of the lobby door, injuring his hand. He was is-sued a YD and taken to —— Hospital as a result.

Each of these incidents began with a student breaking a school rule de-fined by the Department of Education rather than the law. Sarah Watkins was misbehaving; Juan Garcia refused to follow directions during scan-ning; Shane Tompkins attempted to enter the cafeteria when it was not his assigned lunch period. In a number of incidents, although the rule was not explicitly stated in the report, students may have been in the hallways or stairwell when classes were in session, were possibly spotted in an un-likely part of the building, or perhaps were wearing a hat. In fact, none of these behaviors was a matter that warranted a police intervention; in most cases, the inciting behavior is listed in the 2004 DOE Discipline Code as a level-one infraction—the least serious type of offense. An incident usually escalated into a police matter when a student refused to hand over his or her ID card. But even this, "failing to provide school officials with proper identification," was considered a level-one infraction.[6]

Sometimes the inciting moment came when a security agent grabbed a student or pulled the student's hat off his or her head and the student "be-came irate" or even reacted physically. These were the types of scenarios that I observed and that were commonly reported to me by students but were not documented in occurrence reports. It became particularly pal-pable for me, though, one day while I was walking down the hallway at the tail end of the change of periods and a security agent, whose attention was diverted toward two students on the other side of him, suddenly swung his arm up in front of my chest and grabbed my shoulder, thinking I was a student. When he turned and saw a rather stunned adult, he apologized profusely: "I'm so sorry, miss, I thought you were one of the kids." Despite his apology, I was left feeling a little unsettled, knowing that at least this se-curity agent considered it acceptable to grab students.

According to the language in the occurrence reports, the issuance of a summons or an arrest for disorderly conduct appeared to be justified in the eyes of law-enforcement officials and deans by a student's display of "irate," "insubordinate," "disrespectful," "uncooperative," or "uncontrolla-ble" behavior. None of the occurrence reports provided any sort of expla-nation of the student's behavior. There was an implicit assumption that students' irate behavior was completely unprovoked or, in any case, inappropriate, and warranted punishment not only through the school system but also through the criminal- (or juvenile-) justice system.

Several police officers explained to me that a summons was "no big deal." It simply indicated a "violation of the law" and was "virtually no different than receiving a traffic ticket." However, it *was* different, in several important ways. For one thing, when students received a summons in school for disorderly conduct, they had to appear in criminal court, not transit court. The criminal-court experience was markedly different from the traffic-court experience, where there were no escorted handcuffed individuals on display, no officers yelling out people's offenses, no standing before a judge, and no wondering whether this would be the time the judge would say, "Enough. It's time this kid does some time."

When students received summonses and got arrested during situations that began with the breaking of a school rule, the behaviors they displayed for which an officer issued a summons often came only *after* the officer or agent confronted the student. Yet no one asked, at least in official terms, why a student had become disorderly or what it actually meant. Order had become top priority, and "disrespect" was not tolerated within the emerging culture of control.

Violations of the Law: The Predominance of Law-and-Order Practices

At UPHS, 56 percent of all student actions that resulted in a summons, youth referral, or arrest might be subject to criminal-procedural-level strategies in other contexts. In most cases, they would be considered violations of the law (a lesser offense than a misdemeanor) or actual misdemeanors, and in a very small number of cases,[7] the behaviors might be considered felony offenses. The vast majority of these latter incidents involved fighting, weapon possession, or drug possession and, therefore, were punishable by law. Nevertheless, several questions arose for me regarding the efficacy and fairness of arrests and summonses in these cases.

My questions stemmed, first, from the disproportionately high levels of surveillance to which students at UPHS were subjected. Second, I observed that criminal-procedural-level strategies tended to overshadow the use of positive (as opposed to punitive) educational strategies to reduce drug sales and participation in violence. In fact, even when positive strategies, such as counseling, were used, they were auxiliary strategies. The criminal-justice-oriented strategies were the ones that came to define a given incident as a crime.

Finally, particularly in the case of fighting, there was considerable subjectivity in determining whether a behavior was actually a violation of the law. This subjectivity might be explained, in part, by how school personnel contested policing practices and preferred to use their own strategies whenever possible. But, at the same time, minor physical altercations were often defined as criminal acts, and a penal logic tended to eclipse both the efforts toward and the use of more positive or transformative strategies for the reduction of violence and crime, such as peer mediation, comprehensive student-directed antiviolence initiatives, or massive antidrug campaigns.

Drug and Weapon Possession

Inside a school like UPHS, where students had become the subjects of high surveillance and heavy policing, the actions that often resulted in arrest or the issuance of a summons were often not ones that would have been detected in any other circumstance. According to occurrence reports, drug-possession violations, for example, were almost always discovered during the morning scanning ritual, and, in a few instances, controlled substances were found on students during body searches conducted after a student "disrespected" a law-enforcement official during a routine interaction. In other circumstances, say, on the street or in a park or in a typical suburban high school, the police would not have the authority to search a child who did not elicit any suspicion.

Like summonses for drug possession, virtually all summonses for weapons possession were given out at scanning, as students entered the building. In these incidents, the dual impact of zero tolerance and order maintenance became most evident. Many school personnel, for example, regarded the practices around weapons possession as problematic, because students who intended to use weapons in schools were often not the ones getting caught with weapons during scanning. The principal explained: "If a child goes through scanning with a box cutter, it's because they really had no intention of doing anything with it. And I would say [this is true] 99 percent of the time, because otherwise the child would try to hide the blade. There's many ways of hiding a blade very easily to come through scanning."

Many reports in the last decade have presented long lists of absurd arrests made for weapon possession under the national policy of zero tolerance, such as a young child getting suspended for pointing a chicken strip at a classmate as if it were a gun.[8] At UPHS, no report was quite so absurd; in most cases the instrument in question clearly qualified as a weapon. Twenty-four summonses for weapon possession were given out during the school year for the following: five knives, six box cutters, seven razor blades, two cans of mace, one can of pepper spray, one metal pick, and one unspecified weapon. Some may have been carried with the intent to harm someone. However, it was commonly accepted among administrators, deans, and officers that such weapons were carried most often because they were instruments students used at work or for other nonviolent tasks (for example, one of the seven razors was found in a girl's book bag; she claimed that she used it to do her hair), or because they offered students a sense of protection as they walked through their neighborhoods (for example, the mace and pepper spray—common defensive measures against rape—were found on girls). Alvarez lamented,

> There's that zero tolerance in terms of bringing weapons into the building, which I agree with. You know, honestly, however, those policies do not see the young lady or the young man who works for a living to help support the family who has to go into the stock room and open boxes and put them on the shelves, goes home late every day, puts the box cutter in his pocket, forgets about it, comes the next day into school, and the child has to be arrested, suspended, because you have to follow the policy. So that is a very difficult situation for any administrator to be in, to have a child who actually comes to school, who actually does the work, who's doing fairly well, and then you have to arrest the child and suspend him.

None of the incidents involving drugs led to a student referral into a drug-treatment or education program. Students carrying weapons into school were not invited into an antiviolence program and certainly not a self-defense class; nor were the reasons for their having a weapon explored by counselors or administrators in any systematic way. There was also no systemic effort to provide possible alternatives for students, such as tutoring, career counseling, or job training to set them on alternative paths. There were some services provided at the school through the SPARK program,[9] the guidance counselors' office, and the deans' office, but such interventions reached a relatively small percentage of the population and occurred more through the tenacious work of individuals than through any institutionally supported efforts.

Physical Altercations

It is difficult to make definitive claims about the ways in which incidents of violence were handled in the school based on an examination of occurrence reports. On the one hand, I found that not all physical acts of violence were criminalized, despite the fact that there might have been some justification for doing so. On the other hand, there sometimes appeared to be excessively punitive responses to minor physical altercations. According to the occurrence reports, there were forty-one incidents of physical altercations during the school year for which eighty-two students were either arrested or given a summons or youth referral.[10] Of these, fifty-six students received summonses or youth referrals for disorderly conduct. In the remaining cases, students were either charged with assault or the charge was unspecified. Additionally, the reports revealed that there were at least twenty-seven incidents of fighting or other forms of violence in which the police were not involved.

Among the incidents that led to the use of criminal-procedural-level strategies, there was significant variation in the level of severity. Several reports simply indicated that "students were involved in physical altercation." Some were a little more specific, stating something like, "Two girls were fighting in the hallway," or "The verbal argument led to a physical altercation." One report indicated that four students received youth referrals for disorderly conduct for a verbal altercation that "almost led to a physical altercation." Others seemed to indicate a more serious situation. For example, one report described an altercation between six boys that "led to riotous conditions."

There are numerous explanations for the subjectivity that is revealed in these data, including whether or not an incident was gang related and the dissimilarity in students' disciplinary records. Additionally, the inconsistent responses to violence, in part, were due to the persistent efforts of some administrators and deans to contest the use of criminal-procedural-level strategies and to emphasize the use of their own strategies, such as peer mediation and counseling. Nevertheless, minor incidents, even a few that, according to occurrence reports, involved only verbal altercations, sometimes resulted in the use of criminal-procedural-level strategies.

There is another possible reason for the inconsistent use of criminal-procedural-level strategies as a response to violence: the behaviors of students *after* an incident took place. Students appeared to be at risk of receiving a summons when they displayed anger or were unable to calm themselves after an emotionally charged altercation, especially when they appeared to think the intervening officers or school officials treated them unnecessarily harshly. In these cases, it seemed that students received summonses as an outcome of their "disorderly" behavior after a physical altercation, rather than for their participation in it. Occurrence reports did not indicate this specifically, but on several occasions I observed confrontations between students and law-enforcement officials that occurred after a student was "picked up" for fighting where it appeared that the summons was an outcome of the student's conflict with law enforcement (or school personnel).

The Ubiquity of the Threat

The actual number of arrests and summonses issued over the entire school year may not seem excessive to some, considering the total number of students in the school,[11] the length of my study (a full school year), and the nature of urban youth violence and crime. However, the culture of control was not simply a by-product of the use of summonses, arrests, and other criminal-procedural-level strategies; as these policies and practices went into effect, it seemed that a law-and-order discourse emerged within the school, and the use of *threats* of summonses and arrest became commonplace. These threats played a significant role in the establishment of a culture of control in the school.

On several occasions, after altercations took place or when students were brought to B-40 as a result of a confrontation with a law-enforcement official or teacher, I observed students' being questioned. When a student did not present him- or herself in a calm and "respectful" manner, the adult—a dean or officer—would often threaten the student with arrest and a summons, and at times the police would make good on their threat. Typically, these moments would entail heated exchanges between students and school personnel or officers. For example, on a number of occasions I heard both security agents and school personnel say things like, "Keep it up and you'll get a summons," or, "Do you want to get arrested? Calm down."

Even when threats were made as warnings by well-meaning educators who actually wanted to prevent an arrest, the threats ultimately reinforced the culture of control. Threats attempted to squelch dissent. They strengthened the culture of control in that they appeared to grow out of the belief that students had given up their rights in the moment when they broke a school rule or lost control of their emotions. After such an incident, a student was at risk of being handcuffed, charged with breaking the law, and summoned to criminal court if he or she did not quickly become calm and respectful. A brief exchange I witnessed exemplifies this attitude. A student who had been in a fight sat at a desk in the deans' office. It did not appear that the police were set to arrest the other students who had taken part in the fight. They were nowhere in sight. To no one in particular, the student in the office made barely audible comments declaring that he had rights and complained about the way the incident had been handled. A dean admonished him, "Be quiet. You've already abdicated all your rights. The more you say, the more trouble you'll be in. Keep it up and you know what will happen."

Summonses Inside and Out

One morning during spring break, my phone rang while I was getting ready to meet Carlos. It was Officer Bowen from Transit. "Do you know Carlos Mendoza?" he asked.

"Yes," I said and waited for his reason for calling me, although I already realized that Carlos must have been picked up on his way to meet me. The officer told me that Carlos had used his school-issued MetroCard to ride the subway on a nonschool day. The officer needed me to verify Carlos's identity, because Carlos did not have identification on him. (In such circumstances, individuals are brought to a precinct house until their identities are verified. Youth, in particular, are subjected to this process, as they are less likely than adults to have ID with them.)

I explained that Carlos may have thought he was on a school-related excursion to meet me, a researcher. But my explanation came too late and was not relevant to the officer. Carlos was issued a summons for fare evasion, which meant a $65 fine and yet another one-hour trip to Brooklyn transit court and a day of missing school. I had just been to transit court with him a few months earlier. (Unlike criminal court, there were no handheld scanners or bellowing proclamations of people's offenses in transit court—just a large room full of young black and Latino/a men and women and a long set of cashier windows.)

This was a typical experience of many of the students at UPHS that I met. It was not just at school that students received summonses. They accumulated them around school, in their neighborhoods, and in the subway stations. One day in early October, sitting in the detention room with Duane and a group of his friends, I asked them about this. They all had received a number of summonses both inside and outside school. One of the boys, Evan, in response to my question, pulled a crumpled wad of six slips out of his pocket. He smiled sheepishly and explained, "I have to hide them from my father."

But it was not just students frequenting the detention room who were accumulating summonses. Most of the students I interviewed had received at least one summons at some point within the previous year. Kalif, an articulate junior whom I met in the school leadership office, received a summons for fare evasion one night when he used his school MetroCard to return to school after official hours to pick up something he had forgotten. Another student, David, got one for walking through a park after closing hours and another one for loitering in front of the school. One student claimed to have gotten a summons for smoking. Many others reported getting summonses outdoors for loitering, jumping the subway turnstile, disorderly conduct, or littering.

"What kinds of summonses are kids getting outside of school?" I asked eighteen-year-old Wanda.

"Okay, if, like, say I'm on 149th and Grand Concourse; I'm waiting for the number 2 train to come. This happened to me. I spit my gum out on the platform. The cop was, like, 'Excuse me, did you just spit your gum out on the platform?' And, you know, I'm not going to lie, because obviously he seen me. I was, like, 'Yes.' He gave me a sixty-dollar ticket."

"For littering?"

"For littering," Wanda confirms. "I was, like, *a piece of gum!* For a thirty-cent gum I'm gonna get a sixty-dollar fine?"

Later in our discussion, Wanda pointed out that, like many of the students I interviewed, she avoided going outside at the end of the month, because she believed that the police had a quota of summonses to fill. I asked her to explain. She said, "The quota is when the police officers have to give a certain amount of people tickets at the end of the month, and if they don't meet that, they get in trouble."

"So, they're looking for students to . . ."

"Basically," Wanda explained, "and that's when kids don't mouth off to the cops at the end of the month, because they know better."

"Interesting. You think that's a pretty standard thing? Kids know?" (In fact, I had already been informed by an officer that it was not an actual NYPD policy, but officers conceded to me that some cops did need to bolster their numbers and tended to look for kids to give summonses to at times.)

Wanda replied, "Yeah, kids know. Like, right now, from last week till this week, I haven't been outside."

"Why is outside . . . ?"

"It's not that I'm scared to go outside, I just don't want to get a ticket, because them tickets add up, and, plus, if you don't pay the tickets, they come looking for you." And indeed they do. Young people who do not appear in court are eventually found and hauled down to the precinct in handcuffs. I even noted a few instances when students with unanswered summonses were tracked down and pulled out of their classes. Sometimes police caught up with youngsters when they received additional summonses, because their names were already in the police database. On one occasion, Carlos spent almost twenty-four hours in a jail cell when he was picked up for sneaking into a movie theater, and unbeknown to him, there was a warrant out for his arrest for a summons he had received and forgotten about. Upon leaving jail, he was sentenced to one day of community service and fined $95.

Thus, given that the young people in my study were receiving summonses inside and outside school, school-based policing interacted with street policing, creating an intensified level of penal control over their lives. A summons received in school could come back to haunt them in a movie theater, and a summons received on the street could lead to getting pulled out of class.

Penal Control in the Lives of Excluded Urban Youth

In this chapter, I have attempted to show how school disciplinary policies and practices—namely, order maintenance, along with zero tolerance—have the effect of criminalizing noncriminal behavior. My goal was to demonstrate how policies and practices shape school culture, and, more specifically, how order maintenance and the threats that are doled out within the current framework foster a culture of control. Additionally, I have detailed how the students at UPHS were subjected to the same policing strategies around the school and in their neighborhoods. The use of order-maintenance policing in so many of the public domains through which urban youth traverse appears to create situations where they are routinely being confronted by police officers and accumulating court summonses—and if they are not actually getting summonses, they are keenly aware of the possibility of getting them, as Wanda explained. These findings highlight that, although the oft-used metaphor of the school-to-prison pipeline is helpful (and real), the lived experience of many students at UPHS can be better understood through a nuanced description of daily life rather than the pipeline metaphor.[12] Despite a valuable body of scholarly literature on the subject, not all students in these schools are going to prison.[13] In fact, the majority will not likely spend significant time behind bars. To gain sufficient understanding of the everyday life experience of students at the school, it is useful to highlight a more mundane but pervasive phenomenon: how the lives of impoverished urban students are managed by a complex interpenetration of systems. The school, where they are by law required to spend most of their day, becomes an auxiliary to the criminal-justice system. These findings show that urban youth get subjected to levels of surveillance and repression that are not the same as long-term incarceration, but nonetheless, as the school merges with an ideology of street policing, the courts, and even the prison, a particular culture of penal control becomes an aspect of everyday life at school and beyond.

CHAPTER 4

Against the Law

Student Noncompliance and Contestation

R OUTINELY, STUDENTS AT UPHS WERE SUMMONED to criminal court
or got arrested as an outcome of a series of interactions beginning
with the breaking of a school rule. At times, the pivotal moment occurred
when an officer grabbed a student's arm or pulled a hat off a student's head.
At other times, the inciting moment happened when a student was approached by a law-enforcement official and asked for identification. This
process was a defining characteristic of the culture of control inside the
school and a key element in the linking of the school to street policing and
institutions of the criminal-justice system. But culture is not a top-down
process; it is dynamic and dialectical. This chapter explains how students
at UPHS participated in the production of a culture of control (and of
themselves as a criminalized class) through their noncompliance during
interactions with law enforcement. When students refused to hand over
their ID cards to officers or responded to agents' demands with defiance,
they reinforced the institutional perspective that "these kids have to learn,"
and, to some extent, they provided legitimacy for current policies.

Just as the deans and administrators lamented, it sometimes seemed
to me that students could have avoided getting a summons if only they
had cooperated with the police when confronted. Indeed, there seemed to
be some truth to the institutional discourse regarding the process of getting summoned to criminal court as a matter of personal choice—the student's choice. Why couldn't students just hand over their IDs, or answer
the officers' questions, or head to class, or take off their hats, or go willingly to B-40? Couldn't they just comply and avoid getting a summons?
The answers to these questions were a lot more complicated than simple
compliance.

Despite the trouble it caused students, there was an important ideological dimension to their refusal to comply with law enforcement. Their

contestations during interactions with police and agents contained within them a decisive critique of disciplinary practices. Policing practices, especially the demand to see ID, conflicted with students' sense of justice and fairness and their imagined ideal of schooling. That is, students' statements often revealed their ideas of what school *ought* to be but could not be within the prevailing framework. They desired to feel respected, to be listened to, and to be provided with meaningful, relevant learning experiences. In the context of control, these seemed to be things that happened only in "other kids' schools."

During my fieldwork, I identified five factors that were related to and appeared to influence the ways students responded during confrontations with law enforcement. These were (1) students' frustration with classroom experiences and disciplinary practices (and dysfunction); (2) student perceptions of police in their neighborhoods and popular local histories of police abuse and community relations; (3) the development of an intimacy between students and officers and agents due to daily contact; (4) some students' compulsion to maintain a tough posture in front of their peers; and (5) students' sense of indignation, brought about by their sense of injustice and their desire for a different kind of school experience. These five reasons for noncompliance were not separate; they worked together and, at times, were too entwined to analyze separately. The last one, indignation, encompassed all of the others. When I talked with students about noncompliance, almost all of their responses reflected this attitude; although they rarely articulated informed legal arguments or elegant analyses of social injustice, they expressed a sense of injustice and unfairness. Even when students suggested other reasons for noncompliance, they inevitably brought up "unfair" policing practices, poor treatment at the hands of law-enforcement officials, and feelings that they were disrespected. This is, in a sense, what Alison Jagger has called outlaw anger: a reasonable emotional response of a marginalized person[1]—not necessarily a response to the immediate situation in which the student finds him- or herself but a response to the overall symbolic and structural violence done to the student. Thus, noncompliance during an interaction with law enforcement represented several things at once: it provided personal benefits, such as a sense of dignity or social status, and it represented a contest over respect. In fact, the student–law-enforcement confrontation became a crucial "site" of contestation where students refused to legitimize the practices that violated so greatly their imagined ideal of schooling.

Disciplinary Dysfunction

Students' frustrations with disciplinary procedures appeared to have an impact on confrontations. Almost every student with whom I spoke had a critique of disciplinary practices in general. Complaints about disciplinary practices were so prevalent, in fact, that I made an effort to find students who did not have any—but only a few of the dozens I spoke with had nothing negative to say. In a survey that I left for students in the detention room for one week, 73 percent (twenty-seven out of the thirty-seven respondents who addressed the question) indicated that they believed the disciplinary incident in which they had just been involved had been handled unfairly. In itself, this is not surprising or very interesting. But their specific remarks are important for understanding the context in which frustration grew and noncompliance with law enforcement occurred. Students pointed to a host of frustrating experiences. These included incidents that could be described as bureaucratic dysfunction, such as school officials misplacing students' IDs after they had been taken away, resulting in students being forced to remain in the detention room until they could get their IDs returned. Other students complained that their IDs were still "blocked" after the allotted time for a suspension (meaning that when their cards were swiped in the computer, it indicated that the students were still barred from the school and, therefore, must continue sitting in the detention room or leave the building until the problem was rectified).

One day I broached the subject of noncompliance with Zack. We sat at a table in front of a large window in a Jamaican take-out restaurant across the street from the school. I glanced toward the school—a police van was parked in front, as usual, and two security agents conversed on the front steps—and asked why some kids didn't cooperate with the police. As he picked at his chicken and rice, he explained, "'Cause you wind up not getting your ID back. Somehow you don't get your ID back, or you didn't do it. You know what I'm saying? You trying to go to class, or sometimes it's like kids just want to be smart. You know what I'm saying? They just want to be stupid, like, 'Oh, I'm not gonna give them my ID.'"

Students' "being stupid" was a common way their contestation got framed, often by adults in the building but also by other students. It is important to note, though, that Zack expressed indignation at the whole process. Sometimes, he believed, students were innocent of any wrongdoing (or at least they believed their actions did not warrant police intervention).

But the first response Zack gave to my questions was that students were in-convenienced when their IDs were not always promptly returned. I heard this over and over throughout the school year.

Carlos explained that one of his arrests was due to his noncompliance after his ID card had not been returned for several periods while he sat waiting in the detention room: "They never brought down my ID, so I had to [stay] down there, like, every period. [My ID] never showed up." He continued to explain how he left the detention room and encountered some law-enforcement agents. "So then, um, they was, like, 'You gotta go back to B-40,' and I was, like, 'Watchu mean I gotta go back to B-40, be-cause I already spent, like, a lot of periods there because they didn't bring my ID back?' . . . And that's when I got upset, and, um, they said, 'Oh, if you don't go down to B-40, we gotta bring you down in cuffs,' and I said no. . . . I just want to get my ID. I already did my time.' Then they cuffed me and then they gave me a summons for disorderly conduct."

Student responses to my survey also suggested that students experi-enced high levels of inflexibility in the way policies were administered. Five students complained that they were brought down to B-40 for being in the bathroom when the bell rang, and nine students claimed they were "picked up" on their way to class, indicating they were only a few minutes late. In responding to the question "How do you feel about the way the situation was handled?" one student wrote, *They should of let me go to class because I was in front of it.*

Other responses indicated that students felt disrespected (*The dean went off on me; kids don't cooperate because they are disrespected*) or believed they were not being listened to. In describing how he got kicked out of class for talking to himself, one student wrote, *I could have not talked to my-self or curse but I don't think that it means [they had] to have security called on me. . . . [My teacher] could have calmed down for a second and maybe talked to me. That would have been more effective.*

Repeatedly throughout the school year, students made similar com-ments during interviews and conversations with me. For example, one day while I was sitting in an office inside the lunchroom with Takeisha, a sophomore I met in a class I attended on a regular basis, she ex-plained to me, "Teachers never wanna listen." Suddenly, her lips tight-ened, and it seemed to me that she was holding back tears. "They don't wanna hear what you gotta say. They don't take time to *listen.*" Takeisha's teacher described her as a "nice girl." She was not one to get into trouble.

Nonetheless, Takeisha appeared quite pained by her own perception that teachers didn't listen.

All of these statements indicate dysfunction and high levels of frustration with disciplinary practices. They also suggest that there was an implicit desire for another kind of schooling experience: an imagined ideal in which disciplinary practices were reasonable, students were treated with respect, and adults listened to them. The frustration students experienced helped to set the context in which students made sense of and responded to order-maintenance policing.

The Community and the School

Students' perceptions of the police in their neighborhood and popular understandings of community–police relations also appeared to play a role in shaping students' attitudes toward the police inside the school and, thus, their propensity toward noncompliance. When I spoke to students about their relationship with law enforcement inside the school, many made frequent references to police officers in their neighborhoods or stories that they had heard of police abuse. I am not claiming a causal relationship here. I argue instead that students' attitudes toward law enforcement in the school appeared to develop within the larger context of the collective memories of strained community–police relations, especially in the Bronx and other areas of New York City. Whether or not a student had been a victim of maltreatment at the hands of law enforcement, the students in my study were part of a community with a history of distrust and strained police–citizen relations based on stories of police nonresponsiveness, harassment, and brutality. Although my own study was limited to the school population and thus does not document a variety of community members' perspectives of the police, there is significant documentation on the public outrage over police misconduct and abuse associated with the police tactics of former New York City mayor Rudolf Giuliani's "quality-of-life" campaign (on which current school disciplinary policies are based)[2] and the shootings or abuse of such men as Anthony Bias, Amadou Diallo, Abner Louima, and Patrick Dorisman, whose names have become synonymous with police brutality in New York City.

Frequently, students made comments to me in which they alluded to these strained community–police relations. Their remarks revealed resentments and distrust. For example, Jermaine, a student I first took notice of during a confrontation with the police but later got to know when I attended his peer-mediation class during the spring semester, believed that youth, in particular, want to avoid the police. He said that there was no mutual respect between the police and young people in his neighborhood. When I asked him why he thought young people did not respect the police, his response revealed that he viewed police officers as a group in opposition to his own interests as a young black man. He said, "'Cause the cops *say* they're from the streets, but *we're* from the streets. And we're from the ghetto. If you go through this neighborhood or any other neighborhood that's going through the same problems this neighborhood suffers from, you'll hear the same answer. Not probably [from] everybody. Probably senior citizens might be happy, mothers, fathers probably be happy, but as far as youth, you know . . . We don't talk to the cops. We don't associate with the cops. We don't have anything to do with the cops. We don't. We stay away from all that. You understand what I'm saying? We want to live our life."

Jermaine saw the police as outsiders in his neighborhood and noted that young people generally wanted to stay away from the police so that they could "live their lives." Additionally, he believed that the police positioned themselves as if they were from the communities they were policing, but Jermaine implied that he and his fellow (young) community members were the authentic members of "the ghetto." Jermaine took a certain pride in his identity of "being from the ghetto"—one that he constructed in opposition to the police.

At other times, students expressed their distrust of the police in their refusal to turn to the police in a potentially dangerous situation. For example, one afternoon I came across Ms. Jenkins, an English teacher, in the hallway, speaking with a girl who was very upset. A group of female students had threatened to beat her up. Ms. Jenkins tried to calm the girl down and devise a plan. She suggested that the police should be informed and that perhaps a security agent could escort her out of the neighborhood. But the frightened and agitated girl would not accept the plan. "The police don't make me feel safe!" she kept repeating. "They never did *nothing* for me."

Strained relationships with the police were also apparent among some of the students who believed that the police played an essential role in school and neighborhood safety. Alisa, a sophomore who did well in her honors classes and was a member of the student government, for instance, had this to say when I asked her about the police: "The police, I didn't care for the police at all. My uncle was attacked by the police." She paused and then added, "But now I see they're trying to do their job, now that they're here [in the school]."

"How do you feel about them being here?" I asked.

She shrugged her shoulders. "I like them here," she said flatly. "You know, it takes time to get over stuff like [having a relative attacked]. I mean, they're doing their job."

Alisa's ambivalence might have reflected her reluctance to speak too ill of the police in front of the white woman sitting across from her, or it could have reflected the relative safety she felt inside the building. However, her comments may also represent the lived and historical contradictions embedded in the complex relationships between poor and working-class people of color and law enforcement. Anger over abuse and injustice coexists with a desire to feel safe in neighborhoods wrought with violence and a hope that the presence of community police officers might contribute to increased levels of public safety, as they purport to do.

After Carlos received the assistance of the police one night in late January, when he and his girlfriend, Jennifer, were attacked by a group of young people, I was curious to see whether the strong critique I had heard him voice on many occasions had shifted. It had. It had become more nuanced. That is, in light of the incident, he conceded for the first time since I met him that some officers were committed to the good of the public. He said, "There's always crooked cops. But then when something happens to you, they're the first ones you call for help. But I felt like, you know, it's good that they're here. But there's always those cops that do the job because they want to help people, and they want to help the community and maybe change the world. And there's those cops that turn cops because they think that kids are punks, and all they like to do, you know, '[Kids are] all thugs.' And then that's how they treat you. You know, there are two different ways of looking at it."

These statements about the police illustrate how students' attitudes toward school-based policing may have been influenced by experiences they had beyond the confines of the school. These kinds of comments do not necessarily reflect new attitudes based solely on the police presence in school; they reflect a history of distrust and a collective memory of abuse and nonresponsiveness, as well as a desire for—or in Carlos's case, an instance of—police coming to the aid of a citizen.

Daily School-Based Policing

Inside the school, however, the nature of community–police relations and experiences with law enforcement took on unique characteristics. At the same time, daily contact with law enforcement fostered close relationships and created new antagonisms between students and agents and officers. Both the naturalizing effects of daily police and agent presence and the tensions it created appeared to contribute to student noncompliance.

Intimacy and the Obfuscation of Police Authority

Although students frequently complained about the practices of law-enforcement officials, especially those of security agents, observational data indicate that many students had friendly relationships with law-enforcement officials. Students did not directly express their noncompliance in relation to these "friendships." Nevertheless, several deans made comments to me about students not taking the authority of officers seriously at UPHS, and they believed that this was because the students had come to think of law enforcement as an ordinary part of the school community. One dean said to me during a conversation about students' noncompliance, "You see, the students don't think of the cops as cops. They treat them the same way they would treat any adult in the school. They don't realize the power the police have. They don't really learn. So they think they can just mouth off the same way they do to teachers and deans." Another dean made a similar comment. In describing how students ended up with summonses, the dean pointed out, "The kids give PD [police department] the same respect they give anybody else. It's not like they're, like, 'Oh, that's the police department. [I should show more deference.]'"

Within the context of the school, these deans believed that students did not acknowledge police authority. They believed that student–police relationships had become too intimate or too routinized; the officers and agents essentially had become part of the school community. In other words, these deans argued that the students were responding from a cognitive framework in which they lacked the traditional reverence afforded to law-enforcement officials and refused to comply because they had lost sight of the officers' (and agents') state-sanctioned authority.

Additionally, officers and agents often appeared to be caring individuals who saw themselves as part of the school community. At times, they seemed to develop friendly relationships (perhaps even inappropriate ones, although I did not observe any firsthand) with students. This was particularly true with the security agents—the same individuals who were sharply critiqued by students for their shows of disrespect. Virtually all were individuals from surrounding or similar communities. In class status, racial background, educational levels, and at times even age, they resembled the students more than any other adult group in the school (with the exception of the school aides). Given this, and the fact that they had constant contact with the students, some developed relatively intimate relationships with the students.[3] One example of this intimacy was demonstrated one day while I was walking through the cafeteria with a male student. He stopped to converse with a female security agent. Although they both spoke predominantly English, they slipped in and out of Spanish, conveying their shared ethnicity and familiarity with each other. She inquired about his girlfriend, who hadn't been well, the way a concerned neighbor might do, and they spoke of another woman's baby shower.

Another indicator of some students' closeness with security agents was the complaints I frequently heard from students who were never or rarely involved in disciplinary cases. They contended that some students formed alliances with certain security agents, and these students would get away with breaking rules that other students could not break.

For me, over the school year, I also grew accustomed to, and indeed comfortable with, being around police officers and agents. As the months went on, there were a few police officers with whom I began to really enjoy having conversations. Most of the ones that I spoke with (with a couple of glaring exceptions) demonstrated much concern for kids and generally spoke well of them. Officer Hoffmann, in particular, expressed interest in "working with kids." He focused much of his effort on the more serious incidents of violence and gang-related events and showed considerable compassion for young people who joined gangs. "I don't condone it," he assured me, "but I understand it." My conversations with students and observations also suggested that Hoffmann had compassion for the students. One particular vignette demonstrates the kind of rapport he had with some of them.

One day in early winter, during a quiet moment in the deans' office, Officer Hoffmann (who was white) and Duane—one of the highest-ranking Bloods in the school, and black—were having a relaxed conversation about whether or not Duane was a callous individual. Hoffmann jokingly accused Duane, "You wouldn't even care if you found me lying in the street bleeding."

Duane leaned back in his seat and said with what sounded to me like a good deal of sincerity, "No man, you're my nigga [friend]." Hoffmann smiled and gave a soft laugh.

It is impossible to know for certain just how much students' continual contact and closeness with law enforcement in the school influenced levels of noncompliance. My data show only that there was a significant amount of friendliness and intimacy between the two groups, and that many of the deans believed that students lost sight of the authority of the police and treated them "like everyone else." After several months in the school observing and conversing with students and law enforcement, I, like the deans, came to believe that the peculiar situation created through daily policing in the school and the intimacy that developed did indeed influence students' noncompliance. The possibility that students "treated officers like everyone else" existed alongside students' notion that no adult should demand a student's ID (an action associated with street policing) or use criminal-procedural-level strategies to respond to the breaking of a school rule.

Although students' familiarity with law-enforcement officials, their fondness for some of them, and their sense that the officers' presence at UPHS was "normal" may have played a role in noncompliance, these factors do not undermine the significance of student resentment toward law-enforcement officials in the school. It is possible that congeniality concealed other feelings. Perhaps some friendly interactions were strategic moves—public transcripts, of sorts[4]—on the part of students to generate some of their own power in relation to law-enforcement officials. The idea of students forming "alliances" with certain security agents (a theme that regularly came up in conversations) suggests this. It would also not be surprising if individuals who spent day after day together grew genuinely to like each other. Intimacy can coexist with animosity and resentment.

"Like the Knicks at Madison Square"

Students' animosity and resentment, although likely influenced by their existing conceptions of the police in their neighborhoods, appeared to stem largely from the particular treatment they received in the context of the school and from the fact that policing practices conflicted with the hopes and desires students held for what school ought to be.

Jermaine explained that the police in the school were like the basketball team the New York Knicks on their home court at Madison Square Garden, in New York City. One of his narratives serves as an example of how animosity or grudges can build when one is subjected to seeing the same law-enforcement officials every day. His comments also speak to the increased powers that law-enforcement officials had inside the school. Jermaine said, "Now, even when you get into a dispute with the cops, you see the same cop every day. So that grudge is still going to be there, 'cause you still get to see his face. Now, it's different if you get into a problem with an officer on 183d Street and you live on Gun Hill Road [which is several miles from 183d Street]. What's the chances of you ever seeing that cop again? So the grudge is automatically gone. Yeah, this cop arrested me. He punched me in my face, but, whatever. He's out doing his own thing [in the street]."

However, when conflicts occur between a student and an officer in school, the student must face the same officer every day thereafter. Referring to an actual incident that took place between Jermaine and a security agent, he continued, "Now, when I got hit in my face [in school], and I swung back and that fight happened between me and the officer, I got to walk in [to school] every day and say he punched me in my damn face. And I have to sit here and look at him and no, I can't even do anything. When you're in this building rules apply. But now I see the same officer inside and outside in the street. He has the connection inside the school, but I have the connections outside. I step into his world, he steps into my world."

"So, do you see the school as the cops' world?" I ask.

"Yeah. This is their safe spot. This is where they're safe at, regardless of anything, because they're cops. This is their home. This is their domain. This is like the Knicks at Madison Square. Out there [in the streets, it's] a whole different ball game. [The police] don't tell me what to do when I'm out there. [They] can't ask for my ID card. In the streets, I have certain rights. I can turn around and say, 'Get the hell out of my face,' and walk away. And all they can do is sit there and say, 'Hey, what can we do? Our hands are tied. He hasn't do anything wrong yet.'"[5]

Jermaine contended that the school had become the domain of the police, and he implied that the institutional setting provided officers with

a certain kind of protection that they did not have on the streets and an
increased power (to enforce school rules, to demand an ID without suspicion of an actual crime, and to take criminal-procedural-level action
against individuals who were not breaking the law). Jermaine did not
focus on the fact that the increased power infringed on the civil rights of
students inside the school. Instead, he emphasized his feelings of disem-
powerment and frustration within the school and the presence of grudges
that built up as a result of continued contact with the same officers.

Zack also viewed the school as a place where the police had taken over,
and he understood this as a problem. His comments, like Jermaine's, suggest that, given the officers' increased power in the school, they sometimes
treated students poorly or unfairly. One day while hanging out with Zack,
I asked him how things had changed in the school since the implementation of the new disciplinary policies. "They're starting to lock down the
school," he said. "The only thing is, you know, the cops. That's the main
thing right there."

"What about the cops?" I asked.

"You know, the cops in the school is really bad. They talk to you like
you nothing, like you some criminal in the street. But really, you a student
attending high school. And they talk to you, like, 'Oh, fuck that, you ass-
hole, you dumb ass.' They say a lot of words. Well, the cops in the school, is
like they run it. They *are* the school. But if you really look at it, the cops are
supposed to be the law. Cops ain't supposed to be education. You know
what I mean?"

The cops *are* the school. Zack's comment suggests how the presence of
the police in the school and the power they asserted shifted the meaning
attached to the institution for him. At the moment, though, as I listened
to Zack, I was stuck on the language he claimed law-enforcement officials
used. "The cops say stuff like that?" I asked.

"The cops say literally like that. They come out real ugly. They don't
come out as respectful. Now, if you come out ugly, they going to come out
more ugly. If they don't like you already, they going to come out like that.
Or if you come out real, real respectful, you gotta really—excuse my language—you gotta really suck up, you got to kiss ass to do anything. Like,
for the cops to be good to you. I got two friend cops in [the school], Men-
dez and Hoffmann. I'm close to those cops, like, they real friendly. Like,
they don't . . . they talk, you know what I'm saying?"

During my year at UPHS, I never heard police officers or agents curse at students, but on numerous occasions I observed officers and agents antagonize students with both verbal and physical aggression (getting close to their faces and pushing them, for example). And certainly the level of interaction I saw students have with law-enforcement officials was greater than I have seen anywhere else except in my few trips to prisons. So it was no wonder that many students had reconceptualized UPHS as a place run by the cops. But it was a problematic takeover; Zack and others resented that the school wasn't more about education and that the police were free to regulate students' actions so intensely.

Students often reported that law-enforcement officials, particularly the security agents, did not just speak harshly to students; at times, they confronted students physically. Wanda emphasized the physical contact agents made with students as she expressed her frustrations over law enforcement and their practices:

> Don't be pulling on the kids. Because you have one of the kids that's there and you pull on him the wrong way, they can snap. You don't know if that child's been abused, that child has been raped, you don't even know if that child takes medication and you grabbing on that child! Because the same way you grab that child, that child could turn around and say you raped them. "I been raped by a security guard," just saying in general. I've never been raped, but I'm just saying that child could turn around and be, like, "I been raped." Like I said, I don't step in your box, you don't step in mine. And the security guards say, "We have boundaries. You don't step in our box, because when you step in our box, we feel like you're trying to harm us." So you don't step in *our* [the students'] box, because we feel like *you're* [the agents are] trying to harm *us* [the students]. They should have that understanding between the students in the school. If they had that understanding, I bet you there would be no security guard yelling for backup.

"If they just had a little bit more respect, particularly of students' space, or physical boundaries?" I asked.

"Yes, yes! Because you know how many security guards got hit in this school because of that?"

Wanda's statements poignantly suggest that law-enforcement officials were not always sensitive to or equipped to deal with students who had difficult histories of abuse or who took medication. They shouldn't be "pullin' on" students, but they sometimes did, and in Wanda's estimation, that led to physical confrontations or noncompliance. She also noted that security agents demanded that their personal space not be violated, and that the respect that the agents expected from students should be reciprocated.

Almost all of the students I spoke with at UPHS were concerned about being treated with respect and maintaining respect in the eyes of authority figures. But although there may be a commonly held perception that black and Latino/a urban youth are "obsessed with respect" (as I often heard during interviews with teachers), the reality at UPHS was that there was an intense emphasis placed on respecting authority, and students' desire for respect is best understood in relation to the institution's demand for it. Jermaine aptly referred to this dynamic as a tug-of-war; I would call it a contest over respect.[6]

When I asked Jermaine about relationships between students and officers in the school and students' reasons for defiance, he explained that there was a pervasive sense that students were not respected. Defiance, then, became a means to establish respect. He said, "Actually, I'm gonna tell you the truth. A lot of the cops in this school aren't bad in my eyes, because they only get involved when they have to get involved. Everything else is the security guards, but you still have your selective few out of the ten, eleven cops in this building. You still have your few that feel as if they have to prove something. I don't know what it is. I think they want to prove that we're not bad and we're trying to tell them that we are bad. So it's more of a tug-of-war going on between the two."

Initially, I did not understand what Jermaine meant by police officers wanting to prove that students weren't "bad." But as I continued speaking with Jermaine, I realized that what he meant by "bad" is what I think of as "tough." Most students I met at UPHS were invested to some degree in demonstrating their ability to be tough. Toughness was equated with maintaining self-respect and dignity in the eyes of authority figures and peers. In Jermaine's view, the police and agents were attempting to strip students of that dignity by treating them like criminals in the making.

I asked Jermaine why students wanted to convince the officers that they were tough. He said, "So we could have our sense of respect, because they have their respect. They automatically have their respect the minute they say, 'Give me your ID.' That's respect automatically. You look at the ID card. They have their respect. It automatically says, 'This card must be carried at all times. It must be shown upon request.' That's respect automatically. So where do our respect come in? We have no respect. Their respect is on the ID card. Their respect is on the walls. 'No do-rags upon entering class.' That's respect to the teacher. Where's our respect? There is none."

Noncompliance was thus often viewed as a means of maintaining respect through the contestation of an order that represented the "automatic" respect and power of the police. Carlos's framing of noncompliance was similar. He was noncompliant only after he had spent several periods in the detention room waiting to get his ID card returned to him (recall the earlier discussion on general dysfunction). He had "done his time." (Prison metaphors abound!) After being told that his ID had still not been delivered to the deans' office, where he would normally retrieve it, he had gone to look for the agent who had taken it. When he still could not retrieve his ID, he became upset, and that is how he explained his noncompliance. He was tired and indignant, and wanted to go to class. As Carlos and I sat in the courthouse in late November waiting to see the judge for a summons he received (see chapter 3), he told me that there was a time when he had had a good rapport with the police, but that ended a year or so before I met him, at age fifteen, when what he saw as a misunderstanding that took place in the street led to his being dragged to the ground and restrained by three officers. As we talked, he showed me the scar on his wrist left by the handcuffs. Now, Carlos says that he gets angry when the police approach him and speak to him in a way he views as disrespectful. Echoing Jermaine's desire for respect, Carlos said, "To me there's only, like, two choices. Like, stay quiet and go home, or stand up for what you feel is right and wind up in the precinct. And usually I stand up."

When asked about student noncompliance in school, Wanda explained that it was a matter of students "knowing their rights." As we sat in the detention room together one afternoon, she said,

Sometimes the cops, which is a.k.a. the po-po, be harassing the kids, be harassing the students, so you don't give your ID. You know your rights! You know you didn't do nothing wrong, why show ID? Like, I'll be damned if you . . . It's like you're going ten miles an hour, the cop pulls you over. "Why you going ten miles per hour?" You trying to be safe. You're not in the forty lane, you're in the twenty or whatever lane. Wouldn't you ask the officer, "Why you pulling me over?" Wouldn't you tell the officer you know your rights? It's like the students saying, "I know my rights. I didn't do nothing wrong, so there's no reason for me to pull out my ID." That's, like, saying I know my rights. And sometimes the officers will try to talk to you, like, "Give me your ID," like you don't know your rights. I know my rights. I'm not showing you my ID because, number one, I didn't do nothing wrong. And number two, I'm not showing you no ID because I know my rights, I know my rights.

In the school, students were expected to show their IDs whether they had done something wrong or not, but Wanda's comments show how students framed school-based incidents with law-enforcement officials as if they were encounters that took place in the street, in which case they believed an officer would need some kind of reasonable cause to demand to see ID.

These students' remarks are similar to dozens of other student statements I collected throughout the school year. Students frequently expressed their perspective that the cops had gained significant power in the school—like the Knicks at Madison Square—and too often treated students with disrespect. The confrontation with law enforcement and the act of defiance signified students' refusal to accept the way things were. No matter how they framed the issue, as a matter of respect, unfairness, unjust profiling, or civil rights, these students were expressing political indignation. With little or no access to other means of protest, and dissatisfied with the circumstances and the daily (sometimes hourly) confrontation with law enforcement, they felt compelled not to comply.

Perspectives of the "Schoolboys and -Girls"

Whether or not students were academically engaged or had been involved in a disciplinary case, virtually all students I interviewed held some level of critique of the actions of law enforcement in the school, especially those of security agents. Indeed, most students running for student government positions (some of the most academically oriented, engaged students in the school) during that year made a public statement about the need to address police and security-agent "harassment" and to reduce the number of summonses students were receiving. Ronald, a senior and a member of the student government, described a type of "profiling" as he critiqued the practices of law enforcement in the school. He argued that certain students, based on the way they dressed, were treated differently than others when confronted by law enforcement in the hallways. He contrasted his experience of being stopped in the hallway with those of other students: "I believe that it's profiling that's going on in the hallways. Like when I was asked for my ID, I told [the agent] the reason I was in the hallway. . . . I was cooperative, but I believe in asking questions, being assertive and asking questions. Like, I asked, 'Will I be taken down to B-40?' and he said no, he just wanted to see my ID. Then I explained why I was in the hallway, and they listened to me. They weren't, like, . . . The reason that some kids don't show their ID is because [security agents] approach them [in a rough manner] and aggression feeds aggression."

I asked Ronald if he could explain a little more what he meant by profiling. "It's about the way I dress, for example, white buttoned-down shirt. . . . They will look at me and think, 'All right, he doesn't look like a person who will be causing trouble. But if they see a person walking down the hallway with a hat on his head, which is illegal in the school, they will stop this person and approach him in a different manner. I believe there is a profiling going on."

Ronald was the type of student Anne Ferguson would characterize in her ethnography *Bad Boys: Public Schools and the Making of Black Masculinity* as a "schoolboy," as opposed to a "troublemaker."[7] Ronald was constructed by the school as a "good" young man. He was academically oriented and a leader in the school, and he had considerable cultural capital.[8] His mother was a teacher, he spoke in a middle-class register, and he had a middle-class affect. Thus, he was afforded a certain respect that was often not extended to other types of students when they were confronted by law-enforcement officials or school personnel. Ronald understood that, as a "schoolboy," he was treated differently. And even though he was not usually subject to aggressive police behavior in the school, he also recognized that the police and security agents could exacerbate conflict between perceived "troublemakers" and themselves.

Students also made important distinctions between the behaviors of police officers and security agents. Most of the students I spoke with believed that security agents were particularly confrontational with students. Comments made by Lena, Gillian, and Lorenzo, all seniors in good academic standing, were representative of students with whom I spoke. When I asked them about disciplinary policies in the school, Lena brought up the subject of the security "guards" (agents). She said, "Sometimes when the security guards see you, they just want to bother you for no reason. Probably just because that's their job. That's what they do."

"How do they bother you?" I asked.

"They see you walking in the hall, they say, 'Let me have your ID,' for no reason."

Lorenzo added, "They see you with a pass, and they still bother you. The pass is a waste of time."

"And some of them are disrespectful," Lena continued. Her frustration with the situation came through in her voice.

"How are they disrespectful? Can you give an example?"

"Like the other day I was walking down the stairs, and one of my friends touched me on the side, but I thought that it was one of the security guards. So I said, 'Oh, I thought it was him.' So, the security guard walking behind me asked me, 'What? What did you just say?' Like he was gonna argue with me. So I just looked at him and just walked away. And he walked with me down the steps asking questions. 'What did you say?'" She mimicked his confrontational tone.

Gillian interjected, "And sometimes they want to fight the students. I saw it! I saw it!"

Lena: "They step up to you like they want to fight you!"

Gillian: "In your face!"

This exchange exemplifies how students sometimes made distinctions between police officers and security agents. Students were well aware that the security agents worked under the auspices of the NYPD, and they believed that the main difference between the two groups was that security agents had less status and did not carry guns. This is why students commonly referred to them as "toy cops," "wannabes," or "cops in training."

Despite the fact that Gillian, Lena, and Lorenzo did not frequently become involved in disciplinary cases, they, like Ronald, held a strong critique of the ways in which law-enforcement officials approached students. These academically oriented students recognized and pointed out what they viewed to be ill treatment and discriminatory practices.

On Being (or Not Being) a Punk

Some student interactions with the police and security agents were also influenced by students' desire to appear tough in front of peers and in front of law enforcement. The police were, in a sense, a common enemy, or at least a symbol of authority, and it could be beneficial for students to demonstrate to others that they would not "be a punk" in front of an officer. That is, many students believed that they gained social status among peers if they "stood up to" law-enforcement officials. Creating a tough posture (or at least not being "soft," or a punk) also served as a means of protection against bullying and other forms of violence.[9]

One day early in my fieldwork, I sat at a desk in the deans' office, talking with a student who had been given a summons for disorderly conduct after refusing to hand his ID card over to a security agent. He was a small boy who looked as if he could be eleven years old. He was fourteen. He rested his chin on his arms, which were crossed on top of the desk.

I looked down at him and asked, "So why didn't you just give your ID to the agent when he asked for it?"

The boy's eyes widened, and he looked at me as if I had suggested something insane. Without lifting his head, he said with great conviction, "'Cause then I'd be a punk!"

"Would that be so bad? I mean, it would have saved you this trouble with going to court and all?"

But he could not fathom complying. Surrendering his ID was just not something he would have done. I was a little surprised by how certain he appeared. I began asking this question of students I met in B-40, and the notion of not being a punk frequently came up. As I sat with students in the detention room, they often gave me that same incredulous look. "'Cause then I'd be a punk!" they would say, as if nothing was worse than that.

Appearing too cooperative during an interaction with a law-enforcement official, especially one who was already showing disrespect, caused a student to look weak. Students who were gang members and those who were more street oriented were particularly at risk. Appearing too "soft" could make them vulnerable to serious physical peer violence.[10]

On my detention-room survey, one student wrote about noncompliance with authority figures in terms of such peer pressure:

Some students do not cooperate with authority because of the way they are approached. Some students like to act big and bad in front of friends. From my point of view us students are put under peer pressure by peers. Some of us would like to follow rules but can't take the fact that others are watching you and after, the student is mentally or

physically abused by another person. It's more easier to be bad than
good and everyone should know that. Some of us must blend in with
the crew so they won't be picked on. It's like a game. Someone must lose
and someone must win. The losers are the people who do all their work
and follow the rules. The winners are the loud mouth wanna be gangsta
ones. But what we fail to understand is that in this game the losers are
going to make it somewhere. The winners stay where they are or worst.
All I'm saying is that we don't obey rules because in the eyes of others
we don't wanna look like fools.

This young man's analysis explores several of the themes that came up
during my interviews and conversations with students. He started by providing the most common answer I received when I asked students about
noncompliance—students did not like the way they were approached—
but he quickly moved into a poignant description of how students often
felt the need to challenge authority in order to maintain a certain image
among their peers. Kids who did not appear tough or "big and bad"
risked getting picked on or mentally or physically abused by other students. Sadly, this respondent recognized the irony of this behavior—that
the "winners" ultimately stayed where they were or experienced worse
(perhaps prison).

The pressure that the more marginalized students felt to appear tough
in the eyes of peers or to save face in front of adults may help to explain the
difference between the interactions Jermaine and Zack had with the police and the interactions Ronald had. Ronald could calmly ask questions
and get through an incident without getting a summons perhaps partly
because he was initially approached in a more respectful manner (and
continued to receive more respect throughout the interaction), but also
because he was under less pressure to appear tough. Nevertheless, it is important to note that no one had impunity. According to Assistant Principal Juarez and some of the deans, even "good kids" received summonses
for "no reason." I would argue that this is because the good kid / bad kid
binary to which many of the adults in the building referred was misleading. Although there were clear differences between some of the students I
met in terms of their academic performance, disciplinary record, and demeanor, any student who got fed up with policing practices was at risk of
becoming entangled with law enforcement.

Indignation at the Center of Noncompliance

In this chapter, I have attempted to delineate the dynamics and perspectives that appeared to contribute to student noncompliance. Some of what I have detailed provides context for noncompliance: students were frustrated by the complicated and often dysfunctional disciplinary apparatus that they experienced as unreasonable. Other testimonies more directly explained noncompliance: students experienced high levels of indignation and framed noncompliance as an act of maintaining respect, resisting injustice, and standing up for their rights. Students' testimonies also indicated an implicit critique not just of disciplinary policies but of schooling more generally and of the fact that disciplinary practices conflicted with their imagined ideal of school: a place where they might feel respected and listened to. Students' implicit message (as understood through my own sociological piecing together of the sentiments that were expressed to me) went something like this: "You force me to come here and attend irrelevant classes. You don't listen to me. The police disrespect me and try to embarrass me in front of my friends when I haven't even broken the law! I won't cooperate with this."

This type of contestation was also perhaps the most direct example of how students gained command over their presentation of self—a theme I take up in chapter 6—in a context of control. By "standing up" for themselves, as Carlos put it, students literally stood in direct defiance of prescribed institutional norms and made an assertion of self-respect. The psychological rewards for doing so often seemed worth the cost.

Yet, although students' noncompliance might have been a reasonable form of dissent from a critical perspective, such "outlaw emotions" produced students as a criminalized class. Students' noncompliance fueled the perspective of educators and law enforcement that "these kids have to learn." In the public eye, noncompliance helps reinforce representations of low-income black and Latino/a youth as incorrigible and justifies current policies. This is one of the most significant ways that students participated in the creation of the culture of control in the school.

CHAPTER 5

Tensions between Educational Approaches and Discourses of Control

D EANS AND ADMINISTRATORS at UPHS asserted their own disciplinary strategies and even, at times, intentionally subverted the use of criminal justice or school discipline. They often strove for what could be called a culturally relevant disciplinary approach. The strategies I observed, such as counseling, parental contact, mediation, and problem solving (addressing the academic or organizational issue that might be causing the misbehavior), generally grew out of educational or social-psychological frameworks rather than a criminal-justice framework. However, at the same time, the overarching criminal-justice framework produced institutional discourses of control and influenced almost all interactions between school disciplinarians and students during disciplinary incidents.

In his ethnographic study of high schools similar to UPHS, John Devine notes that with the implementation of new security technologies, zero tolerance, and heavy policing, teachers have retreated into their classrooms and no longer take on the role of providing moral guidance to students.[1] In my own study, I found that deans (who were teachers) and school administrators were still personally addressing hallway disorder and attempting to assert a culturally relevant disciplinary practice—doing the difficult work of "reaching the kids"—but, despite their efforts, they, too, had lost their moral authority. Ultimately, school disciplinarians appeared to become invested in the new policing practices (and the language of policing) and would defer to law enforcement or risk getting arrested themselves when even minor incidents became "police matters."

The Educator–Police Relationship

At some of the Impact schools, there has been considerable tension between educators, led by the principal, and police and security agents, and disagreement over which group has ultimate authority in the building.[2] At one Bronx high school, a principal and a school aide were arrested for obstructing justice when they intervened on behalf of a student in what had been deemed a police matter. Several teachers in other Impact schools were also arrested, and a couple of schools received media attention for heated tension between educators and law enforcement.

The relationship between the police and educators at UPHS that I observed was not so strained. Over the school year, I witnessed a growing cordiality that was also reflected in interviews with at least some school personnel and law-enforcement officials.

In September, when I first met Alvarez, the principal, and asked about the administration's relationship with the police, she replied, "We coexist," and reminded me that it was her building and that UPHS was still a school. In those early months, many of the deans expressed frustration with the heavy police presence. "Students are getting summonses for the smallest things!" several complained. In turn, one of the police officers expressed considerable disdain for Juarez, the assistant principal of school safety, and reminded me that, according to his understanding of NYPD regulations, the hierarchy in the school went like this: the police had the most authority, followed by the security agents, and only *then* the school administrators.

In addition, several of the deans I spoke with expressed deep concern over the astoundingly high numbers of black and Latino men, and increasingly women, who are incarcerated or in some way (such as parole or probation) caught up in the criminal-justice system. The heavy police presence in the school made them uncomfortable. Some educators, as people of color from the surrounding or similar communities, alluded to the fact that it affected them personally.

Nevertheless, as the year went on, the two groups forged a seemingly good working relationship. By the end of the school year, the principal pointed out that some educators in other schools could not get along with the police and insisted on interfering in police matters, and one of the police officers made a similarly critical remark about officers at other schools who did not respect the educators' authority enough. By midspring, Juarez informed me in his quintessentially smooth style that he and the police sergeant had been sitting down together for months each morning for coffee to discuss the day ahead. It appeared to me that they had come a long way from the time I witnessed Juarez yelling at the officers to get out of his office during Terrell and James's arrest.

By the end of the year, it appeared that the lead administrators and deans at UPHS generally accepted (or at least resigned themselves to) the conditions of their workplace and had learned to work within the criminal-justice framework, but that did not mean that they themselves had transformed into auxiliary law-enforcement officials. To the contrary, they maintained their identities as educators in myriad ways, and the tensions between their varying levels of critique and their acceptance of the new disciplinary policies remained a prominent theme throughout the school year.

Educational Leaders and Solutions: Alvarez and Juarez

Despite the cordiality I observed, there remained a clear distinction throughout my fieldwork between the driving philosophies of law enforcement and school administrators. And although it is impossible to ascertain which policies and practices had the greatest impact on school safety and order, it is clear from my investigation that the school administrators and their staff played a significant role in instilling some order and reducing violence. Alvarez did not approach violence and disruption as just a "crime" problem; instead, she tended to view disciplinary matters in the broader context of the students' experiences of schooling. With this perspective of discipline, Alvarez, along with her staff, strove to use positive or corrective strategies (conflict resolution, counseling, and the like) rather than purely punitive ones whenever she could to address violence and disruption. She called the work she did "problem solving."

During an interview with Principal Alvarez, she spoke about her approach for addressing matters of school discipline. She emphasized the interrelatedness of discipline, organizational practices, and academics, as well as the importance of building relationships with students. When I asked her about her daily life as a principal, she wrapped up a long list of responsibilities by saying, "And staying in touch with the kids is really very important to me. So I try to spend as much time as I can [with them], whether it's in the cafeteria or in B-40 or in the guidance [office] or in the hallway. I think that's very much a part of the discipline, for them to see that you're there to help them address whatever problems they may have."

Principal Alvarez built on this theme when I asked her to identify the biggest disciplinary problem in the school. Her response transformed our interview into an old-fashioned call down to the principal's office, with me as the student:

> The biggest problem in this building was anonymity. Nobody knew who you were, *Kathy* [placing emphasis on my name]. And since I don't know who you are, you can do what you want. But now I know who you are, *Kathy* [more emphasis], so when I walk the hallway and say, "Kathy, why are you here?" See, Kathy can't hide no more. Kathy can't run away, because Kathy knows that Marissa [the principal] knows that she's there. Now you can't have groups of fifty or sixty kids running around, not knowing who they are. The second thing is, why is Kathy standing in that corner? This is the second time I see her walking this hallway when I come out, so I need to call Kathy. "Kathy, what's going on? Why aren't you in class?" Now we start dealing with Kathy on an individual basis. Let's look at Kathy's transcript. You know, sometimes I'm in the hallway and I see something. I pull a kid, and I'm, like, why don't we have a seat, and I go into my computer and I pull up Kathy's transcript. "Kathy, you failed. Is there a problem?" "Oh, I took that course again." "Let's go call the counselor." Kathy says she's been in this class three times. Well, Kathy's failed this class three times with the same teacher. Why has she been put in that same class with that same teacher? You know, so you start addressing those individual issues.

Alvarez's presence in the public spaces of the school was not constant; she had far too many responsibilities for that. But after only one full year in the school, most of the students I spoke with knew her, and many claimed that she knew them quite well. (It is apparently a powerful message when the principal in a large school calls a student by name.) Alvarez's words illustrate the principal's belief in addressing problematic organizational practices, such as poor programming of students' classes, that undermined students' efforts to remain engaged in the educational process. She demonstrated an understanding that if a student was in an inappropriate class, the student was more likely to be found wandering the hallways.

Alvarez also explicitly connected the issue of discipline to the classroom experience: "And at the same time you start looking at global issues such as what's happening in the cafeteria. What's happening in the classroom? Do I want to be in the classroom? If I walk into the classroom and *I* don't want to be there, there's a problem. That classroom has to call me in. It has to welcome me in."

Juarez, the principal's right-hand man when it came to security, summed up his perspective on effective discipline in terms of listening to students. During a tour of the building one afternoon in September, I observed his style.

As we walked together through the hallways and the cafeteria, Juarez attracted students like a magnet. Students appeared happy to see him; there were lots of handshakes and hugs. He turned to me at one point and explained that it was about listening to kids, showing them that he cared, and getting to know them. If they knew him and respected him, they would listen to him. I might have thought it was all a show for my sake, except that his words were substantiated in the way the students reacted to him. They greeted him excitedly and had stories for him. He smiled and called the girls "sweetie" and patted the boys on their shoulders. Juarez contrasted his own style with that of law enforcement, with apparent indignation in his voice, as he pointed out a few students who were arrested during the previous spring semester for "no reason" and suggested that I interview them. Although ultimately Juarez cooperated with law enforcement, his philosophy and his identity as an educator, like Principal Alvarez's, remained intact.

Because their philosophies were generally based on educational, rather than criminal-justice principles, Alvarez and Juarez could not prevent the police from arresting students or writing summonses, and they tended not to defy openly Department of Education mandates to suspend students or otherwise punish them. How does one who represents the institution maintain an identity that is contrary to the prevailing culture? One way that the principal, the assistant principal, and their team of deans were able to do this was to "put the humanity in the policies."

One day I asked Alvarez how she managed to navigate the mandates imposed from outside the school. Did they mesh with the reality inside the building? Alvarez responded, "I believe that the policy makers are the furthest away from the school building schoolwide, and many times [the policies do] not reflect the reality of the situation. Navigating the system is very interesting and can be done. I think that the people at the building level have to put the humanity into those policies, and if you're able to do that, then it'll be okay, but it is difficult at times but—you know what?" she smiles and adds a bit cheekily, "They're not here. They're not here."

Putting the humanity into the policies sometimes could mean using discretion in how a situation at UPHS was dealt with. This involved such practices as not reporting an incident that could have been viewed as a matter that fell into the domain of the police, instead relying on strategies aimed at transforming student behavior, overcoming obstacles, and rectifying problems.

Putting the humanity in the policies might also refer to the extra effort the principal and some of her staff made to work with certain students. Alvarez and Juarez, for example, took students under their wing and tried to help them become more invested in their classes. These were often the students who were chronically involved in disciplinary cases and had become very alienated from the classroom. In short, the strategy involved showing kindness, helping a student with his or her problems, and working to reengage him or her in the educational process.

On a more passive level, putting the humanity in the policies often referred to nothing more than sympathetically placing one's hand on the shoulder of a boy who sat with his hands cuffed behind his back—as I had seen Juarez do—or in some other way showing empathy for a child under arrest. This occurred because, in the end, educators' actions were constrained by the dominant criminal-justice framework. The principal demonstrated this point as she reflected on how the mandate for zero tolerance of weapons played out on the ground and negatively affected the lives of working youth:

There's that zero tolerance in terms of bringing weapons into the building, which I agree with, you know, honestly; however, those policies do not see the young lady or the young man who works for a living to help support the family who has to go into the stock room and open boxes and put them on the shelves, goes home late every day, puts the box cutter in his pocket, forgot about it, comes the next day into school and the child has to be arrested, suspended . . . because you have to follow the policy. You can't make the exception, because it will come back to haunt you. So then the challenge is, what do you do afterwards? How do you make the process easier—if you can call it that—or more humane for this one person who didn't mean to bring the box cutter, who had no malicious intent?

The principal understood the complexity of such situations and saw the dilemma, but ultimately some rules could not be broken and educational strategies for dealing with disciplinary problems, although not totally disregarded, became secondary to criminal-procedural-level strategies. Putting the humanity in the policies was a palatable way of adhering to policy and working within the culture of control while maintaining a distinction between educators and law enforcement.

Toward a Culturally Relevant Disciplinary Practice: The Deans

The deans were the fifteen or so teachers who were relieved from three periods of teaching each day to assume various responsibilities as part of the disciplinary team (paperwork, hallway monitoring, mediation, and managing the scanning lines, for example). These disciplinarian-educators worked closely with Principal Alvarez and Assistant Principal Juarez. They also had regular contact with security agents and police officers. Some were chosen by the new administration for their ability to connect with students; others sought the change; and still others were told that they could save a teaching position in their department if they would take the job (because a dean's lighter teaching load freed up some classes). The individuals in this group varied widely in their political perspectives and their levels of acceptance of the criminal-justice framework. On the whole, however, deans tended to be more critical than other teachers of the criminal-justice framework, perhaps partly because, as deans, they were more aware of the prevalence and consequences of police interventions. Indeed, no dean with whom I spoke was entirely supportive of policing practices in the school.

Who were these deans? There was Dean Henry, who had graduated from UPHS about twelve years before my study. He was a history teacher, the varsity football coach, and a leader among the deans as he worked on his assistant principal's license. He was tall, with a dark complexion and a warm and polite manner. There was Dean Jackson. He was a twenty-eight-year-old physical-education teacher who was stationed mainly in the special-education wing on the first floor. His energetic style and youthful dress led me to mistake him for a student a few times as we passed in a crowded hallway. Some of the boys from the special-education wing said things like, "We like Jackson. He's from where we're from." And there was Dean Orozco, a sturdy woman with a pleasant face who directed the peer-mediation class; she consistently showed compassion for the students.

The behaviors of these teacher-disciplinarians reflected what could be called a culturally relevant disciplinary style. Culturally relevant discipline, like culturally relevant and responsive pedagogy,[3] necessitates a deep knowledge and respect for students' home cultures and requires educators to engage students in ways that are not divorced from the larger context of their lives. It holds students to appropriately high expectations and attempts to involve parents in meaningful and democratic ways. It is not "soft," but it is always respectful.[4]

Some deans were more intimate with students than others; some teased students more than others; some were more invested in their jobs than others; and each had different strengths and weaknesses. Nevertheless, I noted that many of their actions demonstrated intimate knowledge of their students, including how the students might effectively be engaged. Some of the deans could gain the respect of students by being tough. Students expected these deans to speak roughly at times, carry through on warnings, remain composed while admonishing them, and certainly not back down to a student or let a student get away with making the dean look foolish or weak. At the same time, in keeping with a culturally relevant style, the deans often tried to avoid disrespecting students, especially in front of other people. When they were at their best, the deans held students to high expectations, and they often forged good, almost familial, relationships with students. They could be both stern and loving in an attempt to guide students through life (or at least through school). Their approach, in some ways, was successful. Some deans made progress in putting students "on the right track." Nevertheless, the toughness they displayed, along with their investment in the success of the disciplinary framework, could foster the culture of control.

Several deans reported to me that they believed that the more students became engaged in the educational process, the less likely they would be to cut classes or get into fights. Deans developed different styles, which appeared to be informed by their political perspectives (although sometimes these seemed contradictory), to fit their personality, and to play on their strengths. Many of the deans created categories for me as I asked about different styles. Generally, the categories reflected levels of toughness.

Several of the deans talked about "softies"; a few referred to the "tough love" approach; and Jackson added to the list the colorful term "dictators"—teachers and deans who, in his estimation, might be called by the first syllable of the word. The following sections describe these categories and explicate the deans' reflections on their meanings.

Softies and Dictators

One day, in the office next to the swimming pool in the basement of the building, away from all the chaos, I asked Jackson about the different strategies he and his colleagues used. He provided this critique: "Dictatorship does not work. Authoritarian dictatorship for children does not work at all!"

"And you think that some of your colleagues take an authoritarian approach?" I asked.

Referring to both teachers and deans he explained. "Yeah. It's like a dictatorship. 'This is how it's going to be!' You are not going to get anybody to bow and go the way you want them to. It's not going to work . . . because I've seen it. That, I honestly believe, doesn't work," he said with conviction.

"So, would you call that the dictator approach?"

"Yeah, or being a dick." Jackson then provided examples of both teachers and deans who took the dictator approach. He described several teachers whose classrooms he continually had to visit to pick up students who were being kicked out. He said these teachers took the "it's my way or the highway" approach, and this, he believed, clearly did not work. As for the deans, he recounted an incident when he and a colleague had had a disagreement over whether or not a student who had been in a fight should be suspended. He explained that the student was "not right in the head. . . . She was a special-ed student . . . and she began to act erratic." In this instance, he believed, it was counterproductive to take punitive actions against the girl; it would have been better to try to calm the girl down and talk to her. But his colleague was angry and disagreed. The colleague believed it was better to follow the disciplinary code to the letter of the law.

He continued with his analysis of the categories: "And being a softie does not work either. You can't be a little soft ass, because then [the students] don't respect you when you tell them to do something. They don't follow instructions. They don't respect you. So being a softie doesn't work. Neither does being too nice, because they think that's a weakness."

Jackson went on to explain how his style fell somewhere in the middle—an approach he viewed as "reaching the kids." He said, as if talking to a student, "'I want to help you before it's too late. I'd rather get you now,' and I tell the kids all the time, and they tell me I'm racist. I'm mean, I'm nasty. And I tell them all the time, 'I'm telling you the truth and I'm being honest with you now so when you get my age you will never come back and say nobody didn't tell you ahead of time.'"

"Why do they say you're racist?" I asked.

"Oh, because of my . . . I have a . . . it's a racist joke. And it goes like this: What's the difference between an eighteen-year-old white kid and an eighteen-year-old black kid?"

"What?"

"One's a freshman in college and one's a freshman in high school."

"Oh."

"And they get mad, but the proof is in the pudding. And just two days ago, Wednesday—no, Tuesday—a teacher gave me an article out of the newspaper that said that whites are graduating double the rate of the minorities in this state. And the kid that called me racist, I showed him the article and I said, 'You remember the joke I always tell you, right?' I said, 'Here's the proof in the pudding that maybe it's not a joke but that it's reality.' And they read it and they were totally shocked. . . . They didn't know that. . . . Those kids, when I tell that joke to them, they don't even believe that you're supposed to be eighteen in college. They're so shortchanged that they don't get it. But I have to keep it blunt and in layman terms for them, because that's their wake-up call. I can't sugarcoat it for them."

The young black man who was sitting before me leaned in with a serious look on his face. He continued with a heightened level of passion: "You must understand: *I'm them. They are me. I look like them. They look like me.* We share the same community. And so I have to get them to at least a level of understanding or at least a level of viability, at least, because it benefits me. And maybe I do come out a little venomous at times, but I feel as though that maybe if it hits them now and it hurts them now, that they'll change it so that when they get my age or even older that the situation won't look bad."

Dean Jackson embodied a culturally relevant disciplinary approach. He deeply cared for the students. I observed this in his actions and words. Additionally, the students appeared to be keenly aware of his concern; his style resonated with them. Jackson held students to certain standards and expectations and urged them to stay (or get) focused on academic success and their goals for the future.

Tough Love

It was a quiet morning a few weeks before Christmas break. Duane was sitting all alone in the detention room. He was slumped over a student desk, staring down at his hands resting on the desktop. He wore his large black winter jacket, a do-rag, and a baseball cap. I was struck at how childlike he appeared, sitting alone in the big room. One of the deans came in to tease him, but Duane sat silently, just staring. When the dean exited, I asked Duane if I could sit with him. Without looking up, he nodded. As I took my seat, I asked if he wanted to talk. He shook his head. I sat and waited. The stark basement room so often filled with students now seemed peaceful in its emptiness. Suddenly, Duane released a soft, wounded voice entirely incongruent with his image as one of the highest-ranking and most notorious gang members in the school. "He wouldn't let me in school." He continued to tell me, in a whiny proclamation of unfair treatment, how Dean Henry would not let him in the building, because he didn't have his binder with him—the one Dean Dempsey had bought for him so that he might remain committed to his recent resolution to "get back on track" academically. Duane claimed that he had mistakenly left the binder on the bus. He insisted he had been making an effort, and he showed me the few pieces of loose-leaf paper he brought to school in lieu of the binder. He was given the option of sitting in the detention room for the day, but he was angry that he was wasting his time. "They can't just kick me out. I know my rights," he said. He had a few choice words to describe Mr. Henry.

I was interested to understand Dean Henry's role in excluding from school a student who was making an effort—albeit a feeble one. So, later that day, I approached Henry to ask him what happened. He said, "I need to be strict with Duane to teach him responsibility; otherwise he'll never learn." He added, "He hates me now, but he'll love me next week."

But it didn't take a week. Later in the afternoon, I saw that Duane had transformed back into his gregarious self and was no longer sitting in the detention room. Henry explained with a smile that Duane had decided to forgive him when he asked Dean Henry for five dollars to buy some lunch—a practice I learned was common among a few of the deans and certain students. Mr. Henry performed the delicate balancing act each day of being stern and appearing uncompromising (the students do not respect a "softie," I was reminded again and again), on the one hand, and creating an almost familial relationship with students that often may have been the only thread attaching the students to the school, on the other.

Dean Henry described his approach as "tough love," although I heard Dean Dempsey once refer to this solidly built football coach as "Buttercup," alluding to his soft side. Henry explained that the approach he took depended on the student. He said that he always tried to take into account the student's background and how the student was most comfortable communicating. He was tougher when he needed to be and softer when it was appropriate.

As we sat together in his office one afternoon, he said, "My whole thing is dealing with the [particular] situation [at hand], because some kids need a tougher approach. Some kids need a more loving approach. It all depends on the kid and that all comes through experience, I feel." He went on to talk about getting to know kids from different groups: "I mean, if you can't communicate with the kids who come from Jamaica, you're going to have problems with that group. You know, if you can only communicate with the African American kids, you're going to have problems, because [students are] going to say, 'Oh, he's favoring this group. He's favoring that group.' So you got to find a way to communicate with everyone."

I asked him if the students' culture determined his approach.

"I think it's a combination, because you treat everybody as an individual, but then there's certain groups and they're, you know, not used to being treated one way, because they're from somewhere else. . . . Everyone is an individual, but, like I said, each group comes with its own cultural agenda or identity. You gotta be able to relate to that, you know. It's hard for a lot of people. I mean, I try my best."

I then asked Henry about softies and tough love. He replied,

There are kids that the quote-unquote softie approach is good for them. You know, it'll work for them. And those are the type of kids that don't get in trouble. I mean, when I was a student, I was one of those kids, you know, I was a good student. If I got into trouble for whatever reason, you know, let's say I didn't do my homework. Getting yelled at would turn me off. . . . The way I approach some of the students that go late to class, I don't get on their case. I say, "Listen, you're a senior; you've been here for four years. You know what to do." . . . Or sometimes if you look at them funny, like, you know, you raise your eye like, I can't believe *you* got in trouble. They feel kind of funny because it's, like, wow, he's disappointed in me. And that makes them feel bad. So that's the way you reach those types of students, because a kid who's a good student rarely gets in trouble, you know, they more or less need that coddling. The tough love comes in with those kids that are truly like the tough kids. They're always getting yelled at, all the time maybe at home, and they need that kind of thing to bring [them] back in line, or they come from the tough streets and they need somebody to bring them back in line.

Students' lack of respect for "softies" became evident in most of the interviews I conducted with the students who were chronically involved in disciplinary cases. On a number of occasions, during observations, I heard Duane and other students criticize deans and teachers who were too soft. These students would laugh at teachers and deans whom they perceived as weak, not in control, and easy to manipulate.

I came to understand that Duane and Dean Henry had a good relationship. Indeed, Henry was something of a parental figure in Duane's life. But months later, as I sat across from Duane in the visiting room at Rikers Island (the largest jail in New York City), it was Dean Dempsey whom he wanted me to talk to about raising bail money, perhaps because Duane believed that she was less "parental" than Dean Henry and less likely to confer with Duane's father (whom I spoke with on the phone and who explained that he wanted his son to stay in jail for his own safety and to teach him a lesson). From observation, I would describe Dempsey as quite tough, and she also described her approach as tougher than Henry's. But ultimately, these deans walked the same line, falling somewhere between toughness and love.

Within the categories of softies, dictators, and practitioners of tough love, I found deans who had developed a sense of what they believed to be the most effective ways to work with students, as teachers. All the deans often tried to connect with students and to demonstrate empathy, and they generally saw themselves acting in the best interest of the students. Indeed, they demonstrated considerable interest in finding the most appropriate way of working with students, based, at least to some extent, on students' individual dispositions and their cultural frames of reference.

Institutional Discourses of Control

Although deans and administrators held on to their identities as educators, they generally did not challenge the prevailing culture of control, and they relied almost solely on teaching "personal responsibility" to help students negotiate their interactions with the police. The threat of police action, a summons, and arrest were tools at hand—always reinforcing the culture of control—even when school personnel spent endless time attempting to "reach the kids." Some of the institutional discourses I found were explicitly influenced by the logic of criminal-justice practices, whereas other discourses revealed the tensions between the educators' own critiques and their reliance on penal management.

"He Got What He Deserved": The Discourse of "the Punishment Fits the Crime"

Although the identity of school personnel involved in discipline remained distinct from that of law enforcement, day after day, as police and security agents wrote summonses and made arrests, a penal logic was infused into the school culture. I found myself thinking back to my days as a teacher and noting how the penal logic I observed at UPHS had not been present in the school where I taught. At UPHS, I observed that deans and administrators—even those who opposed the heavy police presence in the school—came to understand the criminal-justice-oriented practices as a normal part of everyday life at UPHS. Everyone, it appeared, became accustomed to the criminal-procedural-level strategies, the heavy police presence, and the use of the criminal-justice language that had seeped into the everyday discourse of educators.

The idea that the criminal-justice framework had become normative in this way came to me one day when I realized that *I* had grown accustomed to seeing teens in handcuffs. I had grown used to kids with a pocketful of summonses. I was used to the tidal waves of blue in the hallways, security agents corralling students during sweeps, and the image of youngsters with their arms stretched out in front of them as agents moved scanners over the contours of their bodies. And I was used to the police lingo that buzzed constantly through handheld radios and the mention of such practices as a "phase two" (body search) or hallway sweeps, for example. I was also used to seeing and eventually interacting with large numbers of law-enforcement officials (security agents and officers) on a daily basis. As a researcher, though, I was mindful of continually "making things strange" and reminded myself that there were other ways of structuring a school. Thus, I never quite got to the point where the practices appeared to be the natural or only way of doing things.

Unlike me, the deans and administrators were not just exposed to these practices, they were required to participate in them, and they were invested in having them work. Every day, they wrote up occurrence reports (like the ones presented in chapter 3) about students receiving summonses and getting arrested for becoming disorderly, justifying within institutional discourse the use of criminal-procedural-level strategies as a response to "insubordination" and "disrespect."

Deans appeared at suspension hearings, where they presented their cases before a "judge" (a lawyer hired by the Department of Education) as representatives of the school. At times, they called upon the police, and often threatened to do so when a child was too unruly. And they were continually interacting and collaborating with the police. As a result of these experiences, such practices became "normal" or "the way things were." They were part of the job.

Part of this normalizing process was the creation of the criminal-justice framework's own discourse—a blend of educational and criminal-justice language. Like any discourse, it shaped the perspectives of individuals working within it. Even when school personnel were appalled by some of the specific events that took place (kids getting summonses for "no good reason," for example), it appeared to become difficult for them to see beyond the overall penal logic. For some, the predominant perspective became what I came to call the "punishment fits the crime" attitude. I often observed this attitude after a student failed to suppress his or her anger during an intervention with a security agent or police officer, or when a student brought a weapon or drugs through scanning and got caught. The rationale went like this: the rules have been set and the students know the rules; they know how the system works. So, if they choose to break a rule or act in a manner deemed inappropriate, then they deserve what they get. In short, widespread awareness of the rules and their consequences justified the disciplinary action, regardless of the fact that school rules and criminal-procedural-level strategies had become entwined to criminalize noncriminal acts.

At one such moment, a dean stood in the office after a student who was on probation had been noncompliant with officers and agents when he was stopped. The incident had escalated to the point where the officers conducted a body search, and the young man was found with a bag of marijuana—a violation of his probation. He would be doing some time in jail. The dean shrugged his shoulders after explaining the situation and said, "He got what he deserved." He said this because the student's actions were "illogical," perhaps even "stupid," given the known consequences. A few days later, I observed a dean shaking his head after a student got arrested. He said, "That was really stupid [of the student]. He got what was coming." These are illustrative examples representative of a common sentiment: students' misbehavior, especially their incorrigibility during confrontations with law enforcement, warranted arrest, because students should have known that arrest was the likely outcome.

"Better Five Days Now Than Five Years Later On": The Discourse of Personal Responsibility

The punishment-fits-the-crime attitude and its supporting discourse was not the only or even the most prominent attitude found among the deans. I observed that as the deans grew accustomed to working within the criminal-justice framework, the relatively low-level criminal-procedural-level strategies, such as summonses and misdemeanor arrests, often came to be seen as a way to teach young people the hard truth about prison. The deans' investment in low-level forms of policing as preventive measures was driven by a sense of urgency; they hoped students would learn from experience in court or jail and "choose another path."

I frequently heard deans and other adults in the building say, "It was his [or her] choice," or, "He [or she] has to learn to take responsibility for his [or her] actions." Nevertheless, sometimes the discourse of personal responsibility that I found at UPHS emerged from a mixture of an internalization of the dominant discourse *and* the fear of the looming presence of the criminal-justice system. The following vignette captures this perspective.

It was early October. I was sitting in the deans' office. A few deans and several police officers were taking care of paperwork or relaxing after a tense moment when two handcuffed students had been escorted into the room and questioned. One of them was sitting directly in front of me, still cuffed and slumped in his seat. He appeared angry and didn't say anything.

The other was to my left. He sat calmly, smiling yet complaining that the cuffs were digging into his wrists. Sitting next to me was Dean Jackson. "See that kid?" he said to me, referring to the second student. "This is all a big joke to him. It doesn't mean a thing to him." He turned and spoke to the young man sharply. "This isn't a joke. You better wipe that smile off your face."

A burly, rosy-cheeked officer leaning against the copy machine and holding a cup of coffee asked if we had heard that the Jamaican kid who was arrested the other day—the one whose mother later stood in the office yelling about how her son had been treated unfairly—got five days in jail.

"Yeah, and I heard the tough guy started crying right there in front of the judge," another cop chuckled. Several people laughed. There was a lull, and in the momentary silence that fell over the room, someone out of my view, in a quiet, reflective voice, repeated, "Five days," to which Jackson added heartily, "It's about time."

I was confused. Based on our previous conversations I believed Jackson was critical of the overuse of the criminal-justice system. Out of earshot of the others in the room, I told him, "I thought you didn't like to see kids locked up."

Without turning to look at me, he said in a matter-of-fact tone, "Better five days now than five years later on."

In keeping with one of the prevailing sentiments driving today's policing practices, Jackson expressed (at least in that particular moment) the common belief that relatively minor punitive measures now *may* help avert students from a life, or at least years, of incarceration. Thus, despite critiques of the overuse of the criminal-justice system, some educators became dependent on its strategies in much the same way that neoliberal criminal-justice administrators have come to rely on low-level forms of repression, such as zero-tolerance community policing, as forms of prevention.

The discourse of responsibility did not preclude the deans' strong critique of policing practices. When I asked Dean Castellano one day why she believed the school was safer than it had been in the past, she cited a list of reasons, including the new principal, the deans, and other changes in disciplinary procedures, but she did not mention the police. So I asked her about them. After a long pause, she said, "Hmm, well, you know what it is. I've seen security agents overreact with kids." Several others also voiced their concerns. For example, on several occasions, Dean Orozco, who facilitated the peer-mediation class, expressed her dismay with policing practices and the growing number of summonses students were getting. Dean White told me the day I met her, "Students are getting summonses for nothing!" Nevertheless, the deans' critiques often coincided with a sentiment that students had something to "figure out." Although the policing practices might not always be fair, they seemed to believe, it was the students' responsibility to change their behaviors, not the police and security agents'. An excerpt from a conversation with Jackson concerning the use of summonses illuminates these kinds of conflicted feelings. He began by telling me that in that school year more students than ever before were receiving summonses and that perhaps it was making them "think twice" before misbehaving.

"So, you think the summons is an effective disciplinary strategy?" I asked.

He paused a moment. "I don't know. Honestly, I think it's a double-edged sword. I mean, it sounds like a good idea, but if it doesn't work, then you just have a whole bunch of kids ending up in the judicial system." He continued:

Maybe they're not going to figure it out [to obey school rules and focus on academic work] now, maybe not tomorrow. Maybe it's going to take them a year or two, but by that time they'll already be screwed in the [criminal-justice] system. I mean, that's why it sucks, because, for instance, I just went into a [class]room to get a student. The PD wanted her, because she didn't go to court for a summons. . . . You know, [the students] take forever to figure it out and get their act together. But meanwhile she has to go to court for something she did here in the building, and now she's going to end up in the legal system dealing with all that and it had nothing to do with anything illegal. See what I'm saying? It wasn't a criminal activity that got her into the judicial system. It was a behavioral issue. . . . [The police] are cracking the whip . . . and whether or not [the use of summonses] has a positive or negative effect, I don't think, for the most part, that they're reaching the kids here.

Jackson's ambivalence over the use of summonses hones in on two important sentiments. First, the summonses might have been useful if they were compelling the students to behave, but they did not seem to be accomplishing that result. Second, students needed to "figure it out," or learn how to behave appropriately, especially when interacting with law-enforcement officials. The idea of needing to figure it out when speaking with law enforcement often led to the practice of coaching, that is, attempting to get students to remain calm, to cooperate, and to act respectfully when confronted by officers and agents. The following is a brief example.

One afternoon, toward the end of the school year, I sat in the deans' office listening to Dean Henry admonish a student who earlier that day had been asked for his ID and claimed to have lost it. The young man sat calmly as Henry intermittently talked to him and filled in some paperwork. "You shouldn't have behaved that way," he said.

"My bad," the young man replied.

"Sorry doesn't help you now; it's too late for sorry," Henry lamented.

Jackson shot a quick look at the young man from across the room. Revealing his strategy of coaching students to defer to authority, he interjected, "You should have used those lines when I told you to!"

The work of "reaching the kids" and coaching students became couched in a discourse of personal responsibility and choice. In this framework, the educator must convince the student to take the right path, to go to class, and to behave. In this sense, the discourse of personal responsibility shares elements with the-punishment-fits-the-crime in that the onus to change is put solely on the student, but it is a distinct position. It demonstrates empathy for the students; it acknowledges larger social forces and the policies and institutional practices that may be viewed as unfair; and it assumes as an ultimate goal the reduction of the use of long-term incarceration.

When It's Too Late

Many times, however, it was too late to coach students to avoid confrontation. When a situation had become a "police matter" (because law enforcement was on the scene), school administrators and deans could not interfere. Any coaching had to be conducted in whispers.

Late one morning on a sunny day in mid-April, I walked down the dim basement hallway toward B-40. I heard a commotion several seconds before I reached the room and took a long, deep breath to prepare myself. It was one of those moments when the deans' office appeared to have been transformed into a police precinct. As I walked into the room, I saw the backs of three officers surrounding a chair where a student sat stiffly on the edge, leaning back with his chin down. His legs were spread wide and planted firmly on the floor. His long, thin arms disappeared behind his back. He was black and lanky and was wearing an oversized navy blue hoodie sweatshirt and jeans. His hair was pulled back from his thin face in simple, straight cornrows. I took a seat next to the door.

"I didn't do nothing," the young man said, half demanding, half pleading. "Take them off me!"

He twisted his body in his seat and raised his cuffed wrists. He repeated his plea of innocence several times. The adults in the room—Assistant Principal Juarez, a couple of deans, and several security agents and officers—appeared to be growing uncomfortable. It was an ugly moment. Juarez bent down and whispered something in the young man's ear.

"What do you mean, calm down?" the student retorted. He looked up toward Dean Henry, who stood a few feet away in the outer ring of adults surrounding his chair, and appealed to the dean to intervene.

"You've been arrested. I can't get involved. You know those teachers who got arrested. This is the same kind of situation," Henry said with a mixture of sympathy and resolution in his voice.

The young man persisted. "The whole thing's on tape," he repeated several times. In time, I realized he had been accused of taking a swing at a security agent. He claimed that the agent had grabbed him and he had been trying to release his arm. Later, the occurrence report would read as follows:

A male student was issued a summons by PO —— of the XX School Safety Task Force for Disorderly Conduct. He refused to show his ID card and swung at SSA ——. He received a principal's suspension.

One of the agents kept making threatening remarks that seemed to exacerbate the situation by further frustrating the young man. The officers demanded that he calm down before the cuffs could come off. "I'll leave the cuffs on till three o'clock," one of them warned.

At one point, the officers stood the young man up, turned him toward a desk, and conducted a body search. One of the deans glanced at me, perhaps wondering what I was thinking in this tense moment. I wondered if the young man's humiliation was intensified by the presence of the lone spectator seated by the door watching all of this. Or perhaps in his anxious state he hadn't even noticed me.

The student was seated again. He was still finding it difficult to calm down while the cuffs were on and the imposing blue figures stood over him. He breathed deeply. "I'm not an angry person," he insisted. He seemed eager to explain himself. "I'm not always angry. I don't wake up all angry. I just don't like getting pushed up against the wall by a big male cop."

"Yeah, I pushed you. It's all on tape. You can report it!" one of the security agents said in a whatcha-gonna-do-about-it tone.

The young man said that he didn't like getting pushed by a big white man. I got a sick feeling in my stomach, assuming that the officer would certainly not accept this as a reasonable explanation for the student's noncompliance.

"Oh, so you don't like white people!"

"Let me rephrase myself." The student realized his mistake. "I have nothing against white people. . . . I don't like cops."

"So why don't you like cops?" the officer asked.

"My neighborhood," the young man replied.

"But I don't work in your neighborhood."

The young man explained how he was tired of walking home to the projects and getting stopped all the time.

The tone of the dialogue had changed. The student got calmer. Everyone seemed to be settling into a waiting mode.

Dean Henry took the seat next to me. Resting his elbows on his knees, he shook his head. "He doesn't know how to be quiet. . . . He shouldn't have been in the hallway." He attempted to make sense of what was going on for me—and, I believed, for himself. I didn't know what to say.

A few days later, I learned the young man's name was Jermaine and that he was a student in the peer-mediation class I had been observing.

This excerpt taken from my field notes demonstrates the authority and the power of the criminal-justice disciplinary model and the penal culture it cultivated. Jermaine's comments about white police officers in his neighborhood also point to the relationship between street policing and school policing and how the two processes could become intertwined in students' minds. The excerpt also exemplifies how educators could do almost nothing to define and redirect a situation once an incident had become a police matter. Their moral authority had been undermined by legal authoritarianism. Dean Henry sat down and shook his head, lamenting Jermaine's inability to calm down, and Assistant Principal Juarez tried whispering in the young man's ear in an attempt to quell his frustration and anger, but ultimately, the prevailing disciplinary paradigm defined the moment.

Working in the Context of Penal Control

In several of the sections in this chapter, I have discussed how educators negotiated the criminal-justice framework by asserting their identities as educators, at times critiquing criminal-procedural-level strategies, and finding ways to make the disciplinary process more humane. The principal confronted, one at a time, a whole history of organizational practices that have created the conditions for violence to flourish, and the deans conducted mediations and counseled students, but these efforts did not significantly affect the existing culture of control that had permeated the school. The limitations placed on the agency of educators were compounded by the weaving together of educational and criminal-justice policy and discourses. In the context of penal management, the deans found themselves (often despite their critiques) expressing such sentiments as "the punishment fits the crime" and "if students understand the consequences, they should be compelled to cooperate." Although the identity of educators remained intact, the criminal-justice-oriented practices became what was expected and even relied upon as educators attempted to "reach the students."

CHAPTER 6

The Underlife

Oppositional Behavior at Urban Public High School

K IDS GOTTA ACT TOUGH AND STUPID when they get here, 'cause,
 you know, they hear about the reputation [of UPHS]. So it's like they
want to make sure they're not picked on," Kericia, a small black girl with
bright eyes and hair neatly pulled back in a tiny ponytail, told me one day
as we sat in the lunchroom.

"Is that what it was like for you when you first came here?"

Kericia, now a sophomore doing well in her classes, giggled and looked
sheepishly at me. "I see a lot of stuff, but I stay out of trouble." Indeed,
there was a lot of "stuff" to see. The most common forms of oppositional
behavior I found at UPHS were classroom clowning and antagonism, cutting classes, hallway disruption, gambling, hat wearing, and fighting. Oppositional behaviors were pervasive, despite heavy policing. They were the
preoccupation of disciplinarians and in many ways helped to justify the
punitive disciplinary approaches.

As an ethnographer, I was interested in the interactions of daily life
and an insider's perspective, as I believed that an understanding of oppositional behavior from students' viewpoints, on a very micro level, would
ultimately allow for a deep analysis of the ways that students' social practices interacted with a particular set of social and institutional forces. I
spent considerable time at UPHS observing students' oppositional behavior and discussing it with them in order to gain insight into how they
made sense of that behavior. I learned that students' perceptions and experiences were indeed influenced by the particular institutional and social
context in which their oppositional behavior took place. Students entered
a school with a "bad" reputation, one associated with high levels of violence and disorder, and they contended with deep feelings of academic
alienation and lack of access to the curriculum. They found many of their

classes boring and irrelevant. They also had to contend with daily policing and the institutional culture of control. Finally, prospects for graduation, higher education, and viable future employment were not great. UPHS students were often painfully aware that opportunities within the informal and illegal economy were ubiquitous within their communities, and other options were scarce. Within this difficult context, students sought certain social and psychological benefits through oppositional behavior. Specifically, they sought to regain a sense of autonomy over the self, create valued identities, position themselves well within social hierarchies, manage and contain violence, have fun, and even make a little cash. Students did not appear to enter into oppositional behavior fully conscious of the benefits they sought or with any explicit intentions, but upon reflection they could explain their rationales and the positive feelings associated with their misbehavior. This is not to say that the institutional and social conditions *caused* oppositional behavior, but the context did appear to have a significant influence on the ways students made sense of their transgressions.

Goffman's classic description of institutional life found in *Asylums* and his notion of an underlife are helpful in gaining insight into the social-psychological benefits students sought in a context of heavy police control.[1] Goffman writes that within institutions "we find that participants decline in some way to accept the official view of what they should be putting into and getting out of the organization and, behind this, of what sort of self and world they are to accept for themselves. Where enthusiasm is expected, there will be apathy; where loyalty, there will be disaffection; where attendance, absenteeism; where robustness, some kind of illness; where deeds are to be done, varieties of inactivity . . . each in its way, *a movement of liberty*."[2] Goffman suggests that institutions, in imposing strict behavioral norms, tend to strip individuals of their "identity equipment," making it difficult for them to maintain a sense of ownership or autonomy over the self. Within this context, individuals make what he calls secondary adjustments, behaviors that go against institutional norms, as a means of constructing the self. The collective and sustained practice of these "movements of liberty" constitutes the underlife.[3]

My observations and students' vivid statements highlighted for me the tremendous significance of the social-psychological benefits students sought and the assertions of the self that they made through oppositional behavior at UPHS, but it is equally important to consider the conceptual frameworks with which students entered the school. UPHS is not known for its scholastics. In fact, within the community and in the media it is considered a very rough school, so tough that it was deemed necessary to flood the school with law-enforcement officials. So what does it mean to be a success or to thrive at such a school? For some incoming students, taken to the extreme, a reasonable goal might be to become the "baddest of the bad." Yet there remained a constant tension between an imagined ideal of schooling and students' hopes to achieve academic success, on the one hand, and making a strong and valued assertion of self at UPHS, on the other.

Classroom Misbehavior

Over the school year, I observed twelve different classes. Each semester, I observed two classes on a regular basis and visited others once or twice. I observed some very sensitive and dedicated teachers, such as Ms. Jenkins, an English teacher who worked hard to create an engaging environment, and Ms. Orozco, whose peer-mediation class was the favorite of many of her students. Nevertheless, in many of the classes I attended, I found students who appeared very bored and were busy doodling, talking, and sleeping. Many appeared to lack access to the material. This was confirmed in dozens of interviews with students who made claims such as, "Teachers don't break it down [explain]," "They don't even know how to teach," and "They don't always explain things." This sense of alienation from course content seemed to me to be the result of a combination of factors, including students' below-grade reading levels, the pressures on teachers to get through an immense amount of material that might appear on the state standardized exam, and a sense of irrelevancy to students. Not surprisingly, when comprehensible and relevant connections to the material were not made for students, rampant misbehavior and disengagement occurred.

The kinds of classroom misbehavior I observed were very similar to the oppositional behaviors that have been documented in previous studies and that I observed as a teacher, but students' classroom antics and the ways in which they narrated their experiences seemed to reflect the current circumstances. They did not usually complain directly about high-stakes testing, but they showed implicit awareness of the tests' impact on classroom practices (see my discussion of this in chapter 2). Content was "boring," and teachers talked too much. Their comments also suggested that their struggles to find meaning sometimes had to do with their lack of adequate academic preparation. (Recall that UPHS was a school with a very high concentration of students reading well below grade level.) Ms. Klein's global history class exemplifies the ways teachers were pressured, by upcoming tests, to plow through material, use a teacher-centered approach, and pay little mind to students' academic needs.

It was late September. Ms. Klein was at the door handing each student entering the room a piece of paper with an excerpt from the *Communist Manifesto* and four questions on it. The students were asked to read the passage and answer the questions. Ms. Klein demanded silence, but many of the students continued to talk. It was not overwhelming boisterousness, just conversations ranging from secret whispers to light banter, with one or two guffaws rising above the steady flow of voices.

"Do I need to read everyone's grade out loud to the class?" Ms. Klein threatened.

Still some of the students continued to talk. Others had settled into their seats and were drawing intricate doodles. A few sat in frustration as they tried to decipher the language of the passage, written in 1847. The warnings continued. "This passage could be on the Regents [standardized state exam]."

Michael, an older-looking student to my left, said in exasperation, "Chill, Miss, just chill." He looked at me and said loudly, "You see who does all the talking?"

Ms. Klein circulated and made comments to individual students. "Did you hear that, Kathy?" a girl called from across the room. "Did you hear what she just said to me?" Another one chimed in, "Yeah, did you write what she said in your notebook?" I tried not to smile. Michael suddenly erupted in open defiance, "*Who's* doing all the talking? *Whose* mouth is going all the time? I only hear *one* person." Ms. Klein ignored him.

Ms. Klein proceeded to give a lecture on Robert Owens and then moved on to Castro's Cuba, and few students seemed to be engaged. Suddenly, toward the end of the class, Dorian, a small boy in the back of the room, threw his hand into the air as if something very important and relevant had just dawned on him. "Oh, Ms. Klein, Ms. Klein," he said. She looked his way.

"My cat died," he said in a serious tone. When the students laughed, he added in a hurt voice, "It's true."

Several days later, the topic was German and Italian reunification. Ms. Klein fumbled with a large map of Europe circa 1871 that she was attempting to hang. She eventually gave up and pulled down a contemporary European map hanging in the front of the room. Many of the students took interest in the map, but some didn't know the European countries. Ms. Klein pointed to Italy. Dorian called out "Puerto Rico!" The others laughed. Ms. Klein rolled her eyes. "Puerto Rico?" She shook her head in disgust. Ms. Klein asked for the name of one of the countries in the former Yugoslavia. The students called out all sorts of answers, Paris and Germany among them. Terrell mumbled, "Serbia," but Ms. Klein did not hear him, and as she turned to the board, he injected an almost inaudible "screw you" into his answer.

By October, the class had moved on to the Opium War. Ms. Klein showed the students a picture of a famous Chinese noblewoman who was addicted to opium and explained how opium addiction was so pervasive at that time, even among the elite, that it interfered with the governance of the country. I found the lecture interesting, but as I had seen during other visits, several students remained almost completely disengaged, immersed in conversations with each other. It was difficult to ascertain whether others were listening or not. The only evidence that any of the students heard Ms. Klein surfaced when a conversation between two boys was triggered by something she said. As the lecture continued, I heard part of the students' conversation. "Opium is heroin, man; crack is cocaine," one young man explained to his apparently less-informed friend. "The Chinese weren't no crackheads."

The calling out, chatting, comments directed toward classmates (or me), and general inattentiveness I have described were the most pervasive forms of oppositional behavior I observed in classrooms. They might be characterized as "apathy where enthusiasm is expected" or a refusal to become an active participant in a process that is understood as irrelevant. Students' comments frequently constituted an assertion of the existence of the self, either by changing the subject to something meaningful to them, as when Dorian declared that his cat had died, or by making irrelevant material relate more to their lives, such as when one boy explained to his classmate that the Chinese weren't addicted to crack. At other times, students' comments indicated outright defiance: an expression of their indignation and a way of constructing their own classroom identity in opposition to the dronelike behavior that was sometimes expected of them as the teacher plowed through the material that might appear on the Regents Exam.

Often during interviews, I detected students' indignation at a teacher's methods or treatment of the students, rather than their categorical rejection of academic work. Students' statements also often suggested that misbehavior occurred when students could not relate to or understand the material. Here is an excerpt from a conversation in the library with a group of students whose science class I visited on a regular basis. Damian, their friend, joined us.

I asked the group to discuss reasons why students got into trouble in classes. Manuel replied, "Kids are acting stupid."

Damian disagreed, but I asked Manuel to continue. "Yeah, they fool around like they have no home training. They think when they come to school they gotta act stupid."

"Yeah, like disrespect," Greg added.

"Okay. But why would a student disrespect the teacher?" I asked.

Greg laughed. "No, the reason why they think they can be disrespectful is because it's that they didn't get no home training—"

Damian, who had been waiting to speak, interjected, "I disagree with all of you!"

"Okay, tell us what you think, Damian."

"I'm telling you it goes back to how the teachers teach, because if the teacher is mad boring and don't have fun with the kids, then the [students are] going to be mad disrespectful no matter what home training they have. Because my little brother, we all home trained, and my little brother still acts up and we all home trained. We got respect for everybody. It's just that some teachers, they don't know how to do their job. . . . If the teacher ain't going to do what she gotta do, then the students ain't going to listen to her or be respectful."

"What do you think?" I asked the others. "Do you agree with that, or do you still think it's about home training?"

"I agree," Greg replied.

Almost simultaneously Darnell nodded his head and said, "I agree."

Throughout my research, I heard many comments like Damian's, suggesting that students' disrespect or misbehavior was a response to the negative experiences they were having in the classroom. But even the idea that students "gotta act stupid" and "disrespect" implies that they may have been compelled to do so as they constructed their identities in opposition to classroom expectations. That is, students understood "acting stupid" as an act of opposition against something, usually an implicit or explicit assault on their self-esteem or identity. They could mock the teacher and the material rather than focus attention on their inability to access the material, express their indignation at having to sit through something irrelevant to their lives, illuminate the farce they believed was taking place, or present a self that did not depend on academic success (even if they actually did desperately want to do better).

Ms. Jenkins, the English teacher whose class was one of the most humane environments I encountered, maintained that much misbehavior was a result of student disconnect from the material and a simultaneous focus on peer conflicts. She shared that "students are constantly inattentive. They just talk out of turn. . . . So, we have a problem trying to hold their attention so that they're not distracted by speaking with their friends and doing all those things while the class is going on . . . and also the squabbling between kids. This one doesn't like that one for nonsensical reasons. 'I don't like that one. She's going out with that one and she thinks she's all that,' and, you know." Other teachers voiced similar ideas about classroom conflict, but I observed additional dynamics in Ms. Jenkins's class as well.

One day while I was sitting in her class, an exchange took place that illustrates a student's social critique and perhaps dissatisfaction with the nature of the class discussion, rather than his inattentiveness and squabbling. The class was reading A Family Apart, a novel set in the United States during the time of slavery. The students took turns reading aloud. Ms. Jenkins periodically stopped the students to give some explanation of the historical context. Not long after they began reading, Shawn and Tyreek—darkskinned young black men slumped in their seats in the back of the room with their coats on—started interjecting comments about racism, disrupting the flow of instruction. At one point, Shawn managed to get the other students' attention. He said, "I think racism still exists, because you walk along Thirty-Fourth Street [a main shopping thoroughfare in Manhattan] and white people look at you like, 'What you doing here, nigger?'" Several students laughed. Ms. Jenkins got angry and said in a serious tone that there was nothing funny about racism and, indeed, it still existed today. The students resumed reading until Ms. Jenkins stopped them to ask them to think about the issues of race in the book. She directed a question about slavery to a light-skinned Puerto Rican boy in the front of the room.

"Why you asking him?" Shawn questioned in an antagonistic tone. "He's white."

Ms. Jenkins's voice grew stern. "Enough!" she said. Another student was called upon to read.

Shawn and Tyreek's commentary, I would argue, not only disrupted classroom instruction but also challenged common classroom discourse on race that suggests that racism is something that happened in the past. Shawn and Tyreek, through their comments, disavowed these notions and insisted that the teacher and everyone else acknowledge what they perceived to be racial dynamics playing out in the classroom. Although Ms. Jenkins supported the boys' view that racism still existed, she was compelled to silence the discussion quickly and get through the material without further interruption.

Another common form of classroom opposition was "the attitude." During interviews, students often admitted to me that they entered the classroom with "an attitude," a posture they saw as a means to preserve their self-respect. Teachers generally interpreted their attitudes as incorrigibility—students walking into the classroom with a hostile demeanor, perhaps pushing a chair out of their way, and taking a seat in the back of the room away from everyone else. Nevertheless, many of these students often saw their decision to go to class as a serious "step in the right direction." They believed they were making an effort but refused to humble themselves publicly. They also often believed that their teachers did not like them, which was probably true in many cases.

Steven, Duane, and Antoine, among others, reported how one teacher simply said, "Get out," when they walked through the classroom door. Others claimed they were "picked on," and when I asked why they thought they were picked on, they often said, "My teacher doesn't like me." So, even if they admitted to having an attitude, they maintained that the animosity began with the teacher. At times, their responses took a more hostile form. They would say something like, "'Cause she's a fucking bitch!"

In sum, showing disrespect and having an attitude could be viewed as ways that students preserved a sense of self-respect in an environment they found oppressively boring, irrelevant, hostile, or humiliating. Other kinds of misbehavior and clowning provided students with an opportunity to attach their own meanings to the classroom experience and to make it more relevant, or at least bearable.

Selective Class Cutting

Although the classroom was certainly a place where oppositional behavior occurred, students' more overt "movements of liberty" occurred when they chose not to attend the classes they found most "boring" or hostile. Both students and deans cited selective cutting, which, in a sense, was the gateway to the underlife, as perhaps the most pervasive disciplinary problem in the school, and it was often when students left the classroom (while remaining in the building) that they were confronted by law enforcement. Some excerpts from my field notes and interviews illustrate how selective cutting worked inside the school and how the very practice of cutting certain classes gave students a sense of autonomy and lent meaning to their experiences inside the school building.

While sitting in the detention room with two students, Alex and Antoine, one day, I brought up the subject of selective cutting. "Do you think there're a lot of kids who spend a good part of the day not in classes?"

Alex replied, "Yeah." Antoine laughed.

"How do they avoid class? You're laughing," I said to Antoine. "Tell me what your day would be like."

"Me personally?"

"As you come into the building and your intention is to not go to class."

"Okay, me personally. All right, the first two periods I go to the auditorium. All right, third period, yeah, I'm in the auditorium again. Fourth, I have lunch. Fifth, I got gym, and then the rest of the time I just go to every gym period. It's not my gym period, but I just go."

"And what does the gym teacher say?" I asked.

"Nothing." (I verified this with a gym teacher, who explained that it happened quite frequently. Some gym teachers reportedly made an effort to encourage students to attend their other classes, but ultimately they rationalized allowing students to stay in the gym, because "at least the kids aren't roaming the hallways getting into trouble.")

"Why do you stay in the auditorium for the first three periods?" I asked.

"That's where everybody be at who's late."

"They put you in there when you come in late, but if you come in second period, you could go to your third-period class," I suggested.

"Yeah, but I don't," he responded.

"You stay in the auditorium?" I wanted to be clear.

"No, I go out, chill, and then back to the auditorium."

"Where do you go to chill?" I had pushed a little too far. Antoine seemed reluctant to answer. There was a short pause.

I tried again. "I'm just trying to understand. Not going to class seems to be a lot of kids' goal."

"It's not my goal," Alex interjected.

Now, Antoine wished to shift the conversation. "It's third marking period," he said. "I go to class now. That's when the credit counts." (He was referring here to the common perception among students that if they pass the last marking period of a semester, they will pass the course.)

I asked both students and school personnel and learned that Antoine's strategies for avoiding classes were ones commonly used by students. But what did students do when they left the auditorium? When the bell rang, all the students in the auditorium were ushered out the back door near the stage. They had been late for their last class, so when the next bell rang, they were released from the auditorium with the expectation that they would head to their next class. Many did, but some did not. I asked Zack, a student I felt I knew better than most and with whom I had developed a considerable level of trust, if he could help me understand what students did when they cut a class. Zack was a good candidate, as I was aware that he was one of the students who frequently cut his classes, although lately he had been making an effort to attend more than usual. Zack invited me to spend a whole day with him. He suggested that I could watch how he navigated the building and negotiated "security." I explained that his proposal presented a problem. If he were seen with me, school personnel and police officers would not engage him in the same way they would if he were alone. So Zack suggested I "hang back," or follow him at a distance, so that people would not realize that I was observing. I decided to try it, aware of the methodological limitations.[4] As it turned out, Zack attended more classes than he cut. Nevertheless, even in the classes he attended, Zack often appeared distant. What follows is an excerpt from my field notes from that day.

On a late May morning, I waited for Zack at boys' scanning. He entered the building in time for his third-period class, swimming. Zack led me through the dank, mazelike hallways of the basement into a section of the school I had never seen. The next forty minutes I spent sitting in the bleachers by the pool. Zack was proud of his swimming ability and waved to me occasionally as if to ensure I was watching. His swim teacher told me he had done better the year before, but Zack suffered from asthma and had gained weight. He also found it difficult at times to concentrate on the workout. Nonetheless, he appeared to be very much in his element in the water, a space where he felt some sense of accomplishment and perhaps even joy.

The bell rang for fourth period. I met Zack at the back entrance to the boys' locker room. We headed upstairs into the special-education wing of the building for English class. Zack introduced me to the teacher, and we sat down.

The class was reading a novel. Zack complained to me that they had been reading the same book for weeks, and he was bored. He told me he had already finished the book. As if the teacher had heard him complain, she began to challenge him with questions. Zack provided vivid details and examples; he had clearly read and understood the text. When the teacher stopped Zack so that another student might participate, Zack started talking with Clarissa, his girlfriend. Then he started rapping. He was beginning to get agitated and bored. He turned to me and said, "I know everything."

The bell rang for fifth period. Zack had a reading and writing class across the hall. He wanted to attend. As the students settled into their seats, the teacher told me that Zack's IQ was higher than his (the teacher's) but Zack's problem was that he had difficulty settling down. That day the class was reading a story about a ten-year-old girl from Maine who writes a letter to the Russian president. It seemed neither age appropriate nor relevant to the students. Zack excused himself to go to the bathroom. I wondered if I would see him again, but he returned in about five minutes. The story ended. The teacher asked the students how they liked it. There was silence. Zack had an empty look on his face. He then pulled his jacket over his head.

In sixth period, Zack had lunch. He convinced me to bend the school rule and take him out to lunch. The security agents, who apparently considered me to have the status of a staff member, did not prevent us from leaving through the front doors. As we returned to the building, Zack was not interested in attending his seventh-period class. We joined the flow of students on the first floor who circled through the hallway during the change of periods. It was easy to get lost in the crowd, but the bell was about to ring and most students had left the hallway. Zack was officially cutting class. I kept my distance and watched Zack with a friend, walking through the hall. A security agent spotted them. At first, the agent ignored them, but then he reprimanded the boys and told them to go to class. He did not threaten the boys with criminal-procedural action. I suspected it was because he knew Zack and was tired of taking action. But another possibility was that, for all the students who got picked up by security, many more were left alone. The boys worked their way around the first floor. Zack walked into Juarez's office, looking for Juarez, the assistant principal who had made a great effort to engage Zack. But Juarez wasn't in his office. In the hallway outside the office, Zack and his friend met up with Clarissa. Zack took his prohibited cell phone out and started playing music. The three students danced down the hallway until they spotted someone coming from the other direction. The three cutters joined a small line of girls who were waiting outside the program office. "Are you all waiting for someone?" the woman in the hallway asked as she passed.

"Yes," Clarissa answered, and the woman kept walking.

Zack continued on to the north corridor, where the principal's office and other administrative offices were located. He lost the others. Ms. Sheldon, a high-ranking administrator, stepped out of her office, walked across the hall, and entered another administrative office. Three police officers were walking in our direction. Zack slipped into Sheldon's empty office. I stood several feet from the office door, pretending to look at the bulletin board. The officers walked by. Zack slipped out of the office and continued toward the auditorium, where he safely spent a few minutes before continuing on his way.

Not all students could get away with what Zack got away with. To some extent, his success in avoiding classes had to do with the cooperation (or resignation) of school personnel and law enforcement. Nevertheless, Zack showed how nonattendance could be accomplished through a variety of strategies—coming late, leaving early, feigning reasons to visit administrators, and even "hiding" right out in the open. In orchestrating his day in such a way, Zack was not simply winning space or asserting a cultural identity; on a deeper level, he was actively regaining a sense of autonomy over the self that heavy policing and alienating classes tended to strip from students. He was declaring and choosing which classes were worth attending and which were not, and his eagerness to show me how strategically he navigated through his day suggested to me that he took considerable satisfaction in the sense of autonomy and control he had created for himself.

Disruptive Behavior

One of the reasons Zack was so successful in avoiding classes and subverting disciplinary action was that he had created a reputation for himself. On several occasions, Zack bragged to me, "I own this school," or, "I'm the boss of this school." Several other students, too, bragged. "Everybody knows me here," as Duane put it one day, with a smile of satisfaction on his face. These reputations came through chronic involvement in disciplinary cases—some serious, some not—and often served students' interests. The behaviors associated with their disciplinary cases included screaming and running in the hallways, arguing with teachers, slamming doors, publicly taunting adults or other students, or otherwise causing some kind of scene. But, in constructing Zack's reputation, like that of so many students regularly involved in disciplinary cases, charisma and sweetness also played a big role. When I mentioned Zack's name or the names of students with similar reputations to the deans and certain administrators and police officers, they rolled their eyes and talked about how "misguided" or "crazy" these kids were, but they also acknowledged their endearing character traits. (I heard students affectionately described as "big babies," "basically good kids at the core," and "loyal.") Thus, some "troublemakers," particularly those who were considered likable, positioned themselves well (by cultivating a soft spot in the hearts of disciplinarians or by wearing them down into resignation) within a context in which students were regularly subjected to alienating, or even humiliating, classroom experiences and police intervention, and they often appeared to relish the control over their situations that their reputations afforded them. That is, students—particularly those most marginalized, with little access to legitimized forms of social approval (for example, making the honor roll or excelling on the football team)—often believed that the benefits that came from disrupting the order of the school outweighed the risks of getting into trouble.

Wearing Hats: Do-Rags and Decorum

The wearing of hats (of any kind, but particularly baseball caps, the hat of choice) and do-rags in school, which was the second-most-common infraction after cutting classes, provides another illustration of how students' transgressions provided a psychological space in which they protected their sense of self and momentarily managed to disrupt imposed standards of decorum. Hat wearing was perhaps the clearest example of how students struggled to hold on to a cultural identity that was not officially welcome in the school but was viewed as providing credibility within the social world of the school.

Some teachers, deans, administrators, and police officers stated that they believed the enforcement of the rule banning head coverings had become so problematic that it should be done away with; it caused more problems than it was worth. One officer and a few deans explained to me that the policy had been put into place because students used hats to signify their gang affiliation. Thus, when all gang paraphernalia (colored bandanas, or "flags," beads, and gang symbols, for example) was banned, so, too, were hats. But these officers and deans explained that students simply found new ways to indicate their gang affiliation. Additionally, I learned that hat wearing was so pervasive that the vast majority of students who wore hats were not gang members. One officer even explained that the NYPD had determined that hat bans were ineffective ways of curtailing gang activity.

Yet the policy persisted. From speaking with deans and teachers, it became apparent that the hat ban was not really about curtailing gang activity, anyway. It was about making students conform to "school values" as opposed to "street values." The theory behind this, as expressed by numerous school personnel, was that one who adhered to a street style of dress did not fit in at school and would not likely do well academically.

Given that so many students were getting into trouble for wearing hats, I started observing students' hat-wearing behaviors and asking them why they continued to wear hats when they knew it was against the rules. Students' responses revealed that wearing a hat was not so much a "defaulting from prescribed activity but from prescribed *being*."[5] Students demonstrated great pride in their hats. (The most popular type was an expensive, fitted Yankees baseball cap.) Their statements also indicated that their hats helped to define them, giving them a sense of self and belonging within a particular sociocultural (and perhaps geographic) group, which many believed had an impact on how they would be treated by others.

"What about hats? Why do students refuse to take their hats off?" I asked Zack, a chronic hat wearer, one afternoon over lunch in the Jamaican restaurant across the street from the school.

"Sometimes they be having bad hair days or fashion. Fashion's a big thing in high school."

"Yeah, it seems really important to kids, like it's part of their identity or something," I said.

"Yeah, it's like part of their identity," Zack confirmed. "The way you look is the way people treat you. In high school, the way you look is the way they treat you and address you."

"It seems to me," I said, "that it's so much a part of the students' identity, like what they wear and who they are and what they feel comfortable in. Is it sort of like being asked to take your shoes off?"

"Yeah, that's how it would be. That's exactly how it would be! Honestly, yeah." My analogy had resonated with Zack. "It would be like walking around here with no shoes," he confirmed.

Wearing a hat appeared to be, in part, an involuntary force of habit not easily broken. This became apparent to me as I repeatedly observed students absentmindedly place hats back on their heads only minutes after they had been told to remove them. But there was something primarily intentional in students' hat wearing. Students continued to bring hats to school, take them out of their backpacks, and place them on their heads. And in some instances, students ended up in confrontations with law-enforcement officials for refusing to remove a hat, at times ending up with a court summons. For Goffman, such an act is about construction of self: "It is . . . *against something* that the self can emerge."[6] This kind of transgression was thus an identity performance through which students strengthened their sense of self in contrast to institutional demands. It also, of course, marked them as members of a particular social group, "a kid from the Bronx," as one student put it.

Gambling

The next example of oppositional behavior I offer, gambling and drug sales in the cafeteria, describes a more clandestine type, what Goffman referred to as a contained secondary adjustment rather than a disruptive one.[7] Additionally, this example entailed a redefining not just of the self but also of a physical space and the creation of "personal territories." These illicit activities apparently occurred regularly in the cafeteria despite the presence of a large security team of deans, law-enforcement officials, and school aides and the presence of security cameras. Although these activities may have involved a small percentage of students, they were frequently mentioned during interviews—often enough to warrant analysis. Additionally, I learned through some of the deans that gambling had become so pervasive in the cafeteria in prior years that game playing had recently been banned.

Gambling, unlike most other school infractions, brought with it monetary incentives: it offered material as well as symbolic rewards for the students. Zack explained to me that the cafeteria was "all about the hustle." In other words, many students, according to Zack, went to the lunchroom to make some money. It was not likely that there was much money to be made, but the excitement of the *potential* to make money was apparently enough.

Jermaine suggested something similar to Zack one day as he explained that UPHS students, unlike students in "better schools," did not come to school primarily for learning. "School for us is more of a way to make money," he said.

"How do you make money in school?" I asked.

"Dice, cards, drugs. You understand what I'm saying? . . . Jobs out here [in the surrounding neighborhood] is not really, um, the job out here is picking up a gun and robbing somebody or getting a package [of drugs] and standing on the corner or even coming to school with a pack and standing in the hallway or playing in the lunch room all day."

Jermaine's statement links the illicit activity in the school to the street and to more extreme forms of illegality and violence that permeated the lives of many students at UPHS. It is also an implicit commentary on how the absence of viable legal work for young men and women of color living in urban areas shaped students' decisions about finding ways to earn money. (Nevertheless, within the context of the school, gambling appeared to be as much a friendly pastime as it was a way of making money, and at no time did it appear to be related to violent incidents.) Jermaine's statement also reveals how he viewed himself as attending a school that was not like other schools. He believed that UPHS was the kind of place where kids went to hustle, not to take academics seriously.

Zack wanted to show me firsthand how students participated in gambling, an activity I could not have observed without his presence. So, one day during his lunch period, he took me on a tour of the cafeteria. His reputation in the school and his knowledge of the social landscape served us well. He seemed to know many of the students, and everyone we approached appeared willing, if not happy, to speak with us. Near the middle of the huge room, a few tables over from the Dominican students, against the wall and intentionally away from the security cameras, Zack pointed to the gambling section. As we approached a table, two boys hid some cards and looked up at Zack, then over at me. Zack nodded his head, indicating that it was OK to continue. The boys took their cards out and resumed their game. Next to the table, a few more boys were playing dice against the wall. We chatted with the boys for a few moments, but they were immersed in their games, so we left. As we walked away from that section, Zack pointed with his chin to a boy pacing near the elevators. "See him?" he asked. The boy to whom Zack referred did not stand out in any way. He was a rather small young man dressed in baggy clothes and a forbidden baseball cap. (Evidently, the hat rule was not strictly enforced in the lunchroom.) He appeared to me simply to be calmly walking in the direction of the exit.

"Yeah," I said.

"He's dealing."

"Drugs?" (I wanted to be sure.)

"Yeah." I was never able to verify this, but, according to the occurrence reports and conversations I had had with deans, it was perfectly believable.

It makes sense that young men who have so few prospects for making money within the formal economy would be attracted to gambling in the cafeteria of their school. Boys claimed that gambling was fun and that it gave them a chance to make a little money. (I did not observe or meet any girls who gambled in the lunchroom, but several told me that they braided boys' hair for money in school.) Students were also creating personal territories within the institution—spaces in which they had generated a certain amount of autonomy, if not in response to, then at least in the context of, their sense of exclusion from formal markets and more conventional uses of schooling. These personal territories allowed students to be in control of their own milieu, something of great significance for young men and women who generally had little or no officially legitimized control over their environments—in or out of school. Those who participated in gambling were giving themselves a sense of purpose, a reprieve from the monotony and boredom of the institution, and even, perhaps, an economic reason for coming to school.

Conflicts and Violence

Inside UPHS, conflict and violence were conceived and framed in two opposing ways. On the one hand, students' conceptions of school violence were shaped by the street and even prison. Students acknowledged the pervasiveness, danger, and for some, the unavoidability of prison. Yet, on the other hand, conflict and violence had a romantic allure, and, in the repressive context of penal management, it provided thrills, excitement, and opportunities to rebel against authority and to construct strong, courageous, and loyal (in relation to friends) identities against prescribed institutional norms. Interestingly, the school, with its high-tech security apparatus and heavy policing, also offered a place to manage street conflicts and limit their potentially devastating effect. This was accomplished through strategic participation in conflict within the confines of the school.

Waking Up to the Same Damn Thing: Street Violence in the Lives of UPHS Students

The vast majority of students reported that street violence was prevalent, but they were rarely involved in *serious* street violence—that which involved weapons or life-threatening situations. Nevertheless, this group often reported being on the sidelines of grave violence, having friends or family members who were involved in serious incidents or witnessing it firsthand. Many also reported being frequently involved in petty conflicts in their neighborhoods, such as verbal disputes and fistfights that did not involve weapons but had the potential to lead to more serious acts of violence. These students, who represented "the average" UPHS student, generally saw any participation in violence as a function of youth. They often reported to me that they intended to go to college and get "a good job." Even if they had some experience in a street clique or gang, they tended not to view themselves as entering a life of illegal street activity.

For other students—a small yet significant and highly visible group— participation in street violence appeared unavoidable. These were generally the students who had joined gangs, some at very young ages, had spent much time on the streets, and at times had been involved in crime and had been incarcerated. Students who were immersed in conflict and violence generally acknowledged their own agency; nevertheless, there was a sense that they had been born into violence and that it surrounded them. Students who were immersed in street violence had perceptions that appeared to be shaped by what might be called an ecology of danger, or a process of socialization in which any social exchange is seen as potentially threatening and can lead to violence.[8]

One afternoon while sitting in his living room, Carlos spoke to me about his history of getting into fights with other young people. I would not describe Carlos as a violent gang member. Contrarily, he might best be described as a street-savvy young man who both had instigated street fights on occasion and had been a victim. He fully expected to go to college and enter the legal workforce with a "good" job.

He said, "I used to see it [fighting] like it was a normal thing, you know. I used to see it like, oh, that's how it is here. Because you know, I'm from New York, so I'm thinking that's how it is. That's how it goes down."

Later in our conversation, he repeated this idea when I asked him to explain why he thought young people engaged in physical violence.

"I mean, it's just how . . . like, I'm a kid from the Bronx, right?" Carlos had trouble explaining exactly why young people fought. He could say only that he believed engaging in fighting was what it meant to be from the Bronx.

Jermaine, like Carlos, viewed daily exposure to street violence and conflict as part of what it meant to grow up in a low-income urban environment. However, Jermaine's reflections also poignantly reveal a feeling of being trapped. One sunny afternoon in early June, while he and I were sitting in a small office off the cafeteria, he said to me, "I mean, I don't like it [street violence and always having to be on guard]. What can you do? I wake up in the same place every morning. It's not like I sleep in and wake up in heaven. I wake up to *the same damn thing every day*." As the sun shone through the office window, he turned from me and peered out into the street. "It's a real nice day," he quietly mused, "a real nice day."

I asked Jermaine whether young people could avoid violence if they wanted to. "I mean, I don't know," he said. "There's rules in the 'hood that aren't rules at all. Like, they never been written down. But every person knows them. You understand what I'm saying?" he asked. "They not rules that say you can't bring do-rags in [to school], but there's rules in the street that say you can't look at a guy like that [in a direct or provocative manner]. Regardless of anything, there's rules to the streets. No matter, if you're from the streets, those rules apply to you no matter where you go, if you go to prison, Catholic school, Harvard, they still apply because that's *in* you."

"So, who makes those rules?" I asked.

"The streets make the rules."

Jermaine referred to a kind of code of the street, an unwritten code of conduct that, in some ways, helps to manage violence.[9] At the same time, however, it perpetuates violence. Only a small number of the young men and women I met at UPHS were embroiled in serious street violence and a true ecology of danger, one which their actions perpetuated but from which they saw no alternatives, because the street made the rules (or, one could argue, because they had no control over the influx and spread of guns and drugs in their communities, and they had little control over the economic and material conditions in which they lived).

Additionally, the students involved in street violence, perhaps as a way of coming to terms with their dangerous lives, often held romantic images of it. Jermaine provided an example of the types of sentiments I heard expressed by the more "hard-core" students. Comparing himself to "suburban" youth, he said, "You never really had nobody that you can say, that's my nigga for life, *for life*. You know what that means?" He then referred to an incident in which he had been involved. "A lot of people don't even know what that means, to have a friend for life, for life, for the rest of your life just because he was standing on the corner when somebody shot at you. That makes you friends for life. 'Cause we coulda died that day. And we would have been friends that same day, so now it's for life. A lot of people don't know what that means. They don't even know what that feels like. That's the greatest feeling in the world. I don't care what anybody says. That's the greatest feeling in the world to know that no matter what happens, no matter what happens in the streets, he's behind me, no matter what."

Jermaine's narrative reveals the complexity of violence in the lives of urban youth: its oppressive presence and its simultaneous romantic allure. His testimony seems to evoke the voice of a wartime soldier telling stories of loyalty, ultimate sacrifice, and the intense emotional rush of friends escaping death together. For most UPHS students, such dramatic tales were absent from their testimonies of street violence. Yet the less serious conflict in which they were involved was often governed by the same street rules and held the same romantic allure and perceived benefits.

Managing Violence and Reaping the Benefits at UPHS

There existed at UPHS what Pedro Mateu-Gelabert has called a bidirectional conflict flow between neighborhood and school.[10] As in the surrounding areas, inside UPHS conflict was pervasive and violence was not uncommon. There was also an underlying sense of fear (although few students admitted being afraid). UPHS was viewed as safer than the streets, but it had a notorious reputation as a violent school. So, inside the school students practiced strategic participation. They could enter into a fight to save face knowing that inside the building there was a certain level of protection, given the security apparatus. Students also chose to participate in conflicts (or even to start them) as a way of not becoming a victim. That is, if they could show toughness, they believed they were less likely to be labeled a punk or to get beaten up.[11] Both of these rationales for participation in violence were about protection and minimizing harm.

Another process at work had to do with the romantic side of violence, the prestige or credibility one could gain by being tough, and the fun or thrill one might experience. Violence and conflict were a terrain where friendships were forged and loyalty was demonstrated and where courage could be proudly displayed, leading to higher social status among peers. Additionally, students could take pleasure in manipulating situations and gaining a sense of control or power by being an instigator or by instilling fear in another. In the following sections, I show how these processes— strategic participation for protection and romanticizing conflict—were intertwined.

"I'm Gonna Get My Respect"

It is important to note that the vast majority of students at UPHS did not rely on a street or prison framework to explain school-based conflicts, nor did they speak about being the instigators of violence or blatantly taking pleasure from it. Testimony by Steven, however, provides one of the most cogent examples of how students understood school violence through the lens of the street and even, at times, prison. It also demonstrates how a policy of mass imprisonment can affect urban schools as significant numbers of formerly incarcerated youth reenter those schools.

Steven, unlike most UPHS students, reported that he had been incarcerated on several occasions. He claimed that he was first incarcerated at the age of thirteen, for kidnapping his younger brother from foster care to bring him home. He told me he did four months "upstate."

Steven explained the importance of gaining others' respect for the purpose of remaining safe, but it is clear that he also romanticized his participation in school violence. He looked back fondly on his participation with a sense of achievement. Indeed, to him, the romantic aspects of violence appeared to be as important as the need to manage violence through strategic participation in it.

One day, while I was sitting at a table at the far end of the cafeteria during a noisy lunch period with Steven and his friend Frankie, Steven reminisced about a "crew" he had started inside UPHS. "I opened up my own crew. You understand? And we fucked up a lot of people. That shit was the best days of my life. We beat the shit out of a lot of people, and my own boys snitched me out. My right-hand man snitched me out."

"Why do you do that?" I asked.

"What?"

"Why do you, um, fuck up other people, as you say?" Steven and Frankie giggled at my uncharacteristic use of language. They struck me as a little goofy.

"Because back then everywhere I'd go all I heard was, yo, you need respect, you need respect, you need respect. If you go to jail, you gotta earn your respect. If you're in the school, you gotta earn your respect. You understand? So I looked at it in a different way. I looked at it like, I'm gonna get my respect."

My eyes scanned the length of the enormous room and the throng of animated and boisterous students. From that distance, the significance of the social maneuverings of seating arrangements, territory marking, lunchtime banter, dice games, and marijuana dealing was obscured. "Why is respect so important?" I asked.

"Because if, like, you get no respect, like this man [pointing to Frankie], people are going to think of him, when you go to jail, when you first get there, you think they're going to look at you and not do nothing? They're gonna do something."

"Respect is protection for jail?"

"No, it's protection everywhere. I got respect here [in the school]. No one will fuck with me."

Steven's narrative highlights the significance of obtaining and maintaining respect among peers. Respect was instrumental; it served as a form of protection. Students like Steven, sometimes coming from prison or other institutional settings, entered a school with a notorious reputation and decided that in order to be safe they had to initiate a physical altercation as a means of reducing the likelihood of their becoming a victim.

Steven also mentioned starting a crew; others joined established gangs. These networks served as another form of protection, as well as a surrogate family for some.[12] Although students who were involved in gangs spoke about protection, they did not often talk about their fear. Nevertheless, their non-gang-affiliated schoolmates did. When I asked students who were not in gangs about the gang presence in their school, they often rolled their eyes. Throughout my interview transcripts, students commented on why students joined gangs: "They're afraid." "They're pussy. They don't want to fight alone." "They gotta hide behind their crew." Thus, fear appeared to play an important role in the decision to join a gang and to participate in the more violent forms of conflict found in the school.

Wanda's comments are perhaps more representative of the students I spoke with, as they emphasize protection over excitement. She spoke about the perceived need to take preemptive action or to be the first one in a situation to present a tough posture. She insisted that "having an attitude" could save a person from being seen as a punk, and this was beneficial for students who wished to avoid a physical confrontation.

As we sat together in an empty hallway one day, she explained it this way: "You have to defend yourself, because if you don't, they [other students] going to take you for being a punk and they going to walk all over you. . . . Let me show [how] attitude [can] work for you. There could be a girl that want to fight you, come up in your face, right. If you be, like, 'Leave me alone, leave me alone,' the girl's gonna think you a punk. If you be, like, 'Whatever, get out of my face, bitch, you nothing. You this. You that' [spoken in a harsh manner], it could help you. The girl's going to be, like, 'Oh, wow. Yo, she really think she hard-core.'"

In Wanda's estimation, having an attitude was about presenting a tough front—a means of protecting oneself against real or perceived violence.[13] She, unlike Steven, did not emphasize the excitement of violence, and she did not appear to take pride in her ability to manage violence through adopting "an attitude." Students who had an attitude hoped that the tough posture would serve as a deterrent. Thus, in Wanda's case, as in others', the focus was more on strategic participation than on romanticizing. Nevertheless, creating a strong self-image (not being a punk) always remained foremost in the students' minds and testimonies. Not being a punk was not just a matter of safety, it was a means of generating self-respect in the context of control.

The School as "a Safe Place to Take Your Beef"

Students recognized that the school offered a certain element of safety. It was certainly seen as safer than the streets. Thus, in their attempt to manage violence, some students would choose to initiate a conflict or respond to a threat inside the school. The school was seen, as one student put it, as "a safe place to take your beef." In other words, the school provided a space where conflicts could be worked out through violence but in a relatively controlled environment.

One day, as I was sitting in B-40 with Officer Hoffmann, I asked him about the specific connection between street violence and what he saw occurring in the school. His response reveals how students used the security apparatus in the school as a form of harm reduction. That is, street conflicts were carried into the school not *despite* the security apparatus but, at times, *because* of it. Hoffmann said,

> Kids will feel safer here [than they do on the street] because, one, they know people are getting scanned coming in here, so more than likely I'm not going to get shot in school. . . . It's like I got beef with this guy. I know he's going to be at UPHS today, so I'm going there to deal with it, because if you notice, a lot of this stuff will materialize inside the school. In my opinion it's because they want to deal with it, but they really don't want to deal with it. They don't want to have to take it the full level, because they know if they start a fight in school, it's going to get broken up. A lot of times, when a kid feels like he got punked by somebody, he'll be, like, "All right, I got to step up to this guy or I'm going to look like a punk." So what he'll do is pick that fight in the hallway in the middle of classes

when there's a school safety agent ten feet away from them, knowing full well that somebody will be there in seconds.

I was not sure students would admit these thoughts to Hoffmann, so I decided to start asking. Jermaine's response was representative. I asked him, "Somebody once told me that they think that kids take their beef inside school because it's, like, restricted, because there's only a certain amount of violence that can occur because there're all these cops here, and there're security cameras. Do you think that's true?"

"Of course," Jermaine responded matter-of-factly.

"So kids will take it to the schools."

"Absolutely. Think about it," he said. "There's nothing in the street that, when you walk over it, it goes 'Beep, beep, beep, beep' to let someone know that you have a weapon on you. So when you're in the streets and you want to smart-mouth, you got to think."

Duane made a similar statement when I asked him whether the school was a safe place to take your beef. He said, "Hell, yeah! Some students is pussy. They're scared. They know anything can go down out there [in the street]."

Students' remaking of the school as a safe place to fight flew in the face of the penal-control efforts in the school. These young people were provided very few and generally grossly undersupported mechanisms for effective and nonviolent conflict resolution. As a result, some opted to manage conflict in the very place violence was most suppressed, so that they could limit the negative consequences. Although there was an element of strategic participation in students' rationales, strategic participation could not be separated from students' attempts to "not be a punk" or, alternatively, to forge "hard" and respected identities.

He Said/She Said and Other Stupid Stuff

Most student conflict developed over mundane and minor disputes—pettiness, snubs, gossip, and misunderstandings or disagreements. These kinds of disputes took on great significance, particularly for students who were alienated from the classroom experience. Like other aspects of the underlife of the school, petty conflict was a domain where social hierarchies were determined, pleasure was sought, and assertions of self were made. Indeed, the domain of petty conflict was an ideal space in which to romanticize violence, as the stakes were generally much lower than with more serious forms of violence.

When asked about the causes of conflict in the school, students usually batted off a list of things that sounded quite mundane. They would immediately bring up fighting on the lines going into the lunchroom or pushing in the hallways or stealing food or teasing. "Kids are always pushing," several students explained, "and cutting in front of other students." Students frequently spoke about altercations starting over "stupid stuff," incidents escalating out of simple misunderstandings or gossip. They also spoke about instigators who found it fun to watch others get into fights.

Sitting with Damian, Greg, and Darnell on one occasion, I asked, "What do you think are the most common causes [of conflict and violence]?"

"Girls," Damian blurted out before I could finish.

"Girls," Greg added emphatically.

"Girls," Darnell agreed.

"Girls?" I repeated. "So when guys are fighting, it's over girls?"

Damian: "Not always, but . . ."

Greg: "Not always."

"It always leads to something like that. And if it's not that, then the second reason is gangs," Damian said.

"Gangs," I said.

"And if it's not gangs, then it's just beef, like from the streets," Damian added.

"Yeah, stupid stuff," Darnell said.

"So stuff carries in from the streets. But what's that related to? Neighborhood fights?

"Just like, yeah. And it just, like, leads into the school," Damian clarified.

During another conversation, which took place in the detention room, Alex described petty conflict in terms of "he said/she said." I asked him to explain what that meant.

"They want to fulfill their needs. They want to see a fight," he said.

"Is it a third person who starts a fight?"

"Yeah, he said/she said," Alex repeated.

"What's that?"

Alex (who usually spoke to me in a relatively formal register and standard form of English) replied, "He said/she said is like a rumor that's made up. Like, say somebody comes to me and says, 'Oh, Alex, Antoine says you a bum-ass nigga. You was wearing his socks the other day,' and then he didn't really say that, but the person that told me then goes to Antoine and says, 'Oh, Alex said you a dirty nigga. You don't wash up.' That's 'he said/she said.' And then we confront each other about it and just be, like, 'Well this girl said that you said that I was a bum-ass nigga.' And then he be, like, 'I didn't say that. But Lindsey told me that you said that I was a dirty nigga and that I don't wash up.' And then it all comes to her. That's 'he said/she said.'"[14]

He said/she said and other stupid stuff constituted a major part of the underlife at UPHS. These incidents were framed very much in the context of urban street violence, and there was always the risk that they would escalate into more serious incidents of violence. Nevertheless, within the context of the school, petty conflicts were relatively contained and offered many benefits. They provided students with the opportunity to present "hard" and respected identities that gave them a sense of (and perhaps real) protection. Through participation in petty conflict, students could make meaning of their school experiences and develop self-esteem in an environment where they had few, if any, legitimate ways of forging valued identities.

Making Sense of Oppositional Behavior at UPHS

Goffman's ideas that within the context of a repressive institution, an underlife emerges and that identities develop against prescribed norms are helpful for understanding how students make sense of oppositional behavior at UPHS. Students tacitly sought a variety of psychological and social gains through their oppositional behavior in the context of a deep sense of academic alienation and penal management. They were able to gain a sense of autonomy, assert a strong image of self, generate fun and excitement, and find ways to contain violence. At the same time, students did not narrowly view UPHS as a tightly controlled place. UPHS, in Carlos's words, was a "social place," unlike the GED program he wanted to attend, where he believed kids took their education more seriously. And UPHS was a school with a "bad reputation." Students continually contended with these constructions of the school as they found ways to establish their identities. It was reasonable, then, as UPHS students, to view oppositional behavior as a fulfillment of expectations as well as a means of socially positioning oneself well.

CHAPTER 7

Living Proof

Experiences of Economic and Educational Exclusion

W HAT DO YOU WANT TO DO when you finish high school?" I asked Stephanie, sixteen, one day as we sat together at a corner table in the lunchroom. Silence. Her face tightened, and after a long pause she frowned and shrugged her shoulders. I had gotten the same response to this question many times before, and it was painful for me to see. Stephanie was one of those students who had stopped dreaming, or at least daring to articulate her dream, of her future. In fact, she did not expect to graduate from high school. She was lacking too many credits and was at that age when counselors started directing students with missing credits into GED programs. College seemed like an insurmountable goal at that point, and any attainable job was not one that Stephanie would dream of having.

Students' relationships to the opportunity structure, through both higher education and viable jobs, were a central part of the context for this study of disciplinary practices. Thus as part of my inquiry, I asked, how was a school like UPHS, with its culture of control, helping to lessen or, more likely, to reproduce inequalities found in the larger society? What kinds of roles were students being prepared to step into as adults? Additionally, how did the ways students made sense of their relationship to the labor market and schooling influence their actions? For me, these were questions concerning the significance of theories of social reproduction and resistance in schooling.

Dreams Modified, Dreams Abandoned:
Students' Relationships to the Job Market

Students at UPHS routinely expressed a deep sense of frustration, ambivalence, or uncertainty about their current and future employment prospects. Indeed, unlike the "lads" of Paul Willis's classic study, who had a vision of working in local factories,[1] dozens, if not hundreds, of UPHS students were quickly losing hope of finding an after-school job and had no solid vision for future employment. Many of those who did have a vision held a somewhat unrealistic one—a third-year student reading at a fourth-grade level, for instance, stating he or she wanted to go to college and become a lawyer. Others, boys in particular, dreamed of being professional ball players or accomplished rap artists. And finally, there were a few students entrenched in a gang lifestyle who imagined as a probability life in the drug trade.

The most frequent question I received from students was, "Can you get me a job?" Carlos, for example, had grown very frustrated in his job search, like many other students in his predicament. He had filled out dozens of applications at local stores and restaurants. When his girlfriend, Jennifer, got a job in a supermarket, he started to believe that it was easier for young women to get jobs than young men, and soon after he gave up trying.

Wanda, who was black, spoke at length to me one day about her job-related frustrations:

> I'm unemployed. I'm at the age that I could work. I'm eighteen. Everybody's telling me, "Go out there and find a job. Do something useful with your life. Help out with your family." . . . I walk into Planet Earth [a young women's clothing store] on Fordham Road [a nearby commercial shopping area]. I come in there dressed up, presentable, going out there looking nice for a job interview. . . . The first thing they look at is my impression, how I look. . . . I ask for a job application. The man tells me . . . he tells me that there's no space available, that he's not hiring. This is a Monday. I wait till Tuesday. I take my friend down there. My friend's Spanish. She's well developed. She gets a job application. The man calls her back. Why is he discriminating against me? Because of my looks? Because the color of my skin? Because I'm not Spanish?

Wanda's statements suggest that young black people can feel discriminated against while inquiring about a prospective job. However, we do not see here the more familiar dynamic in which employers choose white applicants over similarly qualified black applicants. In a working-class shopping district that had a rapidly growing Spanish-speaking population, Wanda believed the competition who were landing jobs were Latinas. She also noted a bias toward young women with a particular kind of aesthetic (sex appeal). These realities were discouraging.

Additionally, Wanda expressed frustration at prospective employers' requiring information about academic performance, even for low-paying, entry-level jobs:

McDonald's asks when you're filling out a job application, it asks you for the last grade you completed or what grade you're in. It asks you your average. McDonald's asks you this, yes, it does. . . . It asks what school you go to. . . . It asks what's your average in math. And it asks you for your age. Say, I'm an honest person. I'm eighteen, but I put tenth grade. I put tenth grade, I'm eighteen, and my math average is average. Now, they look at that, would you hire me? 'Cause, look, they're going to look at why you in the tenth grade and why the hell you eighteen. . . . You thinking, OK, honest and truly, McDonald's is a whack-ass job. You only get paid, what, $6.50? And you get paid every Thursday. That's the only thing good about it. You get paid every Thursday. Why the hell do I have to fill out my grade? I understand about my age, and I understand about the math thing, but why do I have to fill out my grade? Now, what if I was nineteen and still in high school? Do you think I want somebody to know that? You feel me? So I don't think McDonald's should ask those questions. . . . The easy thing is, you know, let me stand on that corner and sell some crack or some weed. Why? I want to have money in my pockets. It won't be a legit job, but at least I have a job. At least I have some money. You feel me?

Overall, Wanda viewed her race, physical characteristics, and school record as obstacles to legal employment. Other students made a connection between exclusion from the job market and having a criminal record. One young man, Alvin, for instance, explained to me that, for him, getting a job was nearly impossible, because he had a record that included numerous petty crimes. He said, "No one's gonna hire me. I can't even get a job at McDonald's." As a young black man with a criminal record, Alvin had reason to be discouraged. Indeed, research suggests that a white man with a criminal record has a better chance of getting a job than a black man with the same qualifications and no criminal record.[2]

Eric, nineteen, was one of the young men I met who dreamed of being a rap artist. He was overage but doing well in school. I met him in his peer-mediation class, where I learned that many of the students and the teacher, Ms. Orozco, believed that Eric was one of the more talented rappers in the school.

One afternoon we sat together in a dark stairwell leading up to the roof of the building, discussing Eric's dreams and frustrations and life in his neighborhood. He shared some of his raps with me to narrate his experiences. His rhymes spoke poignantly of the desperate reality of his neighborhood: young men in their twenties and thirties who had been in prison and were now jobless and living with their mothers:

> I remember the days we'd look at the big boys as heroes.
> Now when we look at them, they nothing but deadbeat zeros.
> Doing nothing but life. So for them, life's a fight,
> praying on their knees to see another night.
> This is why I work hard. I'm not trying to get stuck living off a chick.
> This time I'm trying to get rich quick.

Eric showed considerable determination. He had notebooks full of rhymes, and he was making an effort to graduate. But as we sat together in the stairwell, the lyrics of his raps were cutting and full of despair:

> These days I'm paranoid because I feel everyone's trying to knife my back.
> So, on the lowdown, I'm distant,
> I tell my peeps I got talent but they never listen.
> So I feel my progress is being put on hold.
> I feel like I'm already dead, because mentally my casket's closed.

From the landing where I sat on the floor, I looked up at Eric, four steps above me in the shadow of the building's roof. I became aware of my jaw tightening. Eric and I remained in silence for a few moments, and then, trying to lighten the moment, I commented on his great talent.

Duane, who reported having been a gang member since the age of nine, reflected one day on the idea of graduating from high school and getting a job. As he spoke to me, he revealed how conflicted he felt regarding school and work.

"What do you think a high school diploma could do for you?" I asked.

"Get me a job," he replied.

"What kind of job would you like to get?"

"I don't want to be a cop. . . . To be honest, I never really thought about it."

"No?" I said.

He paused, then said, as if it was a new and rather disconcerting revelation, "*Word*, I never . . . I don't think about it."

"Do you want to go to college?" I asked.

"Hell, no."

"Why not?" I asked, thinking that if he applied himself, he had the academic skills to do well in college.

"'Cause, well, I'm not going to say, 'Hell, no,' because I never been there, but, naw, I don't think so. I don't know. I think about the street too much. You know, I don't really think about my life like that."

Later in our conversation I reminded him that he had mentioned he wanted to get a high school diploma.

"That's all I want," he said emphatically. "If I could get that right now, I'm good."

Suddenly he appeared sad. "Shit," he said with a slight laugh. "I mean, like, I care, yo, but it's like, fuck it." He stared down at his hands resting on the desktop for a moment in silence, then added, "And that's bad, because I'm seventeen. I'm about to be seventeen, and I still don't know what I want to be in my life. All I ever did was gangbang, really. That's about it. I don't know what I want to be. Before, when I was younger, I'm not going to front [lie], I used to want to be a cop, but then growing up I was, like, I saw how they used to act and shit. Fuck the niggas, I don't want to be no cop."

These kinds of remarks from students about their difficulties finding jobs, the micropolitics of who was hirable, their inability to envision a realistic or satisfying future of employment, their ambivalence about the possibility of entering the drug trade, and their feelings toward the police reflect the political economy in which they lived. Moreover, incarceration rates, as I described in chapter 1, have skyrocketed for young black and Latino men and increasingly for women, and the poorer they are and the less education they have, the more likely they will spend time in prison.[3] Thus, more than ever before, the life experiences of young adults—black and Latino/a—in urban centers like the Bronx are shaped not only in relationship to work, or the lack of it, but also (and perhaps in some instances even more so) in relationship to the criminal- and juvenile-justice systems. Some students, like Duane, abandoned their dreams before ever getting to high school. Others, like Stephanie, grew ambivalent in high school, when it became apparent that they were unlikely to find the educational situation they imagined as their stepping stone. And still others, as I came to learn a few years down the line, held tenaciously to their dreams despite the detours through low-wage jobs, dubious training programs, and the complexities of their daily lives.

"If Only . . .": Students' Relationships to Academic Work

Changes in the political economy, along with the institutional context, also appeared to influence young people's relationship to academic work. During my data collection, I was particularly interested in the perspectives of students who participated in oppositional behavior, like those discussed in chapter 6. Previous studies on this topic have focused on oppositional behavior as a kind of implicit social critique and a celebration of a nondominant culture (working-class culture or black culture, for example).[4] These studies have also viewed oppositional behavior as a form of resistance to schooling, or to mental labor generally, stemming from students' implicit understanding that the educational system is not structured to benefit their group as a whole. Such analyses often predated the deindustrialization of so-called first-world cities and the dramatic growth of the criminal-justice system. So it was not surprising that what I encountered at UPHS was somewhat different. Oppositional behavior certainly embodied elements of critique, but times had changed. There was no shop-floor culture like the one Willis wrote about in the 1970s, for example, for UPHS students to embrace. Prison and street life played a larger role than factory life in shaping young people's cultural productions and notions of masculinity. And despite the fact that so many students in my study could not articulate a viable career goal, virtually every student with whom I spoke maintained the perspective that a high school education was an important step in the process of going to college and attaining "a good job." This attitude was reflected in Duane's statements in my conversation with him, and in dozens of other student narratives about schooling and employment.

There were moments when I wondered whether students felt some fear that being too academically oriented would be viewed by peers as "acting white."[5] However, these sentiments were never reported to me explicitly. If I brought up the issue of acting white, students would give me curious looks as if it *might* be a factor, but they didn't think about their oppositional behavior in those terms. This may be because I am a white researcher, but, based on my numerous conversations with UPHS students (as well as my experience as a high school teacher), I believe that fear of appearing white, particularly in a context where there were virtually no white students, was not a strong motivation for oppositional behavior. Likewise, the fear of being "too soft" was only one of the ways in which students made sense of their opposition. There were some academically engaged students in the school, like Ronald (chapter 4) or Kalif (chapter 3), who either avoided participation in the underlife, in particular the terrain of conflict, or were able to be "hard enough" when the situation called for it. They appeared to become "multicultural navigators," able both to conform to expected institutional norms and to adopt a kind of street style when it was called for.[6]

Roslyn Mickelson's classic study of concrete and abstract attitudes toward academic work for black youth offers a better construct for making sense of my own data.[7] Students at UPHS often expressed abstract attitudes of desire for school success and an understanding that finishing school could be beneficial. However, their concrete attitudes (and behaviors) often reflected the daily experiences and feelings of alienation from classroom work and their sense of exclusion from both better school experiences and satisfying legal employment. Within the current political economy, it appears that many students tended to hold hopeful values and, at the same time, resisted against alienating experiences and the treatment they received.

Daily life between abstract and concrete values, I learned, constituted a middle ground, a social, psychological, and often physical space between efforts toward academic success and dropping out (a path some 60 to 70 percent of UPHS students ultimately took). That is, students who were alienated from their classes and participated in various forms of oppositional behavior did not drop out immediately. It appeared that they often did not leave until school administrators began encouraging or forcing them to do so. Instead, they spent sometimes a couple of years attending high school on a fairly regular basis. During this time, these students expressed a desire to "turn things around" or "do better" once they found the "right" program or school. They spoke poignantly of their imagined ideal of schooling, in places they believed existed elsewhere, perhaps even in the Bronx, where they could learn a valuable skill for the job market, have a flexible schedule, benefit from state-of-the art computers, be away from the negative influences of certain peers, or take courses where content seemed relevant and respectful of their life experiences. Essentially, what I found was that students' relationship to schooling, in particular that of students occupying this middle ground, was framed—if I might draw from my interest in grammar as a former ESL teacher—by the unreal conditional. Students generally contended that the realities of schooling and the experiences they were offered would have to change in order for them to fulfill their goals. They were critical of their current situations, but they did not reject schooling. Contrarily, they yearned for something better. They described their goals and dreams in what I call their "if only" statements.

Duane's "if only" scenario entailed being transferred to a high school in another part of the city where he believed there would be fewer negative peer influences and he would see his father more often. One day, I asked him what he thought it would take for him to get a high school diploma. He replied, "It would take me to stop the bullshit I'm doing and go to class. I could go to class . . . I'm capable of doing my work. I'm not a stupid kid." This I knew to be true. On occasion, Duane would show me a novel he was reading, not something assigned in class but something he chose to read. And although some teachers may not have been able to hear past his frequent use of a nonstandard variety of English and street slang, in our many conversations I found him to be insightful and analytical as he discussed such things as books and the complexities of gang regulations.

"It's just that it's hard with all this shit going on," Duane continued. "If I get into the next school [referring to a high school in Brooklyn to which he expected to be transferred], I'm gonna get my grades up." Duane desired to do well in school despite the fact that he was immersed in gang life. Like many students, he held on to some hope that he could graduate from high school—if only he could be given a fresh start at a different school. Beyond that, he did not appear to have any vision.

Andrew, a sophomore I met one day in the hallway of the special-education wing, had this to say when I asked him whether or not he liked school: "I like it OK, but, you know, the classes are wack. I mean, like, it would be better if I could learn a skill or something." Andrew, who had a learning disability, did not find much meaning or use in classroom activities such as learning how to produce the formulaic essays one had to write to pass many of the Regents Exams.

Wanda, who was more engaged in her classes than Duane was, explained to me that she was holding on to the hope of entering some kind of accelerated program so that she could graduate on time. She, like many students I met at UPHS, described "messing up" in the past but trying to do better in the present. Although she was occasionally still getting into trouble, Wanda was attending her classes and struggling to find a way to graduate on time. But time was running out. She was eighteen, well past the age when many students are directed out of traditional high schools and into GED programs. She said, "This is my fourth year at UPHS. I'm supposed to graduate this year, but unfortunately since I messed up in my ninth-grade year, I won't be graduating this year. I'll be graduating next year. But [the] thing I wanted to do [was] a program to get more credits so I wouldn't have to be one of the kids that drop out and get a GED, because I really don't want to get a GED. There's nothing bad about a GED, but it's not for me, since I know I have the potential of [graduating]."

Like Duane, Wanda took some responsibility for the situation she was in. She also recognized her own potential, but experienced the frustration of being caught in an institutional setting that had not served her well. If only she could get placed in a program that would help her graduate before she got pushed out. She frequently spoke to her counselor about her goals, as well as to Assistant Principal Juarez, who did what he could to help students, but, given the dearth of alternative opportunities for young people in her situation, nothing appeared to be happening.

Carlos and Jennifer also expressed "if only" sentiments. Carlos believed his best bet for entering college would be to get into a GED program. He did not feel he got the individualized attention he needed for success at UPHS. "I learn better one-on-one," he told me several times. He also said on a number of occasions that UPHS did not offer an atmosphere

conducive to learning. He believed a GED program might offer a more serious, academically focused learning environment. After Christmas break,
Carlos dropped out of UPHS and enrolled in a GED-preparation program
for students who did not have the academic skills required for entrance
into a GED program.

Jennifer, who did not usually get into trouble in school but had difficulty making it there on time or at all, hoped to transfer to a school closer
to her new foster home so that she could establish better attendance.
When I met her, she was fifteen and wanted to become a doctor. She left
her supermarket job and took a job in a pharmacy. She did well with the
bookkeeping end of the job and received some training. She got laid off
but was hired at another drug store. She thought she might pursue a career
in keeping accounts in a pharmacy, something she viewed as related to the
medical profession and a "step toward" her ultimate goal. Jennifer finally
transferred to another school but claimed she didn't like it. She dropped
out and enrolled at a proprietary trade school, which had promised her
both a GED and a credential that would help her attain a more advanced
position at a pharmacy. In fact, the school guaranteed her a job upon completion of the program. By that time, my study at UPHS had ended, but I
continued contact with her. Jennifer was back living with her mother, and
she and Carlos had broken up. She was juggling work and a long commute
to her new school.

Proprietary schools, also known as for-profit trade schools, like the one
Jennifer was attending, have seen tremendous growth through the 1990s
and early 2000s. Indeed, they have become a multibillion-dollar business
that allures students with promises of well-paying jobs upon completion.
However, they have been widely critiqued for their deceitful and aggressive recruiting practices. They take thousands of dollars from each student
in federal loan money, but students often do not finish the programs or
when they do finish, they frequently end up in minimum-wage jobs with
significant debt. Consequently, the vast majority of defaults on federal student loans involve individuals who attended these proprietary schools.

Although her path to becoming a doctor may have been modified, Jennifer never quite let go of her "if only" dream. Instead, she viewed the proprietary school as a way of getting closer to her goal. At the time, I en-
couraged her to take a more conventional path, apply for her GED, and go
straight into a public community college, but the promise of acquiring a
GED while simultaneously gaining a credential that guaranteed her a job

was too appealing. Jennifer managed to juggle her job, her classes, and her difficult home life for several months, but the situation became too much for her to handle and she dropped out of the proprietary school with significant debt.

Along with institutional and job-market realities, students' lack of academic preparation contributed to the erosion of their "if only" dreams. UPHS students, particularly those who were caught in patterns of oppositional behavior, expressed deep levels of frustration concerning particular classroom experiences. This was not surprising. The vast majority of students entering UPHS read well below grade level and often had difficulty accessing texts and standardized-exam questions. Additionally, many had spent years in special education before exiting out and entering ninth grade as general-education students. Students who had trouble understanding the content in their classes generally described classwork as boring, or they complained that the teacher didn't know how to teach, or "break it down." They wanted to learn. They wanted to succeed academically, and they were angered by the kinds of experiences they encountered.

Rethinking Reproduction and Resistance

As students' relationship to the job market changes and schools become restructured in accordance with economic exigencies, the meaning of reproduction and resistance shifts and becomes more complicated. Although urban schools still have a reproductive function (frequently preparing children of low-wage workers for less lucrative jobs in the service sector while preparing children of middle-class parents for higher-paying professions and managerial positions), the concept of reproduction as traditionally rendered in the industrialized Fordist era, when the large neighborhood public high school predominated, may be less germane than it was twenty-five or even ten years ago.[8] The vast system of sorting and tracking that I described in chapter 1 leads to varied and sometimes unpredictable outcomes. The process begins very early in a student's academic life. A first grader may be tracked into special-education classes or a failing school or, if he or she is lucky, a new, more academically rigorous and well-resourced school—one of the better charter schools, perhaps. At the high school level, there are myriad experiences created through sorting and tracking and school-choice schemes. In higher education, there are a number of paths to pursue, from elite four-year universities, to four-year and two-year colleges, both public and private, that target "nontraditional" and low-income students, to institutions like the proprietary school Jennifer attended.

As Lois Weis points out, the concepts of reproduction and resistance in the form of oppositional behavior are in flux as the consequences of resistance within our current political economy have changed. The reproduction of a working class is not the only or necessarily the most likely outcome. For Weis's white working-class research subjects, the consequences of resistance within the new political economy were not what one might have predicted. Some of her subjects who had resisted schooling ultimately were able to take advantage of the expanding tertiary college system that now prepares students for various segments of the labor market and for secure, viable jobs.[9]

My primary interest, however, has been the kinds of educational experiences and employment prospects that exist for the thousands of low-income students of color living in cities all over the United States who have reached their teen years academically underprepared, often with tenuous and troubled relationships to school. Additionally, I am interested in these students' creative processes of self-making within their social and institutional context. These students are frequently concentrated in certain "low-performing" schools, and those schools—like UPHS—are the ones most likely to adopt an extreme form of zero tolerance that includes order-maintenance policing. In their daily lives, what do the processes of social reproduction and resistance look like?

Social Reproduction and the Criminalization of Excluded Youth

The restructuring of schools has created a more complex system of sorting and tracking and more possibilities for unpredictable outcomes. As an educator, I remain optimistic that some new urban schools are creating better opportunities for low-income students and that it is possible, through radical change, for the vast majority of schools to do much better than they are doing now. But in confronting our present situation, whose interests are being served by schools like UPHS that have instituted the most extreme forms of zero tolerance? What role do these schools play in social reproduction?

David Garland's description of our societal culture of control that I described in chapter 1 is useful in analyzing how the kinds of disciplinary policies and practices one finds at UPHS influence or interrupt processes of social reproduction in schooling.[10] Garland explains that crime-control responsibilities have moved beyond the boundaries of the criminal-justice system and into the fabric of everyday life and institutions of civil society. One such institution likely to assume crime-control responsibilities is the racially segregated urban public school, with a high-tech security apparatus and heavy police presence—a school like UPHS. Such schools are located at the intersection of the two prevailing ways of thinking about crime control that I outline in chapter 1, one that emphasizes containment of "the dangerous other" and the other that emphasizes social-control strategies in everyday life. In other words, the school becomes a key site for the implementation of "preventive" low-level forms of repression, while at the same time, truancy laws and school-based policing help to contain and control low-income urban youth of color within the confines of the school. Additionally, as order maintenance becomes the established paradigm and the culture of control permeates the school, the educational mission is diminished—or takes a backseat—as it is assumed that order must be enforced through the law before academic innovations can be implemented.

In everyday life, the scenario looks something like this: students have daily exchanges with law enforcement and become accustomed to policing and prison terminology. They get threatened with arrest and summonses, and many actually are arrested. They get hauled down to the police station in the middle of the school day. They accumulate summonses and miss school to attend court. The summons, thus, becomes a central part of daily life—either as a reality or as a looming threat—and a key mechanism through which order is enforced (although not necessarily maintained). Additionally, in hegemonic fashion, the institutional discourses of "the punishment fits the crime" and "personal responsibility" dilute the power of critique and construct policing practices inside the school as normative. Put simply, for schools like UPHS, their primary function is perhaps not the reproduction of a *working* class but the *production of a whole population of criminalized, excluded youth.*

Oppositional Behavior as Resistance and the Contradictions of the Middle Ground

In the preceding chapter, I provided a microanalysis of student oppositional behavior, building on the work of Erving Goffman; here I will place that analysis in a critical framework in order to engage and reconsider previous theories of oppositional behavior as a form of resistance. The work of early theorists of oppositional behavior as resistance in schooling constitutes a major contribution to critical educational theory and, in particular, our understanding of student nonconformity.[11] These theories offer a compelling challenge to deterministic structural analyses of schooling (which characterize students as drones or dupes) by highlighting human agency and revealing the political implications embedded in oppositional behavior. Paul Willis, for example, explains in *Learning to Labor* that he begins with the cultural productions of "the lads" to illustrate that a theory of social reproduction directs us only toward the general process by which the relationship between classes is replaced, which implies that the cultures of the different classes are also merely replicated. But an analysis of the lads' cultural practices reveals the creative self-making processes of young people. It also illustrates the dynamic nature of social reproduction and points to possibilities for social change.[12]

Equally important, theories of oppositional behavior as resistance reveal the flaws in overly psychological analyses that pathologize students and remove their oppositional behavior from its larger social-historical context. However, as times have changed, so, too, have the significance of oppositional behavior, students' motivations, and their rationales for participation in it. The kinds of transgressions that I observed at UPHS were not qualitatively very different from those documented in previous studies, and to some extent the meanings remain the same. Oppositional behavior in school can still be viewed as an implicit social critique and an assertion of a particular cultural identity, for example.[13] However, as I spoke with students and observed their actions, it appeared to me that the current political economy, the societal culture of control, the structure of schooling, and students' daily experiences inside the school all influenced the meanings attached to oppositional behavior.

At UPHS, as I have illustrated, oppositional behavior did not indicate a total rejection of schooling, as resistance theorists of previous decades have suggested. The critiques of students who participated in oppositional behavior appeared to be directed less toward the institution as a whole, or white middle-class culture in general, and more toward particular practices and policies that conflicted with their imagined ideal of schooling. As Zack claimed, for example, "The cops ain't supposed to be education." Even when students held some antischool sentiments, they expressed poignantly their interest in doing well in school, if only they entered the right program or transferred to a "better" school or if their teacher "broke it down" for them. Such attitudes toward schooling appear to be a reflection of the changed political economy and the punitive turn in crime control. Even if students could no longer imagine attaining a viable job, almost all the students with whom I spoke wanted to finish school, avoid the drug trade, and stay out of prison. With more young black men in prison than in college today (and high rates of incarceration for Latinos and women of color), prison may have been viewed as a probability, but it certainly was not a goal of any student with whom I spoke. Getting an education, they understood, would increase their chances of carving out a "good" life for themselves and avoiding incarceration.

Nevertheless, although students generally desired academic success, their behaviors often suggested resistance to it. The apparent contradictions in their words and actions, though, were not contained within their own cognitive frameworks; the contradictions were lived and historical, and existed within institutional structures and the political economy. UPHS students who occupied the middle ground between graduating and succumbing to difficult social and institutional realities were keenly aware of the benefits of educational credentials and yearned for different kinds of classroom experiences. Yet, at the same time, many were academically underprepared. They were tracked into a school with an almost nonexistent focus on academics, an irrelevant curriculum, and very little investment in academic enrichment and support services. They also contended with high levels of conflict and violence and daily policing both inside and outside their school.

These students knew, perhaps even more explicitly than Willis's working-class lads, that, in their particular situations, they were not being prepared for success in higher education and, thus, their prospects in the labor market would be seriously hindered. Some students, like Duane and Stephanie, began to lose hope and could no longer articulate a dream. For these students in the postindustrial world, oppositional behavior as a form of resistance could spin freely without the context of any socially imagined future.[14] What did it matter how "bad" Duane was, for example? He had no tangible vision of life beyond high school.

Still, at UPHS I found that students were often able to discuss the future. They did so in terms of their "if only" dreams, keeping some faith in the imagined or real institutions that they believed existed for their betterment, a compelling perspective when the most visible alternative was entering a life in the illegal economy, prison, and an early death. This was the lived contradiction of the middle ground between success and dropping out, where oppositional behaviors often made good sense and served important purposes.

As I illustrated in the preceding chapter, students sought and often found social and psychological benefits through oppositional behavior despite the high price they paid for their actions. Understanding the many and complex advantages to participation in oppositional behavior within the current context, I would argue, is central to a revised theory of oppositional behavior as resistance. Gaining insight into students' experiences and motivations moves us beyond the framework of oppositional behavior as resistance against schooling and teases out the deep and personal meanings embedded in these behaviors.

I do not mean to imply, however, that students were calculating in their oppositional behavior or that they acted solely in their individual self-interest outside a cultural framework. Students did not usually decide to start a fight or curse at a security agent or enter the building with a hat on, consciously seeking the particular benefits those acts might afford. As Goffman describes, the underlife of the institution is the *collective* and sustained practice of secondary adjustments, or oppositional behaviors.[15] At the same time, Goffman posits that secondary adjustments become central in the process of being or becoming and thus hold deep significance for the self. Similarly, Willis argues that many oppositional behaviors, particularly those that involve assuming tough postures, prove to be highly intractable, especially when formed through the winning back of identity or dignity.[16] Thus, students acted very much as part of a cultural group, and their oppositional behavior, I would argue, often reflected a racialized class consciousness as well as a sense of being limited by their cultural milieu. This became evident in students' reported rationales for their behavior when they made statements such as, "This is how it goes down here [in low-income urban neighborhoods]," or, "We're from the 'hood," or, "The street makes the rules." Nevertheless, upon reflection, students were able to articulate the personal benefits that oppositional behavior provided, and they could describe the positive feelings associated with those behaviors.

The advantages of participation in oppositional behavior were multi-faceted. Students' oppositional behaviors appeared to be expressive and, at the same time, instrumental. The expressive and the instrumental were closely linked and at times almost indistinguishable. The use of Goffman and the notion of an underlife, discussed in the preceding chapter, help to demonstrate the interconnectedness and significance of self-expression and instrumentality. Disruption, wearing hats, gambling, and fighting, to name some of the most prevalent forms of oppositional behavior I found, became a vehicle through which valued identities as members of a particular social group were constructed against prescribed school norms (expressive). At the same time, in the context of academic alienation and penal control, students were able to make other kinds of personal and symbolic gains (instrumental). Students' actions could reward them, for example, with a renewed sense of autonomy or control over themselves in a repressive setting. Moreover, young people who participated in oppositional behavior could reposition themselves within social hierarchies, gain a level of protection against peer violence, and perhaps even make a little cash. A host of benefits woven together made oppositional behavior attractive.

Disruptions, at times predominantly cathartic moments of "letting loose" in a repressive environment (I have vivid images of the expressions of sheer delight on the faces of some students as they yelled and sang while running through the hallways), also could lead to momentary shifts in power relations in which students who struggled in their classes and often felt "not listened to" could feel that they "owned this school." Wearing a hat could be understood as a way of expressing one's pride of "being from the Bronx"—an identity not welcomed within the school but certainly one that evoked images of strength and toughness on the street (expressive). Simultaneously, hat wearing, as part of the desired aesthetic, could boost one's status among peers (instrumental). Fighting and gang membership were expressive in that they could be romanticized, at least some of the time, through displays of loyalty and bravery (recall Jermaine's tale of the bond formed between two young men who "could have died" together on the street); at the same time, they were instrumental in that strategic participation in violence could limit its negative consequences in a situation where disciplinary practices did not adequately keep students safe. Additionally, many oppositional behaviors appeared to be implicit expressions of students' moral outrage and frustration over the circumstances to which they were subjected. Anger and indignation were certainly evident in students' narrations of their oppositional behavior.

Noncompliance with law-enforcement officials, like other oppositional acts, was motivated by myriad factors. It could for a fleeting moment shift relations of power, help students regain a sense of autonomy, and help save face by a student's displaying toughness against a widely disliked authority figure (law enforcement). Some students seemed to gain considerable satisfaction from giving law-enforcement officials a difficult time, as if it were almost a sort of game. Nevertheless, acts of noncompliance were also the most explicit expressions of indignation and were often enacted in anger over what was viewed as unfair treatment. Students expressed the desire to "stand up for themselves" and they made declarations of "knowing their rights."

The more I spoke with students who existed in this middle ground, the more I came to see the logic in their actions. Ultimately, their oppositional behavior often served in the production of themselves as members of a criminalized class, but the immediate benefits were palpable and enticing. At times, oppositional behavior in the particular context I examined appeared almost necessary or, at the very least, worth it. This is not to say that the oppositional behavior I observed was caused by economic and social conditions or institutional practices. It was, instead, enacted within the context of a deep sense of economic and educational exclusion and penal management, and in this context, it often appeared advantageous.

My goal here is not to refute previous theories of oppositional behavior as a form of resistance. But I would argue that it is perhaps more fruitful to shift the lens onto what individual students get out of oppositional behavior on a personal level. This shift in focus helps to illuminate the logic of students' actions in the current context and, by illuminating how social forces are mediated through everyday institutional practices, it can provide insight into points where policies do disservice or injustice to students. As Goffman states in regard to the sociological significance of secondary adjustments, "[It] is not what this practice brings to the practitioner but rather the character of the social relationship that its acquisition and maintenance require. That constitutes a structural as opposed to a consummatory or social psychological point of view."[17] In other words, students' oppositional behavior can serve as a diagnostic of power and as an indicator of where social policies and institutional practices fall short.[18] For educators interested in critically assessing their institutions, this perspective can be most useful.

Recommendations for Effective Urban Schooling and Sound Discipline

P ERHAPS THE MOST IMPORTANT INSIGHT that emerged from this study is that within the framework of zero tolerance and order maintenance, students end up getting summoned to criminal court for incidents that began with the breaking of a minor school rule, not the law. Cutting class, wearing a hat, or being disruptive did not directly lead students into the criminal-justice system; instead, the behavior that resulted in an arrest or summons often came only *after* the student was confronted by law-enforcement officials. Frequently, when students chose not to comply with law enforcement or attempted to explain themselves, their "disrespect" or "insubordination" was constructed as disorderly conduct and subsequently resulted in arrest or the issuance of a summons. At other times, students' behaviors may have been considered a violation of the law or a crime (such as fighting), but many of these incidents could have been handled internally by school disciplinarians, as they often had been in the past. In either case, it became clear that aggressive policing practices and police surveillance prevailed over other types of responses to disorder and often created a flow of students into criminal court.

My observations also revealed that it was not the sheer number of police–student confrontations resulting in arrest or summonses that concretized the culture of control; the culture also had much to do with the appropriation of a wide range of criminal-justice-oriented disciplinary practices and their supporting discourses. Such practices included hallway stops, sweeps, and getting threatened with a summons. Additionally, security technologies (metal detectors, cameras, and scanners) were physical manifestations of the culture of control.

In the new framework, school personnel lost their traditional moral authority during disciplinary incidents and often accepted order-maintenance-style discipline not necessarily as *ideal* but as the *norm* and the legitimized response to disruption. Similarly, students grew accustomed to daily policing and the language associated with policing practices and prison life. In essence, I observed that, despite some resistance among school personnel, the discourses and moral rationales that support aggressive street policing and zero tolerance within the larger society had permeated the school, and it appeared that the culture of control would exist no matter how many students were actually tracked into criminal court or jail.

This finding suggests a complex relationship between the school, street policing, and institutions of the criminal-justice system. In the framework I have described, students do not simply go from school to prison as police make arrests inside the school. They are instead subjected to heavy policing in various domains of their lives—in the streets, on public transportation, and in the hallways of their school—as the criminal-justice system comes to operate through civil institutions and public space. As young people accumulate summonses for minor violations of the law and school misbehavior, they grow accustomed to spending time sitting in court, and a significant number spend time in jail or prison. These once-separate domains—the school, the street (with both its logic of violence and its aggressive policing practices), and institutions of the criminal-justice system—become instantiated in each other, and the boundaries between them become blurred in students' minds.

The policing practices to which students are subjected can lead to years of routine trips to criminal court, traffic court, probation, and a night or two in jail for a series of offenses, including such behaviors as walking through a park after dark, loitering, public drinking, and jumping the subway turnstile—the kinds of behaviors in which young, unemployed men and women can easily become involved. Additionally, there is the ambiguous offense, both in school and out, of disorderly conduct.

We do not fully know the impact of long-term, daily interaction with police and subjection to heavy police monitoring. On the one hand, most men and women who spend significant time in prison have prior histories of low-level offenses. On the other hand, most young people who have received a number of quality-of-life summonses do not spend years in prison. In fact, in accordance with "criminologies of everyday life,"[1] order-maintenance policing is meant to be preventive. It was designed as a cost-efficient approach to crime control that keeps the prison population down, as its goal is the reduction of major crime. Whether or not order maintenance really does prevent more serious crime has been widely debated among criminologists. What we can reasonably say is that order maintenance and mass imprisonment have a kind of symbiotic relationship. Although they grow out of different ideological perspectives and criminological thinking, order maintenance and mass imprisonment mesh well together and are the major manifestations of our societal culture of control.[2]

As an educator, my concern is what happens to young people when they become accustomed to daily interactions with law enforcement and court involvement and at the same time are confronted with few viable job prospects and lack of access to relevant educational experiences that would adequately prepare them for productive roles in society. Some young people may "age out" of disorderly behavior; they may get tracked into some kind of credentialing program and manage to secure legal work, at least for some period of time. But for many others, getting "picked up" has already become a routine and normalized experience, something that eventually goes unquestioned, and these young people may embrace criminalized identities as it becomes more and more difficult for them to change their life courses.

Additionally, I would argue that although the culture of control inside the school appeared to mirror the culture of the larger society, within the context of the school there were unique consequences. As the culture took hold, attention seemed to be diverted further than ever away from educational concerns and constructive responses to violence and disruption. Indeed, there seemed to be little, if any, room within the prevailing paradigm for serious and productive discussions about implementing a holistic set of transformative solutions. If things didn't take a dramatic turn, it seemed the matter would simply come down to the removal of troubled and gang-affiliated students, placing them elsewhere in the school system or pushing them into a life on the streets.

In using a dialectical construct of culture, I have also attempted to show how students, along with external and institutional forces, influenced the school culture through their contestation with law-enforcement officials and oppositional behaviors. In chapter 4, I demonstrated that students' contestation during interactions with law-enforcement officials often facilitated their entrance into the criminal-justice system and, to many adults, often seemed unnecessary. (Couldn't they just "remain calm" and "show respect"? educators moaned.) But when viewing these acts of contestation from the students' perspective, they can be understood as reasonable responses to the circumstances to which they were subjected.

Students received certain benefits through contestation. Although their motivations were quite complex, it was clear that their defiance was at least in part a stand against something they thought unnecessary, unfair, or unjust. The contests that often ensued during police–student interactions were often over issues of respect. Authority figures demanded it, and students sought to preserve a sense of self-respect in an atmosphere that provided few legitimate opportunities to gain a sense of it. The police–student interaction, then, became an important "site" of contestation where students proclaimed their "rights," as Wanda suggested, or "stood up" for themselves, as Carlos explained.

Oppositional behavior was also a terrain where students tacitly sought social, psychological, and other personal benefits in the context of a deep sense of educational and economic exclusion and penal management. The behaviors I observed, from hallway antics to wearing a hat to speaking back to a security agent, were motivated by a wide variety of factors. On the one hand, students' oppositional behaviors were expressive in that they allowed students to construct valued identities and present a particular image of themselves—strong, deserving of (or at least insistent on) respect, and belonging to a particular community, for instance. Their actions were also expressive in that they were implicit proclamations of the students' indignation and frustration over the kinds of schooling experiences they were provided. On the other hand, their oppositional behavior was instrumental as it provided a variety of personal benefits, such as increased social status, safety, and thrills. These ways of framing oppositional behavior took on heightened significance in the context of a school with a notorious reputation for disorder and violence.

Finally, I revisited critical educational theory and discussed the significance of reproduction and resistance today. In brief, schools continue to serve a reproductive function. One's educational experiences at this historical juncture appear to shape one's future socioeconomic status and life chances much in the same ways they did decades ago, but the process of reproduction has become more complicated. As schools are restructured to meet new economic exigencies, new kinds of sorting and tracking mechanisms are put into place. Gone are the days when the bulk of urban students attended large neighborhood high schools with either a college-preparatory or vocational focus. Instead, a wide range of school experiences can be found. For example, some working-class and poor students may receive preparation for service or technical jobs that require some college, whereas others, like many of those at UPHS, will not even finish high school. They will get transient, low-wage work in the formal economy, and many will likely pick up some work in the informal or illegal economy. Subsequently, these latter students may become some of the hundreds of thousands who develop a long history of sporadic, or perhaps regular, involvement with the criminal-justice system.

Like reproduction, the notion of oppositional behavior as resistance also needs to be placed in the current context. Low-income black and Latino/a students face more serious consequences than ever before for their oppositional behavior in school. When they misbehave, they participate in the production of themselves as a criminalized class. Nevertheless, as I mentioned earlier, it is important to note the benefits, real or perceived, that students implicitly seek and the meanings they attach to their behaviors. In the context of penal control and a deep sense of exclusion from economic and educational opportunities, students find ways to develop identities within their own cultural frameworks that they can be proud of, to identify as part of a particular community, to manage the violence in their lives (which official policies do little to mitigate), to make a little money, to have fun, and to "stand up" for themselves as an act of preserving their sense of self and their dignity.

I would argue that it is vital for educators to acknowledge these benefits for two reasons. First, my findings suggest, as have others', that students' oppositional behavior does not represent a wholesale rejection of schooling.[3] The students I met at UPHS, while spending often a few years in what I have called a middle ground, could be successfully reengaged before dropping out if they were presented with the social and academic supports they need, with meaningful and relevant educational experiences, and with some tangible possibilities for their future. Although these students in my study often turned their attention elsewhere, their desire for a meaningful educational experience and a diploma could be described as nothing short of deep yearning.

Second, students' rationales for their transgressions suggest that they seek benefits and create meaning within the void that external forces, policies, and institutional practices have created. They hold on to an imagined ideal of schooling, but what they have been offered deeply violates that ideal. In this context, students seek ways to develop a strong sense of self through transgression, given that there are few, if any, sanctioned paths to "success" and dignity available to them. They also attempt to limit the impact of conflict and violence in their lives through strategic participation in that conflict when the adults in their lives have failed to provide a dominant culture of nonviolence or even comprehensive nonviolent conflict-resolution programs.

There are no quick and simple solutions for mitigating disruption and violence while at the same time providing fulfilling educational experiences that help to set students on a course toward higher education and, ultimately, satisfying (or at least viable) work. I have suggested that myriad factors have set the conditions for and given rise to the culture of control that I found at UPHS. Therefore, the solutions must also be wide-ranging and comprehensive.

Rethinking the Zero-Tolerance, Order-Maintenance Framework

A vast literature demonstrates the negative consequences of zero tolerance. There has also been a considerable public outcry following the most absurd and alarming incidents of punishment under zero tolerance. In response, some states have modified their policies to give more discretionary powers to school personnel. Yet zero tolerance remains the prevailing framework for school discipline, overshadowing more holistic, constructive, and preventive forms of discipline. Additionally, inside certain targeted urban schools, zero tolerance is intensified through the use of order-maintenance-style policing. This is a growing trend with considerable political support, although it is widely contested by some parent groups, legal-advocacy groups, and community-based organizations.

UPHS serves as an example of how zero tolerance and order-maintenance school discipline play out in the daily lives of low-income black and Latino/a youth. Indeed, schools like UPHS, with their heavy police presence and culture of control, have become a kind of hybrid institution where the educational mission takes a backseat to the control mission. This needs to change, but it cannot happen simply by dismantling the security apparatus and getting rid of the police inside schools. Instead, we must begin to think differently about discipline and embrace models that focus on the moral, social, and academic development of youth rather than on punishment and exclusion. It is also important to establish a new paradigm as we move away from current strategies, as it is unwise to dismantle a system of discipline, however faulty, before knowing what will take its place.

My findings point to a number of possibilities. First, we must restore the moral authority of school disciplinarians—teachers and administrators—who have an understanding of adolescent development and are trained in educational approaches. The school disciplinarians I observed were not "soft" on disorder or violence. They knew how to gauge a situation, and most attempted to take a holistic approach: enforcing rules, encouraging students to get to class, buying them binders and notebooks, engaging parents, and counseling students who were often confronted by immense difficulties. If the right supports were in place, their approaches would become significantly more effective, more comprehensive, and more widely used.

At UPHS, there would be little work for security agents if the role of the deans were expanded. If the team of deans, who are trained as teachers, were enlarged and if they were given more release time from classroom duties, they could do the jobs of the security agents, patrolling the hallways and engaging rule breakers. The work the deans were already doing in my study suggested its effectiveness and its potential if it were given more institutional support. Their approaches may have been the single most significant factor in the reduction of violence and disruption that had occurred at UPHS. Indeed, many students, administrators, and deans attributed the reduction of violence directly to the approaches the deans were using. The culturally relevant disciplinary approaches involved, in part, developing a deep understanding of students' home cultures and lived experiences and "reaching the kids" through "tough love" conversations. With the proper supports and a major reduction in the use of police intervention, the deans could make further strides toward a culturally relevant and responsive approach. They could spend less time on coaching students on how to avoid trouble with cops and more time on helping them develop strategies for making healthy and positive decisions. They could also make more meaningful and lasting connections between the school and parents and community groups.

Although there need to be clear consequences for misbehavior, disciplinary approaches must also provide students with a sense of respect and dignity. Students involved in disciplinary cases should have the sense that they are entering into a process of problem solving. Principal Alvarez believed strongly in this idea, and it was successful—but only to the extent that institutional structures allowed. In other words, her approaches were undermined and overshadowed within the prevailing disciplinary paradigm and educational context.

My argument here is consistent with previous research that indicates that the restoration of the moral authority of school personnel is essential to transforming schools and maintaining discipline. John Devine, for example, warns that "paramilitary-style" school discipline leads to the "marshmallow effect," a phenomenon in which students push the limits of the rules and then teachers, lacking the moral authority to confront students, give way.[4] Similarly, Richard Arum provides a nuanced and eloquent analysis of how the courts' attention on student rights has eroded the moral authority of teachers and school administrators, but he is equally critical of zero-tolerance approaches, which he maintains are counterproductive and undermine the legitimacy of school discipline.[5]

Other teams of school personnel could also be buttressed, such as the guidance counselors. Guidance counselors, social workers, and individuals from community-based organizations working within schools could play expanded roles in institutionalizing comprehensive conflict-resolution programs and student-led antiviolence initiatives and in providing the other kinds of supports students who are frequently involved in disciplinary cases need. I observed counselors and other service providers helping students in constructive ways, but as with the deans, their efforts did not have full institutional support. They were overworked, carrying huge caseloads of students, and were implicitly viewed as playing an auxiliary role.

In New York City, as elsewhere, the rules themselves also need to be reconsidered. What would happen if students were allowed to wear hats in school, for example? Most deans seemed to think the effort it took to enforce this rule made it counterproductive. They often pondered the absurdity of a student ending up in handcuffs for an incident that began with an adult telling a student to take his or her hat off. Letting students wear their hats in school might have the added advantage of creating the feeling among students that the institution respects their identities.

Finally, the only occurrences for which deans or school administrators need the assistance of the police are actual crimes and violent incidents. Police officers may also be able to work successfully and positively with young gang members. I observed Officer Hoffmann doing this kind of work, for example. He engaged gang members with respect and showed tremendous concern and empathy for them. But the structure in which he and his colleagues worked was designed for the suppression and expulsion of gang activity, through heavy surveillance, arrest, forced transfers to other schools or GED programs, extended suspensions, and expulsions. These punitive tactics do not address the needs of students in gangs; nor do they address students' desires to succeed in school or leave a gang. There is no structure in most urban schools to deal with youth in gangs and other youth immersed in violence in systemically and comprehensively positive ways and to address the problems and obstacles they face. Developing such programs systemwide is a necessary step toward mitigating violence.

Interesting alternatives to zero tolerance and effective research-based disciplinary models already exist, but they have not generally received the attention or support they need for nationwide implementation. One such model is known as Schoolwide Positive Behavior Support.[6] In contrast to zero tolerance, the focus of this model is on the positive behaviors that students manifest. Teachers actively teach, expect, and acknowledge appropriate behavior; they involve families and community, and focus on the prevention of disciplinary problems. Research on Schoolwide Positive Behavior Support indicates that the model leads to reductions in serious disciplinary problems and helps to create a positive school climate. Of course, in urban schools like UPHS where violence is a serious problem, any program must go beyond behavioral issues and explicitly address the kinds of conflict and violence that are present in the lives of so many urban youth. Based on his extensive research on school violence, Pedro Noguera argues that approaches to mitigate violence must be attached to youth development programs that provide comprehensive services to low-income youth. He also recommends involving youth in long-term efforts to reduce violence.[7] Ronald Casella offers a specific model that incorporates many of these aspects. He suggests adopting restorative justice, a concept developed in the field of criminology as an alternative to mass imprisonment that proposes that perpetrators should make right their wrongs.[8] Offenders are thus held directly accountable for their actions and for restoring losses to their victims. These recommendations would allow students to take some ownership over creating a safe school for themselves. They may also provide new outlets for alienated students to gain respect and develop valued identities as leaders in the school's antiviolence initiatives.

Such approaches also help to restore the moral authority of school personnel, who would take active roles in the development and implementation of the new programs.

Of course, a paradigm shift in school discipline seems nearly impossible within the larger context I've described. Current policies are supported by public and political discourses that place tremendous faith in law enforcement as a solution to social problems in urban communities. Students at schools like UPHS are seen as needing to be policed, so the current policies often make good sense to the general public. Additionally, as I argued in chapter 1, the disciplinary policies mesh well with current reforms and restructuring schemes. And finally, the policies make good fiscal sense, as security agents working for the police department are paid considerably less than teachers and counselors. However, schools must work to maintain their integrity as educational institutions, not hybrid educational-penal institutions. Educators and counselors, not law-enforcement officials, should engage students in matters related to school discipline. The goals of educators should be to help young people develop academically, socially, and morally, facilitating their full and productive participation in society. It seems so simple, yet too often structurally marginalized urban students are prepared instead for continued entanglement with the criminal-justice system.

Educational Solutions

Classroom Practice

It is a moral outrage that we would take such a punitive stand in matters of urban school discipline when so little is offered to urban students. Radical changes are needed in today's classrooms, particularly those in urban areas serving the most marginalized and alienated students. Here, I focus on a small number of key changes that may have the most direct bearing on matters of classroom engagement and alienation. I start with the contention that classroom alienation is in large part an institutional process *done to* students, especially low-income urban students of color.

The educational-reform efforts of today and the recent past tend to give very little attention to the dynamics and conditions of everyday life in the classroom. The discourse around education is full of catchphrases that imply a focus on the classroom level. For example, we hear quite a bit about "high standards" and "research-based practices," and there has been a renewed focus on teacher preparation. Nevertheless, policy makers rarely seem to consider deeply the implication of testing and curricular mandates and the resulting social and interactional dynamics found in low-performing urban classrooms.

In urban schools, we often find a predominance of high-stakes test preparation and highly controversial, often scripted programs in reading and math, limited focus on other content areas, and often none at all on art and other kinds of enrichment. Even when district leaders attempt to institute more student-centered approaches, such as cooperative learning or writing workshops, teachers find them very difficult to implement effectively, given myriad institutional constraints. Subsequently, too often we find bored, alienated, and indignant students who at times cannot fully articulate their indignation, but they usually indicate somehow that something is dreadfully wrong. These students may reach the ninth grade not fully prepared for high school–level academic work. As a result, they are often confronted with teacher-centered instructional practices and content to which they lack full access.

Testing is not the sole culprit of classroom alienation, but, as the central focus of school reform for more than a decade, it has drawn considerable attention away from the everyday realities of the classroom. The use of tests as a sole measure of success does not enhance the classroom experience in any way. Indeed, there is mounting evidence that standardized tests weaken curriculum and exacerbate the already high dropout rate among poor and working-class students. As I have illustrated, my data similarly show a situation in which a tremendous amount of material is (sometimes frantically) transmitted to students without allotting any time or attempting to make connections to their life experiences or even to check for comprehension. At the same time, other studies suggest that culturally relevant and responsive pedagogies improve the academic success of children of color.[9] Put simply, such classroom experiences validate students' knowledge base, include familiar and meaningful cultural reference points, build on their particular learning styles, and contain a sociopolitical dimension that encourages students to critically analyze the world in which they live. These pedagogies empower students intellectually, socially, emotionally, and politically. Many successful teachers already have a deep commitment to these pedagogical approaches, but it is sometimes extremely difficult to infuse locally and culturally relevant content into such tightly controlled contexts.

Then, of course, there is the reality that not all teachers are oriented toward culturally relevant and responsive pedagogies. To remedy this, teacher-education programs, besides ensuring excellent content knowledge and instructional skills, must take seriously the notion of helping to develop the proper kinds of dispositions in preservice urban teachers. It has been documented that misconceptions and negative teacher attitudes lower student achievement.[10] Research also illustrates that teachers' lack of cultural competencies can lead to bias against students of color in disciplinary cases,[11] whereas Sonia Nieto's work suggests that teachers' love for their students and active role participating in issues of social justice may have lasting positive effects on student learning.[12] Students at UPHS were at their best when their teachers were respectful, firm, and welcoming. Teachers tend to work more effectively with urban students when they have had the opportunity to develop considerable knowledge of their students' communities and an understanding of the social and economic forces that shape their students' lives.

We also need to prepare urban students for the realities of these new times. For instance, students should have ample opportunity to develop critical media literacy and Internet research skills. They should be given the chance to study their communities and their location in the world through inquiry-based, collaborative projects. Additionally, urban students should be given the chance to develop multiple cultural and global perspectives. This idea gets considerable attention in reform discussions, but in the urban classroom, the opportunity to view issues from multiple perspectives often gets undermined as teachers are compelled to move quickly through course content, and nothing is discussed in any real depth. Finally, while urban teachers hold students to high expectations and provide rigorous academic experiences, resources must be made available to allow them to address the needs of individual students through differentiated and individualized instruction, scaffolding approaches, and other supports. One of the gravest injustices today is allowing whole cohorts of urban students to graduate or drop out of high school with fifth- or sixth-grade reading levels and little in the way of critical-thinking skills, leaving them unprepared for entrance into college or the workplace, because an inadequate level of support was provided along the way to remedy this.

Of course, these kinds of recommendations necessitate an increase in and a redirection of funding. The issue of school funding is extremely complex and reaches beyond the scope of this discussion. Nonetheless, the funding issue is essential to the institutional transformations I am suggesting. Suffice it to say that there are gross funding disparities that favor suburban schools and specialized urban schools serving middle-class students and that disfavor urban schools serving low-income students. Moreover, federal funding has dwindled dramatically over the last several decades and, for several years, what funding there is has been based on a scheme that penalizes, rather than supports, low-performing schools.

Of course, conservatives often counter the call for more spending by arguing that it doesn't help to "throw money at the problem." Many of these same conservatives have no problem justifying the huge funding disparities between the suburban schools their own children often attend and urban schools attended by other people's children. The issue of how money is spent also does not get addressed in the simplistic conservative "throwing money" sound bite. Will we invest in enrichment programs, new instructional technologies and other material resources, smaller class sizes, and the like, or will we keep "throwing money" at private testing companies, for-profit corporations in the business of running schools, and the latest prison-like security technology?

School Restructuring

As I argued in chapter 1, restructuring schemes in urban school districts have been conducive to the adoption of zero tolerance in its beefed-up form. There is much promise in the creation of small schools, but small schools can succeed only when they avoid replicating the same inequities and problems found in traditional large public schools and when all small schools receive the resources and freedom to adopt the kinds of educational and disciplinary practices that meet students' needs. Michelle Fine argues that in our efforts to create successful small schools, we should institute a "standard of social justice."[13] This standard gets ignored in all the talk of standards. It asks, does a school offer a sense of respect and dignity? Such a standard is met through the establishment of democratic, collaborative relationships with parents and communities, engaging classroom experiences, and appropriate academic and social supports. When schools meet this standard, violence and disorder are likely to decrease.

The traditional large urban public high school of the past was often a disorderly and violent place that failed to prepare students for full participation in society. We have reached a time in which such schools are in dire need of revitalization, if not some form of restructuring. However, within the prevailing paradigm, reformers place far too much emphasis on accountability, punitive sanctions, and school closings, and too little on the creation of places where urban students (and their parents) feel welcomed, supported, and respected.

Unfortunately, under President Obama and U.S. Secretary of Education Arne Duncan, we seem to be getting an intensified No Child Left Behind program, rather than an alternative. As part of the 2009 American Recovery and Reinvestment Act, a competitive grant program, called Race to the Top, has been established. The reform effort places strong emphasis on the creation of charter schools and performance pay for teachers, and standardized testing will continue as the measure on which success of these reforms is based. Such a plan is disconcerting in light of the mixed research on the success of charter schools and the abundance of research on the negative consequences of high-stakes testing. Indeed, the plan is detrimental to the very survival of public education, as more and more decisions regarding education are placed in the hands of for-profit corporations. To make circumstances even more challenging, in the midst of continued punitive reforms, districts around the country are laying off unprecedented numbers of teachers because of budgetary constraints caused by the recent recession. Thus, fiscal realities will make it extremely difficult to implement the kinds of classroom-level reforms needed to re-engage alienated students and prepare them for success in higher education and the job market.

Macrostructural Factors and a "Bottom-Up" Social Movement

As I have argued, recent education reform has not been the primary factor leading to zero-tolerance disciplinary policies. The kinds of zero-tolerance and school-based policing practices we find in many urban schools are a direct outgrowth of our punitive crime-control policies, which are supported by both conservative and neoliberal ideologies and are rooted in economic structures. Thus, in rethinking urban school discipline, we need to consider urban economic development, crime-control policy, and social policies aimed at urban youth. Jean Anyon argues compellingly that, "unless we make some changes in the way the macro-economy works, economic policy will trump not only urban school reform but the individual educational achievement of students as well."[14] She goes on to state that economic and social policy must include strategies to increase the minimum wage, invest in urban job creation and training, and provide funds for college completion to those who cannot afford it.

We also need more investment in community- and school-based programs that support youth, rather than target them. Young people growing up in urban centers need better access to a whole range of services, such as health (including mental health) services, arts programs, life skills and literacy programs, and antiviolence initiatives that teach nonviolent conflict resolution and provide real possibilities for avoiding gangs. Duane and Zack, like so many low-income urban youngsters, were both initiated into gangs before their tenth birthday. What could have been their futures had the structures been in place to intervene at that pivotal moment in their lives?

As we strive for better economic and social policies, we also need to consider the impact of current crime-control policies on the lives of individuals and families in low-income urban communities. Mass imprisonment weakens the social fabric of urban communities and hurts families. It creates new obstacles for people in entering the job market, in gaining entrance into higher education, and in housing. Yet, despite the negative consequences of mass incarceration, a significant shift in policy does not appear to be on the horizon. The Obama administration has yet to take on the issue of the mass incarceration of young black men and other people of color. Perhaps the greatest impetus for change in the first decade of the new millennium has been states' budgetary constraints and the limitations those constraints place on the building of prisons. But even with the slowdown of prison construction, incarceration rates remain high, and more black men head to prison than to college.

The other major phenomenon in crime control, order-maintenance policing, driven by the ideology of cost efficiency, only stands to gain more political and popular support in our current economic context. It would be grossly imprudent to argue against strong street-policing programs altogether. Some developments over the last couple of decades in community-based policing have helped to create safer neighborhoods in urban communities around the country. However, we must examine critically the practices of order maintenance and their outcomes. The tough discourses and harsh practices that explicitly target certain individuals (such as black and Latino/a youth, homeless individuals, and jobless individuals) have generated significant distrust of the police within urban communities and have greatly infringed on the civil rights of individuals. These policing practices, with their focus on low-level arrests, have also worked in conjunction with punitive sentencing and parole policies to dramatically expand the prison population and the criminal-justice system more generally (through the use of local jails, probation, and parole). My vision includes crime-control policies that would rely far less on the use of prisons and would utilize policing strategies that respected the human and civil rights of individuals and fostered healthy police–community relations.

Punitive urban school discipline springs from a broader context of racial oppression, economic inequality, and our subsequent reliance on penal control. In a grossly inequitable school system and stratified society, punitive urban school disciplinary policies serve the interests of the white middle and wealthy classes, as poor youth of color are demonized through the discourses of zero tolerance and subjected to heavy policing. In the struggle for better urban schools and more just disciplinary practices, "small wins" in favor of low-income urban youth, such as more funding for student-led antiviolence initiatives and institutional support for culturally responsive classroom practice, are worth striving for. However, a massive "bottom-up" social movement that links policy and the daily experiences of youth to macrostructural forces is needed to effect more lasting and broad-reaching change. Numerous community, youth, parent, and advocacy groups are organizing around urban education, fighting for better schools and making connections to larger social issues with the hope of creating better opportunities for low-income youth of color. Some groups have added to their agenda the issue of punitive school discipline. School discipline, particularly school-based policing, is a promising focal point for mobilization, because it exists at the nexus of a range of educational, criminal-justice, and social policies and allows those involved in organizing efforts to make the necessary connections between various levels of lived experience, institutional practices, and social structure. Educators can become directly involved in social-justice movements. They can also play an important role in organizing young people by facilitating relevant classroom discussion and collaborating with students who are subjected to penal control and who already express their indignation in less constructive ways.

What Happened to UPHS and Its Students?
A "Turnaround" School and Its Legacy

In June 2008, almost one hundred years after its establishment, UPHS graduated its last class. The entire building had been transformed into several small, theme-based schools. Together, they are known as the UPHS Campus. The mayor's office boasted that UPHS was an example of the city's successful "turnaround" schools. The transition to small schools appears to have had a positive effect on school environment. Rates of violence and disorder at the new UPHS Campus have reportedly gone down, and according to the most recent student survey (2009–2010) conducted by the Department of Education and posted on the various schools' websites, the majority of students in the building reported that disciplinary practices were "fair" and that they felt safe in hallways, bathrooms, and stairwells. It was a small majority, but that is an improvement over the situation I encountered a few years earlier, when I was hard pressed to find anyone who thought disciplinary policies were fair. Yet, despite the improvement, the vast majority of students from all the small schools reported high levels of bullying, and approximately 10 percent of the students in the building reported never feeling safe in areas outside the classroom. There also appeared to be a significant gang presence in the building; the majority of students reported gang activity from some to all of the time.

In response to a number of highly publicized incidents of police abuse throughout the New York City school system, many community organizations and student groups have organized around the issue of aggressive police force in schools. This appears to have had some positive impact on policing practices, or at the very least it has put a spotlight on law-enforcement practices in schools, which should lead to decreased misconduct and abuse. But Mayor Bloomberg's policing program is still in effect, and incidents that stir public outcry continue to occur. At the UPHS Campus, police vans can still be found parked in front of the building, and there is still a significant law-enforcement presence inside. In 2010, a major incident in the lunchroom apparently began as a conflict between two feuding small schools that shared the enormous room. When the massive fight came to an end, a few people were brought to the hospital and several were arrested.

As I read about the purported success of education reform in New York City and elsewhere, I cannot help but think of a recent study that illustrates that the improvement in academic performance at UPHS is likely due to a changed population. The study shows, for example, that approximately three times as many students entering the various small schools as freshmen today read at grade level, which tells us that current UPHS Campus students are better prepared for high school and most likely less marginalized altogether than the students who attended the now-defunct UPHS. But what has happened to all the alienated and struggling students like the ones I met at UPHS? It is difficult to imagine that current reforms have made such a tremendous difference within elementary education that there no longer exists a population of underprepared, alienated high school freshmen. Given available data, it seems more likely that those students still exist, and many of them would be counted among our astoundingly large population of dropouts or push-outs.

And what has happened to the students whose stories and perspectives have filled the pages of this book? Unfortunately, I fell out of touch with most of them. Several of them gave me cell phone numbers, only to have their phones disconnected in the months or years that followed, and many moved to new addresses, as is common among urban residents living in poverty; their lives are disrupted by eviction for nonpayment or displacement due to rent hikes and gentrification or the need to relocate in search of employment. I also experienced changes in my life and eventually moved away from New York.

When I last had contact with Wanda and Zack, they were still students at UPHS. I remained in contact with Carlos and Jennifer after they left the school. At the time of this writing, Jennifer is now twenty-one and living in the Bronx. She had been living with her mother until her mother was hospitalized in the latter part of 2008. Jennifer was evicted from the apartment and entered the shelter system, along with her one-year-old daughter. She has been in a shelter for almost two years and is now waiting to move into her own apartment with public assistance. Jennifer's mother died last Mother's Day, after a long illness, with Jennifer at her side. Although Jennifer and Carlos no longer date, they remain good friends.

After Jennifer dropped out of the proprietary school, she worked temporarily as an assistant in a child-care center. Instead of defaulting on her loan, which has been deferred, Jennifer recently returned to the proprietary school to get her GED and continue her training in medical billing and coding. Currently, she is not working. She said to me, "It's like a contradiction. I need to work, but I want to go to school so I can get a better job. But you can't really do both." For now, she is looking for a weekend job. She plans on finishing the program and then starting at a community college to pursue the dream she has fiercely held on to since she was a young schoolgirl—becoming a doctor. Through all the misery she has experienced, that dream has become like a child's security blanket, offering her something tangible to hold so as not to feel lost.

In a recent conversation we had, Jennifer blamed herself for not taking school seriously enough in the past, but her attitude has changed now that she is a mother. "I need to take responsibility for my daughter," she told me.

Carlos, now twenty-two, continues to live with his mother. Carlos's mother bought a house in a quieter section of the Bronx, in a neighborhood that Carlos believes has fewer negative influences than his previous neighborhood had. The GED-preparation program he began after leaving UPHS closed down after his first year there because of lack of funding, so he had to transfer to another program. Carlos grew frustrated and did not attend regularly. Eventually, at eighteen, he dropped out and began to work full-time. Carlos, like Jennifer, now admits that he did not take school seriously enough back then, but, given the frustrations he was experiencing and the lure of a full-time job, his decisions appear reasonable. In 2008, he returned to a new GED program at a campus of one of the City University of New York's four-year colleges. The person in charge of the program understood he was working full-time and allowed him to take the GED exam without attending classes. He passed and then entered a college-preparatory program on the same campus. That program assisted him in enrolling in the community college he now attends. He would eventually like to become a social worker, and, just as he told me when he was at UPHS, he wants to work with children. He says that all the time he spent holding Jennifer's hand as she went through the foster-care system inspired his career choice.

Jennifer and Carlos are two examples of young people from UPHS who remain determined to pursue higher education and find good and satisfying work. They have navigated the myriad institutions through which they've passed as best they could. Between balancing work and school (and a baby, in Jennifer's case), their paths to satisfying work have been arduous and circuitous, but they remain steadfast on those paths.

Duane moved to Brooklyn to live with his father and to attend a new school where he hoped he'd be able to stay out of trouble. His new neighborhood was about an hour and a half by subway from the Bronx. But Duane was unable to avoid gang life in his Brooklyn neighborhood. He and a few other gang members knocked down and beat up a boy on the street and stole his neck chain. Duane was arrested and subsequently convicted for assault. He spent a few months in jail. I visited him there and attended his hearing with his girlfriend, who was a UPHS student. He received five years' probation.

The last time I met with Duane was almost a year after he had left UPHS. We met one late afternoon at the subway station near his home. Our plan was to see a movie, Saw II—his choice—and to have dinner at McDonald's. Later in the evening, as he walked me back to the subway, we discussed his latest involvement in the criminal-justice system. Duane explained to me that he felt trapped. He knew he had made some poor choices, but he could not envision an alternative. He did not believe that he could last five years. He was afraid he'd be sent to prison for a probation violation and would have to face an even more threatening and violent life behind bars. He was considering leaving the state, and he asked me for money. Luckily, there was no decision to be made, as I didn't have any to give. We hugged, and I passed through the subway turnstile. I did not hear from Duane again.

I do not see a direct causal connection between disciplinary practices at UPHS and the life courses of young people like Duane, Carlos, and Jennifer. They encountered numerous circumstances before and after attending UPHS that shaped their life courses. As I have argued, we must look beyond the school into the lives of low-income urban youth and their social and economic realities to have any real sense of their struggles and the logic of their choices. But the heavy policing of low-income youth of color in and out of school is perhaps one of the most potent reflections of the ethos of exclusion that inspires today's policies. Zero tolerance and order maintenance are striking examples of our societal response to social problems caused by inequality and poverty. Duane, Jennifer, and Carlos are the "living proof," as Carlos liked to say, of the struggles urban youth confront within the current social and educational-policy context. Each has taken a different life course, but their paths are common among young people growing up in places like the Bronx. They begin at young ages with bright dreams, like Duane, who at eight years old wanted to be a police officer. Then, as they near the proper age for high school graduation, they hang on to their "if only" dreams—to be placed in a better or more suitable program, to have teachers that will listen, to get a transfer that might make a difference, to get out of the gang life. As we watch the painful erosion of or the desperate clinging to their dreams, some of us may judge harshly the choices young people make, but we must understand those choices within the deep sense of educational and economic exclusion many urban youth experience. When we do this, we begin to see where institutional and social policies have failed them.

Acknowledgments

THIS PROJECT began as my doctoral dissertation in the Urban Education Program at the City University of New York Graduate Center. Many mentors and friends there provided tremendous support from the very early stages of the project. Among these individuals, I am most grateful to my dissertation chair, Jean Anyon, who has remained an invaluable mentor over the years. Our countless conversations greatly enriched this project. I was also extremely fortunate to have Michelle Fine on my dissertation committee; she always had a wonderful way of listening when I was lost in my theory or my data and then brilliantly helped me make sense of it all. Special thank-yous go to dissertation committee member David Brotherton, who was always available for a thought-provoking discussion on methodology and street life, and to Stanley Aronowitz, who offered me an invaluable independent study in critical theories in education.

Several friends and scholars read the dissertation or drafts of the book manuscript and gave me invaluable feedback and encouragement. Their expert insights and advice tremendously improved the quality of this book. I am honored, humbled, and deeply grateful to have had their support and help: Greg Dimitriadis, Edgar Rivera Colón, Robert Courtney Smith, Howard S. Becker, Carol Stack, Paul Willis, Alice Goffman, and Harvey Moloch. I also thank Howie Winant, who believed in this project and helped me find a home for it at the University of Minnesota Press.

A heartfelt thanks to the wonderful students, former and present, in the Urban Education Program at the CUNY Graduate Center whose paths crossed mine; they make me proud to be an educator. Special thanks to my friends Liza Pappas, Michael Dumas, Eve Tuck, Jen Weiss, Lori Chajet, Janice Bloom, Emily Shnee, and Toni Miranda.

My deepest appreciation goes to the students of Urban Public High School. I am especially grateful to the beautiful young people who gave so much of their time to me and shared details of their lives: RB, MM, CP, MM, JF, and JR. I have a tremendous love and admiration for them, and I am honored to know them. A special thank-you goes to "Principal Alvarez," "Assistant Principal Juarez," and all the deans, especially "Mr. Jackson," "Mr. Henry," "Ms. Orozco," "Ms. Dempsey," and the secretary, "Lorraine," who welcomed me, generously gave their time, and supported my efforts. I am grateful to the teachers and other school personnel who granted me interviews or welcomed me into their classrooms. Finally, sincere thanks to "Officer Hoffmann" and other law-enforcement officials who shared their thoughts and perspectives.

I extend sincere gratitude to the staff at the University of Minnesota Press and to its faculty board. The book's editor, Jason Weidemann, was encouraging through the long review process and generous with his thoughtful feedback as I prepared final revisions. Many thanks, as well, to Danielle Kasprzak, Laura Westlund, and Daniel Ochsner for their part in getting the manuscript ready for publication, and my sincere appreciation to Tammy Zambo, for her excellent copyediting, and Eileen Quam, for her great job with the index. I appreciate the work of three reviewers (David Garland, Pedro Noguera, and one who remained anonymous), who provided extremely useful feedback; their excellent insights added immensely to the final version of the manuscript.

Others offered different kinds of support that made this book possible. Un mil gracias a la familia Perez Ortiz: este libro no podría haber sido escrito si no fuera por Nieves Ortiz y su familia que son una familia segunda para mi hijo cuando yo no puedo estar con él. Heartfelt appreciation goes to my own family for their tremendous and unwavering support and encouragement: to my parents, Gerard and Shirley Nolan, and to my brothers Jim, Tom, and Bob, my sisters-in-law, and my nieces and nephews. Finally, for steadfast encouragement and support, my deepest gratitude goes to my partner, Mitch Duneier, and our son, Liam, who brings us constant joy.

Notes

Introduction

1. Brown, *Derailed* and *Education on Lockdown*.
2. Althusser, *Lenin and Philosophy*; Anyon, "Social Class and the Hidden Curriculum of Work"; Apple, *Ideology and Curriculum*; Bourdieu and Passeron, *Reproduction in Society, Education, and Culture*; Bowles and Gintis, *Schooling in Capitalist America*; and Willis, *Learning to Labor*.
3. Willis, *Learning to Labor*.
4. See for example, ibid.; Fine, *Framing Dropouts*; MacLeod, *Ain't No Makin' It*; and Valenzuela, *Subtractive Schooling*.
5. Marcus, *Ethnography through Thick and Thin*.
6. Piven and Cloward, *Regulating the Poor*.
7. Garland, *Culture of Control*.
8. Brown, *Derailed* and *Education on Lockdown*.
9. See A. Goffman, "On the Run."
10. E. Goffman, *Asylums*.

1. How the Police Took Over School Discipline

1. Herbert, "Six-Year-Old under Arrest."
2. Stallworth, "High School Security Guards Accused."
3. Melago, "Cuffed Kid's Family Sues."
4. R. Campbell, "Throw the Book at Him."
5. Saulny, "Twenty-Five Chicago Students Arrested."
6. Holloway, "Mother Raises Concerns."
7. Katz, *The Irony of Early School Reform*; Waller, *The Sociology of Teaching*; and Friedenberg, *Coming of Age in America*.
8. Katz, *Irony of Early School Reform*; and Rothman, *The Discovery of the Asylum*, 262.
9. Waller, *Sociology of Teaching*, 10.
10. Katz, *Irony of Early School Reform*.

11. Garland, *Punishment and Welfare* and *Punishment and Modern Society*.

12. J. Anderson, *The Education of Blacks in the South*.

13. Sentencing Project, "Facts about Prisons and Prisoners."

14. Western, *Punishment and Inequality in America*, xii.

15. Wilson, *When Work Disappears*.

16. Fiscal Policy Institute, *New York City in the Great Recession*.

17. Western, *Punishment and Inequality in America*.

18. Murray, *Losing Ground*.

19. Garland, *The Culture of Control*, 184.

20. Ibid.

21. Harcourt, *Illusions of Order*, 1.

22. McArdle and Erzen, *Zero Tolerance*.

23. Harcourt, *Illusions of Order*; Levitt, "Understanding Why Crime Fell"; and Western, *Punishment and Inequality in America*.

24. Zimring, *American Youth Violence*, 183.

25. Correctional Association of New York, "Juvenile Detention in New York City."

26. DiIulio, *How to Stop the Coming Crime Wave*.

27. Noguera, "Reducing and Preventing Youth Violence."

28. National Council on Crime and Delinquency, *And Justice for Some*.

29. Correctional Association of New York, "Juvenile Detention in New York City."

30. Citizens Crime Commission of New York City, "NYC Juvenile Justice Statistics."

31. Center for Constitutional Rights, *Racial Disparity in NYPD Stops and Frisks*.

32. Apple, *Educating the "Right" Way*, 42.

33. Ravitch, *The Death and Life*, 9.

34. Ibid., 20–21.

35. Ibid., 29.

36. Ibid., 93.

37. Sirin, "Socioeconomic Status and Academic Achievement."

38. Biddle and Berliner, *What Research Says about Unequal Funding*.

39. Previti and Schill, *The State of New York City's Housing*.

40. Drum Major Institute for Public Policy, *A Look at the Impact Schools*.

41. Skiba, *Zero Tolerance, Zero Evidence*; and Casella, "Zero Tolerance Policies in Schools."

42. Advancement Project, *Test, Punish, and Push Out*.

43. Noguera, "Preventing and Producing Youth Violence"; Brown, *Derailed* and *Education on Lockdown*; American Bar Association, *ABA Zero Tolerance Report*; and Skiba and Peterson, "The Dark Side of Zero Tolerance."

44. Skiba, *Zero Tolerance, Zero Evidence.*

45. Gregory, Skiba, and Noguera, "The Achievement Gap and the Discipline Gap."

46. Brown, *Derailed* and *Education on Lockdown;* and Skiba, Michael, Nardo, and Peterson, *The Color of Discipline.*

47. Arum and Beattie, "High School Experiences"; Sweeten, "Who Will Graduate?"; and Hirschfield, "Another Way Out."

48. Advancement Project, *Test, Punish, and Push Out.*

49. "Mayor Michael R. Bloomberg and Schools Chancellor Joel I. Klein Announce New School Safety Plan."

50. See, respectively, Gendar, "Security Cams to Watch Horror Highs" and "Crackdown at Mayhem High"; and Campanile, "Thugs Run Wild in Troubled HS" and "Stop the Violence."

51. Pleasing Mayor Bloomberg, the New York State Legislature in May 2010 voted to lift a cap on charter schools, more than doubling their number in the state in an effort to win federal grant monies under the new Obama-Duncan Race to the Top program.

52. Klonsky and Klonsky, *Small Schools.*

53. Hemphill and Nauer, *The New Marketplace.*

54. Ravitch, *Death and Life.*

55. Tuck, "Gate-ways and Get-aways."

56. McNeil, *Contradictions of School Reform;* Lipman, "Making the Global City"; and Orfield and Kornhaber, *Raising Standards or Raising Barriers?*

2. Signs of the Times

1. E. Goffman, *Asylums,* cited in McCormick, "Aesthetic Safety Zones," 181.

2. Later in the school year, Juarez moved to an office on the first floor and Dean Henry took over his desk in B-42.

3. Instituting the Culture of Control

1. "Criminal-procedural-level strategies" was a term used by officers to distinguish their own approaches from the approaches used by educators for dealing with discipline problems. Such strategies include body searches, handcuffing, interrogating, arrests, and the issuance of court summonses.

2. Garland, *Culture of Control,* 124–29.

3. According to aggregate data reported by the police department, which appear on the school report card (see New York City Department of Education, School Report Cards), 240 incidents led to police action (arrest or summons). The discrepancy may exist because deans may not have written up all incidents. This

possibility is supported by the fact that there were at least two police incidents that I was aware of that took place inside the school for which I did not find occurrence reports. It is also possible that school personnel did not write up incidents that took place outside the school despite their being considered school-related matters.

4. There were three more summonses issued for disorderly conduct for unspecified reasons. In the case of physical altercations, there were other incidents in which it was not clear whether students received summonses for disorderly conduct, assault, or harassment. In cases where students received summonses for "misbehaving" or "insubordination," I included these in the "disorderly conduct" category.

5. Statements are quoted verbatim and in their entirety. Only names were changed, to pseudonyms.

6. New York City Department of Education, *New York City School Discipline Code*, 10.

7. On the School Report Card for the 2004–2005 school year (New York City Department of Education), the number of "crimes against persons" in the "major crimes" category was eight. Occurrence reports offer no information as to the classification of criminal offenses, and information as to what these crimes were is unavailable. From the data I did collect, however, it appears likely that these incidents were gang-related fistfights or assaults. Although there was documentation for several incidents of weapon possession, only one occurrence report indicated the use of a weapon during a fight. In this incident, a female student hit another student in the head with a combination lock. The offender was arrested for assault. Another report indicated that a student was transported to a hospital.

8. American Bar Association, *ABA Zero Tolerance Report*.

9. SPARK is a program that provides services related to the social aspects of schooling. SPARK staff counsel students and engage them in discussions on the consequences of risky behavior.

10. In some cases, only one student received a summons. During other incidents, as many as six students received summonses.

11. The total population of UPHS was about 3,000. The total number of police actions (arrests, summonses, and youth referrals) was 240, according to police records. There were occurrence reports for 221 of these actions.

12. Brown, *Derailed* and *Education on Lockdown*.

13. American Bar Association, *ABA Zero Tolerance Report*; Brown, *Derailed* and *Education on Lockdown*; and Ziedenberg, Brooks, and Shiraldi, *School House Hype*.

4. Against the Law

1. Alison Jaggar, "Love and Knowledge," quoted in Meiners, *Right to Be Hostile*, 29.

2. New York State Office of Attorney General, *New York City Police Department's "Stop and Frisk" Practices*; and Davis and Matue-Gelabert, *Respectful and Effective Policing*.

3. See Brotherton, "Contradictions of Suppression"; and Devine, *Maximum Security*, for similar analyses of student–security-guard relationships.

4. Scott, *Weapons of the Weak*.

5. Jermaine's account captures the relatively accurate basic understanding of his legal rights, but is somewhat misleading. The U.S. Supreme Court case *Terry v. Ohio* (1968) dictated that for a police officer properly to effect a "terry" stop on the street, the officer must be able to articulate "reasonable suspicion" that a criminal activity is "afoot" (New York State Office of the Attorney General, *"Stop and Frisk" Practices*).

6. The security agents' concern with respect may stem from a cognitive and cultural framework similar to the students', because the two groups are often structurally located in similar ways. However, the institutional fixation on respect appeared to be associated with the dominant culture's fixation on "law and order" and the school's perception that students (children) must learn to respect authority figures (adults).

7. Ferguson, *Bad Boys*, 10.

8. Bourdieu and Passeron, *Reproduction in Society, Education, and Culture*. See also ibid.

9. See Janelle Dance's *Tough Fronts* for a detailed analysis of this phenomenon.

10. E. Anderson, *Code of the Street*; Brotherton and Barrios, *The Almighty Latin King and Queen Nation*; Carter, *Keepin' It Real*; and ibid.

5. Tensions between Educational Approaches and Discourses of Control

1. Devine, *Maximum Security*.

2. Bronx Borough President's Office, *Who's in Charge?*; and New York Civil Liberties Union, *Criminalizing the Classroom*.

3. Ladson-Billings, *Dreamkeepers*, 19–20.

4. Bireda, *Eliminating Racial Profiling in School Discipline*, 59–60.

6. The Underlife

1. *Asylums* is best known for its description of the "total institution," to which its inmates or patients are confined. However, Erving Goffman makes reference frequently throughout the text to a variety of social establishments, such as the workplace and the day school, that are not total institutions. Especially in his chapter entitled "The Underlife of a Public Institution," Goffman tends to broaden his analysis to include many kinds of institutional settings that have "clear-cut standards against which to examine details of life within the establishment" (176).

2. Ibid., 304–5 (emphasis mine).

3. Ibid., 189-99.

4. I could not be sure how my presence influenced Zack's behavior that day. Having spent considerable time with Zack, heard others tell stories about him, and observed people's reactions of his behavior the day I followed him led me to believe that some of his behavior that day was for show, but for the most part it was consistent with his usual behavior and did not constitute anything extraordinary. Additionally, I could not be certain that school personnel and officers were completely unaware of my presence, but for the most part my presence was not acknowledged, and their behaviors appeared typical of others I observed on my various walks through the hallway.

5. E. Goffman, *Asylums,* 188 (emphasis mine).

6. Ibid., 320 (original emphasis).

7. Ibid., 199.

8. Fagan and Wilkinson, "Guns, Youth Violence, and Social Identity."

9. E. Anderson, *Code of the Street.*

10. Mateu-Gelebert, *School Violence.*

11. See Janelle Dance's ethnography *Tough Fronts* for an analysis of this aspect of school violence.

12. There is a considerable literature on why young people join gangs and the functions gangs serve in their lives. See, for example, Brotherton and Barrios, *Almighty Latin King and Queen Nation*; A. Campbell, *The Girls in the Gang*; Chesney-Lind, *The Female Offender*; and Kantos, Brotherton, and Barrios, *Gangs and Society.* The statements I collected from students who reported being members of gangs or crews were consistent with these studies.

13. Dance, *Tough Fronts.*

14. Deans and police officers addressed some of these kinds of conflicts, during which students were subjected to criminal-procedural-level strategies. At other times, these kinds of conflict went under the radar. See Casella's *At Zero Tolerance* for an analysis of how zero-tolerance policies often obscure the various forms of violence and conflict that have the greatest impact on students' lives.

7. Living Proof

1. Willis, *Learning to Labor.*
2. Pager, "The Mark of a Criminal Record."
3. Western, *Punishment and Inequality in America.*
4. See, for example, Willis, *Learning to Labor*; Giroux, *Theory and Resistance in Education*; McLaren, "The Ritual Dimensions of Resistance"; Foley, *Learning Capitalist Culture*; and Solomon, *Black Resistance in High School.*
5. Ogbu, *Minority Education and Caste*; and Fordham and Ogbu, "Black Students' School Success."
6. Carter, *Keepin' It Real*, 17.
7. Mickelson, "The Attitude-Achievement Paradox."
8. See Anyon, "Social Class and the Hidden Curriculum"; Apple, *Ideology and Curriculum*; Bowles and Gintis, *Schooling in Capitalist America*, Bourdieu and Passeron, *Reproduction in Society, Education, and Culture*; and Willis, *Learning to Labor.*
9. Weis, *Class Reunion*, 181.
10. Garland, *The Culture of Control.*
11. See Willis, *Learning to Labor*; Giroux, *Theory and Resistance in Education*; and McLaren, "Ritual Dimensions of Resistance."
12. Willis, "Cultural Production is Different."
13. Willis, *Learning to Labor*; and Ogbu, *Minority Education and Caste.*
14. Willis, "Foot Soldiers of Modernity," 400.
15. E. Goffman, *Asylums.*
16. Willis, "Foot Soldiers of Modernity," 395.
17. E. Goffman, *Asylums*, 201.
18. See Ewick and Silbey, "Narrating Social Structure," 1330–31.

Conclusion

1. Garland, *Culture of Control.*
2. Ibid.
3. Michelson, "Attitude-Achievement Paradox"; Carter, *Keepin' It Real*; and Dance, *Tough Fronts.*
4. Devine, *Maximum Security*, 108–10.
5. Arum, *Judging School Discipline.*
6. Skiba and Sprague, "Safety without Suspensions"; and Skiba, Ritter, Simmons, Peterson, and Miller, "The Safe and Responsive Schools Project."
7. Noguera, *City Schools and the American Dream*, 130–40.
8. Casella, "Zero Tolerance Policies in Schools."

9. Ladson-Billings, *Dreamkeepers*.
10. Delpit, *Other People's Children*.
11. Bireda, *Eliminating Racial Profiling*, 59–60.
12. Nieto, "What Keeps Teachers Going?"
13. Fine, "A Small Price to Pay," 169.
14. Anyon, *Radical Possibilities*, xv.

Works Cited

Advancement Project. *Test, Punish, and Push Out: How "Zero Tolerance" and High-Stakes Testing Funnel Youth into the School-to-Prison Pipeline.* Los Angeles: Advancement Project, 2010. http://njjn.org/media/resources/public/resource_1462.pdf (accessed August 20, 2010).

Althusser, Louis. *Lenin and Philosophy, and Other Essays.* New York: Monthly Review Press, 1971.

American Bar Association. *ABA Zero Tolerance Report.* Washington, D.C.: American Bar Association, February 2001.

Anderson, Elijah. *Code of the Street: Decency, Violence, and the Moral Life of the Inner City.* New York: Norton, 1999.

Anderson, James D. *The Education of Blacks in the South, 1860–1935.* Chapel Hill: University of North Carolina Press, 1988.

Anyon, Jean. *Radical Possibilities: Public Policy, Urban Education, and a New Social Movement.* New York: Teachers College Press, 2005.

———. "Social Class and the Hidden Curriculum of Work." *Journal of Education* 162, no. 1 (1980): 67–92.

Apple, Michael. *Educating the "Right" Way: Markets, Standards, God, and Inequality.* 2nd ed. New York: Routledge Falmer, 2006.

———. *Ideology and Curriculum.* New York: Routledge & Kegan Paul, 1979.

Arum, Richard. *Judging School Discipline: The Crisis of Moral Authority.* Cambridge, Mass.: Harvard University Press, 2003.

Arum, Richard, and Irene Beattie. "High School Experiences and the Risk of Adult Incarceration." *Criminology* 37, no. 3 (1999): 515–40.

Biddle, Bruce, and David Berliner. *What Research Says about Unequal Funding for Schools in America.* Education Policy Reports Project, Tempe, Ariz.: Arizona State University, Winter 2002. http://epsl.asu.edu/eprp/EPSL-0206-102-EPRP.doc (accessed August 13, 2010).

Bireda, Martha. *Eliminating Racial Profiling in School Discipline: Cultures in Conflict.* Lanham, Md.: Rowman and Littlefield, 2002.

Bourdieu, Pierre, and Jean Claude Passeron. *Reproduction in Society, Education, and Culture.* Beverly Hills, Calif.: Sage, 1977.

Bowles, Samuel, and Herbert Gintis. *Schooling in Capitalist America: Educational Reform and the Contradictions of Economic Life.* New York: Basic Books, 1976.

Bronx Borough President's Office. *Who's in Charge? A Report Related to Disputes over Authority between Police and School Administrators in Bronx Schools.* New York: Bronx Borough President's Office, July 2005.

Brotherton, David. "Contradictions of Suppression: Notes to a Study of Approaches to Gangs in Three Public High Schools." *Urban Review* 28, no. 2 (1996): 95–118.

Brotherton, David, and Luis Barrios. *The Almighty Latin King and Queen Nation: Street Politics and the Transformation of a New York City Gang.* New York: Columbia University Press, 2004.

Brown, Judith. *Derailed: The Schoolhouse to Jailhouse Track.* Washington, D.C.: Advancement Project, 2003.

———. *Education on Lockdown: The Schoolhouse to Jailhouse Track.* Washington, D.C.: Advancement Project, 2005.

Campanile, Carl. "Stop the Violence: Fearful Teachers Protest Students' Reign of Terror." *New York Post,* November 23, 2002. http://www.nypost.com/p/news/stop_the_violence_fearful_teachers_2r9gl5doKufWN5bGvyjoK (accessed August 2, 2010).

———. "Thugs Run Wild in Troubled HS," *New York Post,* December 16, 2003. http://www.nypost.com/p/news/thugs_run_wild_in_troubled_hs_6V3Q C37ZByTyEzoRE6xrN (accessed August 2, 2010).

Campbell, Anne. *The Girls in the Gang.* 2nd ed. Cambridge, Mass.: Blackwell, 1991.

Campbell, Rich. "Throw the Book at Him, or the Maalox." *TC Palm,* November 30, 2008. http://www.tcpalm.com/news/2008/nov/30/rich-campbell -throw-bookhim-ormaalox (accessed August 28, 2010).

Carter, Prudence L. *Keepin' It Real: School Success beyond Black and White.* New York: Oxford University Press, 2005.

Casella, Ronald. *At Zero Tolerance: Punishment, Prevention, and School Violence.* New York: Lang, 2001.

———. "Zero Tolerance Policies in Schools: Rationale, Consequences, and Alternatives." *Teachers College Record* 105, no. 5 (2003): 872–92.

Center for Constitutional Rights. *Racial Disparity in NYPD Stops and Frisks: The Center for Constitutional Rights Preliminary Report on UF-250 Data from 2005 through June 2008.* New York: Center for Constitutional Rights, January 15, 2009. http://ccrjustice.org/files/Report_CCR_NYPD_Stop_and_Frisk_0. pdf (accessed August 27, 2010).

Chesney-Lind, Meda. *The Female Offender: Girls, Women, and Crime*. Thousand Oaks, Calif.: Sage, 1997.

Citizens Crime Commission of New York City. "NYC Juvenile Justice Statistics." Citizens Crime Commission of New York City, 2010. http://www.nycrimecommission.org/initiative2.php (accessed August 27, 2010).

Correctional Association of New York. "Juvenile Detention in New York City." Fact sheet. New York: Correctional Association of New York, 2010. http://www.correctionalassociation.org / publications / download / jjp / factsheets/ detention_fact_sheet_2010.pdf (accessed February 21, 2011).

Dance, Janelle. *Tough Fronts: The Impact of Street Culture on Schooling*. New York: Routledge Falmer, 2000.

Davis, Robert C., and Pedro Mateu-Gelabert. *Respectful and Effective Policing: Two Examples in the South Bronx*. New York: Vera Institute of Justice, 1999.

Delpit, Lisa. *Other People's Children: Cultural Conflict in the Classroom*. New York: New Press, 1995.

Devine, John. *Maximum Security: The Culture of Violence in Inner-City Schools*. Chicago: University of Chicago Press, 1996.

DiIulio, John. *How to Stop the Coming Crime Wave*. New York: Manhattan Institute, 1996.

Drum Major Institute for Public Policy. *A Look at the Impact Schools: A Drum Major Institute for Public Policy Data Brief*. New York: Drum Major Institute for Public Policy, 2005.

Ewick, Patricia, and Susan Silbey. "Narrating Social Structure: Stories of Resistance to Legal Authority." *American Journal of Sociology* 108, no. 6 (2003): 1328–72.

Fagan, Jeffery A., and Deanna L. Wilkinson. "Guns, Youth Violence, and Social Identity in Inner Cities." In *Crime and Justice*, vol. 24, *Youth Violence*, ed. Michael Tonry and Mark H. Moore, 105–88. Chicago: University of Chicago Press, 1998.

Ferguson, Anne A. *Bad Boys: Public Schools in the Making of Black Masculinity*. Ann Arbor: University of Michigan Press, 2000.

Fine, Michelle. *Framing Dropouts: Notes on the Politics of an Urban Public High School*. Albany: State University of New York Press, 1991.

———. "A Small Price to Pay for Justice." In *A Simple Justice: The Challenge of Small Schools*, ed. William Ayers, Michael Klonsky, and Gabrielle H. Lyon, 168–72. New York: Teachers College Press, 2000.

Fiscal Policy Institute. *New York City in the Great Recession: Divergent Fates by Neighborhood, Race, and Ethnicity*. New York: Fiscal Policy Institute, December 2009. http://www.fiscalpolicy.org/FPI_NeighborhoodUnemployment_NYC.pdf (accessed July 8, 2010).

Foley, Douglas. *Learning Capitalist Culture: Deep in the Heart of Tejas.* Philadelphia: University of Pennsylvania Press, 1992.

Fordham, Signithia, and John Ogbu. "Black Students' School Success: Coping with the Burden of 'Acting White.'" *Urban Review* 18 (1986): 176–206.

Friedenberg, Edgar. *Coming of Age in America.* New York: Random House, 1965.

Garland, David. *The Culture of Control: Crime and Social Order in Contemporary Society.* Chicago: University of Chicago Press, 2001.

———. *Punishment and Modern Society.* Oxford: Oxford University Press, 1990.

———. *Punishment and Welfare: A History of Penal Strategies.* Brookfield, Vt.: Gower, 1985.

Gendar, Alison. "Crackdown at Mayhem High: Dozens of Safety Agents Sent to Seven Troubled Schools." *New York Daily News,* November 22, 2002. http://www.nydailynews.com/archives/news/2002/11/22/2002-1122_crackdown_at_mayhem_high__do.html (accessed August 2, 2010).

———. "Security Cams to Watch Horror Highs." *New York Daily News,* November 23, 2002. http://www.nydailynews.com/archives/news/2002/11/23/2002-1123_security_cams_to_watch_horro.html (accessed August 2, 2010).

Giroux, Henry. *Theory and Resistance in Education: A Pedagogy for the Opposition.* South Hadley, Mass.: Bergin and Garvey, 1983.

Goffman, Alice. "On the Run: Wanted Men in a Philadelphia Ghetto." *American Sociological Review* 74, no. 3 (2009): 339–57.

Goffman, Erving. *Asylums: Essays on the Social Situations of Mental Patients and Other Inmates.* Garden City, N.Y: Anchor, 1961.

Gregory, Anne, Russell Skiba, and Pedro Noguera. "The Achievement Gap and the Discipline Gap: Two Sides of the Same Coin?" *Educational Researcher* 39, no. 1 (January–February 2010): 59–68.

Harcourt, Bernard. *Illusions of Order: The False Promise of Broken Windows Policing.* Cambridge, Mass.: Harvard University Press, 2001.

Hemphill, Clara, and Kim Nauer. *The New Marketplace: How Small-School Reforms and School Choice Have Reshaped New York City's High Schools.* New York: Center for New York City Affairs, Milano The New School for Management and Urban Policy, June 2009.

Herbert, Bob. "Six-Year-Old under Arrest." Opinion-editorial. *New York Times,* April 9, 2007. http://query.nytimes.com/gst/fullpage.html (accessed August 2, 2010).

Hirschfield, Paul. "Another Way Out: The Impact of Juvenile Arrest on High School Dropout." *Sociology of Education* 82, no. 4 (2009): 368–93.

Holloway, Karel. "Mother Raises Concerns after Special-Needs Son Is Fined for Cursing at Richardson ISD School," *Dallas Morning News,* October 15, 2009. http://www.dallasnews.com/sharedcontent/dws/dn/education/stories/Nrichcuss_15met.ART.Central.Edition1.4c04e1c.html (accessed August 2, 2010).

Kantos, Louis, David Brotherton, and Luis Barrios, eds. *Gangs and Society: Alternative Perspectives.* New York: Columbia University Press, 2004.

Katz, Michael. *The Irony of Early School Reform.* Cambridge, Mass.: Harvard University Press, 1967.

Klonsky, Michael, and Susan Klonsky. *Small Schools: Public School Reform Meets the Ownership Society.* New York: Routledge, 2008.

Ladson-Billings, Gloria. *Dreamkeepers: Successful Teachers of African-American Children.* 2nd ed. San Francisco: Jossey-Bass, 2009.

Levitt, Steven. "Understanding Why Crime Fell in the 1990s: Four Factors That Explain the Decline and Six That Do Not." *Journal of Economic Perspectives* 18, no. 1 (2004): 163–90.

Lipman, Pauline. "Making the Global City, Making Inequality: The Political Economy and Cultural Politics of Chicago School Policy." *American Educational Research Journal* 39, no. 2 (2002): 379–419.

MacLeod, Jay. *Ain't No Making It: Leveled Aspirations in a Low-Income Neighborhood.* Boulder, Colo.: Westview, 1995.

Marcus, George. *Ethnography through Thick and Thin.* Princeton, N.J.: Princeton University Press, 1998.

Mateu-Gelabert, Pedro. *School Violence: The Bi-directional Conflict Flow between Neighborhood and School.* New York: Vera Institute for Justice, 2000.

McArdle, Andrea, and Tanya Erzen, eds. *Zero Tolerance: Quality of Life and the New Police Brutality in New York City.* New York: New York University Press, 2001.

McCormick, Jennifer. "Aesthetic Safety Zones: Surveillance and Sanctuary in Poetry by Young Women." In *Construction Sites: Excavating Race, Class, and Gender among Urban Youth,* ed. Lois Weis and Michelle Fine. New York: Teachers College Press, 2000.

McLaren, Peter. "The Ritual Dimensions of Resistance: Clowning and Symbolic Inversion." *Journal of Education* 167, no. 2 (1983): 84–98.

McNeil, Linda. *Contradictions of School Reform: Educational Costs of Standardized Testing.* New York: Routledge, 2000.

Meiners, Erica. *Right to Be Hostile: Schools, Prisons, and the Making of Public Enemies.* New York: Routledge, 2007.

Melago, Carrie. "Cuffed Kid's Family Sues City, Ed. Dept." *New York Daily News,* June 18, 2008. http://www.nydailynews.com/ny_local/education/2008/06/18/2008-0618_cuffed_kids_family_sues_city_ed_dept.html (accessed August 27, 2010).

Mickelson, Roslyn A. "The Attitude-Achievement Paradox among Black Adolescents." *Sociology of Education* 63 (1990): 44–61.

Murray, Charles. *Losing Ground: American Social Policy, 1950–1980.* New York: Basic Books, 1984.

National Council on Crime and Delinquency. *And Justice for Some: Differential*

Treatment of Youth of Color in the Justice System. Oakland, Calif.: National Council on Crime and Delinquency, January 2007. http://www.nccd-crc.org/ nccd/pubs/ (accessed June 15, 2010).

New York City Department of Education. "Mayor Michael R. Bloomberg and Schools Chancellor Joel I. Klein Announce New School Safety Plan." New York: New York City Department of Education, December 23, 2003. http://schools .nyc.gov/Offices/mediarelations/NewsandSpeeches/20032004/1223-2003 -13-2-36-874.htm (accessed July 15, 2010).

———. *New York City School Discipline Code*. New York: New York City Department of Education, 2004.

———. School Report Cards, 2004–2005. http://schools.nyc.gov/daa/ SchoolReports/ (accessed September 18, 2006).

New York Civil Liberties Union. *Criminalizing the Classroom: The Over-policing of New York City Schools*. New York: New York Civil Liberties Union, 2007.

New York State Office of the Attorney General. *New York City Police Department's "Stop and Frisk" Practices: A Report to the People of the State of New York from the Office of the Attorney General*. Albany: New York State Office of the Attorney General, 1999.

Nieto, Sonia. "What Keeps Teachers Going?" *Educational Leadership* 60, no. 8 (2003): 14–18.

Noguera, Pedro. *City Schools and the American Dream: Reclaiming the Promise of Public Education*. New York: Teachers College Press, 2003.

———. "Preventing and Producing Youth Violence: A Critical Analysis of Responses to School Violence." *Harvard Educational Review*, 65, no. 2 (1995): 189–212.

———. "Reducing and Preventing Youth Violence: An Analysis of Causes and Assessment of Successful Programs." *In Motion Magazine*, April 28, 1996. http:// www.inmotionmagazine.com/pedro3.html#Anchor-Conclusion47383 (accessed August 28, 2010).

Ogbu, John. *Minority Education and Caste*. New York: Academic Press, 1978.

Orfield, Gary, and Chungmei Lee. *Racial Transformation and the Changing Nature of Segregation*. Cambridge, Mass.: Civil Rights Project at Harvard University, 2006.

Orfield, Gary, and Mindy Kornhaber, eds. *Raising Standards or Raising Barriers? Inequality and High Stakes Testing in Public Education*. New York: Century Foundation Press, 2001.

Pager, Devah. "The Mark of a Criminal Record." *American Journal of Sociology* 108, no. 5 (2003): 937–75.

Piven, Frances F., and Richard A. Cloward. *Regulating the Poor: The Functions of Public Welfare*. Toronto: Random House, 1971.

Previti, Denise, and Michael Schill. *The State of New York City's Housing and Neigh-borhoods, 2003.* New York: Furman Center for Real Estate and Urban Policy, New York University, 2003.

Ravitch, Diane. *The Death and Life of the Great American School System.* New York: Basic Books, 2010.

Rothman, David. *The Discovery of the Asylum: Social Order and Disorder in the New Republic.* Piscataway, N.J.: Transaction, 1971.

Saulny, Susan. "Twenty-Five Chicago Students Arrested for a Middle-School Food Fight." *New York Times,* November 10, 2009. http://www.nytimes.com /2009/11/11/us/11foodfight.html (accessed July 7, 2010).

Scott, James C. *Weapons of the Weak: Everyday Forms of Peasant Resistance.* New Haven, Conn.: Yale University Press, 1985.

Sentencing Project. "Facts about Prisons and Prisoners." Washington, D.C.: Sentencing Project, 2010. http://www.sentencingproject.org/doc/publications/ publications/inc_factsAboutPrisons_Jul2010.pdf (accessed August 28, 2010).

Sirin, Selcuk. "Socioeconomic Status and Academic Achievement: A Meta-Analytic Review of Research." *Review of Educational Research* 75, no. 3 (2005): 417–53.

Skiba, Russell. *Zero Tolerance, Zero Evidence: An Analysis of School Disciplinary Practice.* Policy Research Report #SRS2. Bloomington: Indiana Education Policy Center, 2000.

Skiba, Russell, Robert S. Michael, Abra C. Nardo, and Reece Peterson. *The Color of Discipline: Sources of Racial and Gender Disproportionality in School Punishment.* Bloomington: Indiana Education Policy Center, June 2000.

Skiba, Russell, and Reece Peterson. "The Dark Side of Zero Tolerance." *Phi Delta Kappan* 80, no. 5 (January 1999): 372–76, 381–82.

Skiba, Russell, Shana Ritter, Ada Simmons, Reece Peterson, and Courtney Miller. "The Safe and Responsive Schools Project: A School Reform Model for Implementing Best Practices in Violence Prevention." In *Handbook of School Violence and School Safety: From Research to Practice,* ed. Shane Jimerson and Michael Furlong. Mahwah, N.J.: Erlbaum, 2006.

Skiba, Russell, and Jeffery Sprague. "Safety without Suspensions." *Educational Leadership,* September 2008, 38–43.

Solomon, Rovell P. *Black Resistance in High School: Forging a Separatist Culture.* Albany: State University of New York Press, 1992.

Stallworth, Leo. "High School Security Guards Accused of Excessive Force." KABC-TV, Los Angeles, September 27, 2007. http://abclocal.go.com/kabc/ story?section=news/local&id=5677461 (accessed August 10, 2010).

Sweeten, Gary. "Who Will Graduate? Disruption of High School Education by Arrest and Court Involvement." *Justice Quarterly* 23, no. 4 (2006): 462–80.

Tuck, Eve. "Gate-ways and Get-aways: Urban Youth, School Push-Out, and the GED." PhD diss., City University of New York, 2008. ProQuest (AAT 3325386). http://www.umi.com/.

Valenzuela, Angela. *Subtractive Schooling: U.S. Mexican Youth and the Politics of Caring.* Albany: State University of New York Press, 1999.

Waller, Willard. *The Sociology of Teaching.* New York: Wiley, 1932.

Weis, Lois. *Class Reunion: The Remaking of the American White Working Class.* New York: Routledge, 2004.

Western, Bruce. *Punishment and Inequality in America.* New York: Russell Sage Foundation, 2006.

Willis, Paul. "Cultural Production Is Different from Cultural Reproduction Is Different from Social Reproduction Is Different from Reproduction." *Interchange* 12, nos. 2–3 (1998): 48–68.

———. "Foot Soldiers of Modernity: The Dialectics of Cultural Consumption and the 21st Century School." *Harvard Educational Review* 73, no. 3 (2003): 390–415.

———. *Learning to Labor: Why Working Class Kids Get Working Class Jobs.* New York: Columbia University Press, 1977.

Wilson, William Julius. *When Work Disappears: The World of the New Urban Poor.* New York: Vintage, 1996.

Ziedenberg, Jason, Kim Brooks, and Vincent Shiraldi. *School House Hype: Two Years Later.* Washington, D.C.: Justice Policy Institute, April 2000.

Zimring, Franklin. *American Youth Violence.* New York: Oxford University Press, 1998.

Index